learning in the
middle years more
than a transition

Susan Groundwater-Smith
Jane Mitchell
Nicole Mockler

learning in the middle years more than a transition

THOMSON

Australia . New Zealand . Canada . Mexico . Singapore . Spain . United Kingdom . United States

Level 7, 80 Dorcas Street
South Melbourne, Victoria
Australia 3205

Email: highereducation@thomsonlearning.com.au
Website: www.thomsonlearning.com.au

First published in 2007
10 9 8 7 6 5 4 3 2 1
10 09 08 07

Copyright © 2007 Nelson Australia Pty Limited.

COPYRIGHT

Mitchell, Jane Margaret, 1960–.
    Learning in the middle years: more than a transition.

    Includes index.
    For educators of middle school students.
    ISBN 978 0 17 013299 2.

    ISBN 0 17 013299 4.

    1. Learning – Study and teaching (Middle school).
    2. Thought and thinking – Study and teaching (Middle school).
    3. Learning, Psychology of. I. Groundwater-Smith, Susan.
    II. Mockler, Nicole. III. Title.

370.15

Publishing manager: Michael Tully
Publishing editor: Elizabeth Vella
Project editor: Louise Powell
Developmental editor: Susan Heale
Production controller: Ruth Coleman
Text designer: Olga Lavecchia
Cover designer: Olga Lavecchia
Editor: Gill Smith
Permissions researcher: Pamela Underwood
Indexer: Julie King
Cover image supplied by Masterfile
Typeset in Minion 10/13 by KnowledgeWorks Global Ltd.
Printed in China by China Translation Printing Services

This title is published under the imprint of Thomson.
Nelson Australia Pty Limited ACN 058 280 149 (incorporated in Victoria)
trading as Thomson Learning Australia.

The URLs contained in this publication were checked for currency during the production process.
Note, however, that the publisher cannot vouch for the ongoing currency of URLs.

CONTENTS

Pt I

Learning in the Middle Years

Pt II

Teaching in the Middle Years

PREFACE

From the beginning, we wish to affirm that this is an optimistic text – one that sees the benefits and joys of learning and teaching in those critical years of schooling, the Middle Years. We have capitalised the phrase deliberately because we make a case that, indeed, the Middle Years are particularly important in the context of school education. We acknowledge the difficulties in definition and the claims made against distinctiveness, but these years have great possibility for pedagogical transformation not only in terms of what it is that learners do, but also what it is that their teachers do. We assume that you, who may be undertaking an initial teacher-education course or may already be working in classrooms and schools, are anxious to move beyond an instrumental view of teachers' work towards one that is transformational. We also are cognisant of the many different environments in which you work, ranging from city and regional campuses of universities through to metropolitan or rural and remote schools across states and territories.

Without labouring the point, we want to be clear that the thinking behind this text is based on notions of pedagogy with the intention of transforming learning in a range of contexts. We could call it 'good pedagogy', but this does not sufficiently distinguish it in terms of its potential to be liberatory: that is, liberating all participants from taken-for-granted practices. We could call it 'authentic pedagogy', a term that is now so widely used as to lose some of its meaning. We toyed with the idea of calling it 'critical pedagogy', but believe that it would set an agenda that may be beyond what many schools are able to achieve, given the very real bureaucratic constraints within which they work. So, the term that we feel most embodies our intentions is 'transformative pedagogy' – we hope that its effect is to provide insights, arguments and tools that have the potential to transform not only students' learning in the Middle Years but also the professional learning of their teachers.

We consider how young people can learn in conditions that respect them and give them a sense of their own agency, and how teachers can work such that they have authentic dialogic relationships with their students and with each other. By this we mean that there should be opportunities for teachers to have conversations with one another and their students about the conditions for learning – going beyond the kind of talk that is directed to organisation within the classroom and moving towards genuine and mutually respectful discussion. With this goal in mind, we have organised the book upon the principles of transformative pedagogy: the chapters discuss the many issues, concerns and problems that swirl around Middle Years education and contain extended case studies. The case studies provide the opportunity for dialogue, as each prompts a discussion in which participants must consider and reveal their position on both the substance of the case and the taken-for-granted ways they have thought about education.

A number of years ago, an American educator, Ira Shore (1980), brought to classrooms the concept of exploring themes from everyday life, stripping them of their superficiality and examining closely the sub-strata that contributed to their being. He drew upon the work of Paulo Freire, who enjoined educators to use dialogue as a catalyst for learning and to explore the 'what', 'when', 'where' and, importantly, the 'why' of phenomena and events. Freire saw education as inherently political, and so do we – a matter to which we shall return. He used the metaphor of 'banking' education (Freire 1972) whereby students are the depositories and teachers the depositors – instead of communicating in a reciprocal way, the teacher issues communiqués and effectively makes 'deposits' that the students then passively receive, memorise and repeat. He argued for a move away from this approach towards education as problem-posing as opposed to problem-solving. This focus upon problem-posing is a core thread throughout this book. Indeed, an initial problem is that of defining when and what are the Middle Years of schooling.

DEFINING THE MIDDLE YEARS

Different accounts of schooling for the Middle Years embrace different age spans. For our part, the range that we consider covers Year 6 – in most states and territories the last year of primary schooling – through to and including Year 9. Our reason for deciding on this span is that these years correspond to the developmental period of early adolescence and include the period of transition from primary to secondary schooling. As we argue in the chapters that follow, young people in this phase of their lives have a range of affective and cognitive needs arising from the changes that are occurring in their bodies, minds and circumstances. It is a time when they are adjusting to profound physical, social, emotional and intellectual change; when they are beginning to construct their sexual identity; and when they are building new, different and sometimes quite troubling relationships with adults as they seek to establish their independence.

As Barratt (1998) has argued, the Middle Years are also a time when we have to rethink how we are going to meet these complex needs in ways that go beyond current arrangements. It is no longer sufficient to present young people with a slightly upscaled primary curriculum or a downscaled competitive academic curriculum. However, it is also not sufficient to merely sequester this group without considering the continuity of their education. Creating separate schools for the Middle Years may well contribute to further problems of adjustment – primary to middle school and middle to senior school. What is most desirable is a relatively seamless transition from one to the other.

Rod Chadbourne (2003) has worked extensively in the field and in preparing teachers for the Middle Years. He is careful to point out that while the philosophy of good schooling in these years is not distinctive but is shaped by sound generic educational principles based on student-centred learning, its application in the context of young adolescents is. It is precisely the nature of early adolescence that makes the application of schooling to suit adolescents' needs distinctive, because it is a time when they are most likely to become alienated and disengaged and develop habits that lead to low self-esteem and lack of resilience.

Our emphasis then is upon the kinds of practices that contribute to and enhance the learning of these young people. Some of these practices have already been spelled out by writers such as Carrington, who describes 'signature practices' (2004: 34), among them interdisciplinary school teams, appropriate transitions between primary and secondary contexts, an integrated curriculum, exposure to smaller numbers of teachers, and so on. These practices and more are discussed throughout this book.

THE SCOPE OF THIS BOOK

In order to orient you to this book, we first outline the processes that we have used to write it. Our collective decision was to use two intersecting voices: the first of these speaks directly to you – not just 'you' as an individual reader, but 'you' as a collective of students and practising teachers who have chosen to grapple with the challenging questions related to learning and teaching in the Middle Years. We hope that you will use this book as a resource to provoke your thinking and beliefs about how young people learn and how schools can best provide for their learning. The book takes you beyond recipes and looks at the underlying reasons behind those matters that are so taxing for those working with adolescent learners. Which brings us to the second voice: throughout the book, we draw upon recent scholarship and research from Australia and overseas and report this research in the third person to differentiate what is our own stance and what is the work of the academic field.

In effect, using both voices is one of the pedagogic features of the book. The book itself can be seen as the curriculum, with all of its attendant complexities; the curriculum is at the pedagogic interface, where teaching and learning intersect around what is to be taught and what is to be learned. Our writing and your reading can be seen as analogous to these other components of the pedagogic act, the teaching and the learning. As with sound pedagogy we are concerned with engagement – your engagement. We expect you to be active readers who will use the text as a platform for further investigation and debate. An important pedagogic feature of the book is the extended case studies with accompanying provocations and questions. The cases are not closed examples *of* a particular event or phenomenon, but are examples *for* professional learning as you reflect upon the various issues that are raised. In this way it should become clear that theory and practice are not separate entities – each works on the other in complex and compelling ways. This book is neither a manual nor a strictly academic work; it is one designed to challenge and engage. All too often, texts about teaching become 'tips for teaching', while academic resources are couched in obscure and inaccessible language. Our hope is that the book sits between these two extremes.

Deep understanding, another sound pedagogical aim, cannot be engendered by a text that does the work for you. As you read, you will not be told what to think.

Instead, we expect that you will organise and reorganise your thinking as a result of analysing and evaluating what you read, what you bring to your reading and what your colleagues contribute.

As you work your way through the contents, you will encounter many issues: What are the features of learning in the Middle Years? What is adolescence? How do we differentiate groups of learners and what are the consequences of addressing diversity? What are the effects of living and learning in greatly different contexts? How do teachers themselves learn? We have no pre-packaged solutions or aphorisms, rather we bring to your attention the many and sometimes contradictory ways that these issues have been investigated and require you, as intelligent readers, to clarify your own understanding and the ways you might address these issues. This is not to say that the text is a relativist one whereby any solution counts. While not preaching to you, we do make clear that your chosen solution should be grounded in ethical practice that honours and respects all who participate in the educational setting.

Below we provide you with a series of signposts as to the direction of each chapter. Thus the overall map is set out, but the route and the means of travel is in your own hands.

THE CONTENT

In the chapters we indicate how the propositions about the nature and construction of the text can be made practical and how teachers can develop well-grounded strategies to meet the needs of students in the Middle Years. The book falls into two main sections: the first focuses on students and their learning in the Middle Years, while the second considers the professional learning of teachers working in the Middle Years. For you to see more clearly the route the book takes, an outline of each chapter follows.

Part I – Learning in the Middle Years

Chapter 1 Adolescent learners: social and psychological contexts of schooling

This introductory chapter brings to the surface some of the concerns that make problem-posing about Middle Years education such an interesting and worthwhile activity. Among these challenges we discuss the sociopolitical milieu in which education is provided, the cultural context of schooling and learning, and diversity in the social geography of Australia.

Issues surrounding adolescence and student engagement from both psychological and sociological perspectives are discussed. We consider the consequences of disaffection upon student achievement and examine ways that schooling structures may be developed to enable a more effective transition from primary to secondary schooling. We emphasise the need for academic care of students as essential to the delivery of an effective curriculum through appropriate pedagogies.

The case studies focus upon transitions and the voice of students. They draw on studies in which students have been consulted and engaged in the design and implementation of inquiries to address their concerns around schooling in the Middle Years. Central to planning is making transitions and student wellbeing.

Chapter 2   Young people: identity, diversity and inclusion

This chapter builds on concepts from Chapter 1 to examine differences among students in the Middle Years and how school practices can respond to these differences. Difference is defined in terms of gender, socioeconomic status, ethnicity, Aboriginality and social geography. Central are social justice and equity questions pertaining to how schools shape and reflect differences between students.

The case study focuses on the principles for teaching developed by a teacher working with Indigenous students in a remote school. The case highlights important ways that teaching practice can recognise and respond to the needs of students in a particular community.

Chapter 3   Rethinking curriculum for adolescent learners

Here we explore how curriculum reform can enhance student engagement and achievement. We examine some of the state and territory curriculum policies and how they can facilitate or inhibit student learning in the Middle Years.

The case study is concerned with curriculum integration, often considered one of the important aspects of a middle school curriculum. 'Real world' problems are presented that require students to draw on various disciplinary skills to understand issues and build knowledge. An example is used of staff development around the design of an integrated unit and the associated challenges. You will consider how integrated units are designed, how curriculum design is translated into practice and some of the pros and cons of curriculum integration.

Chapter 4   New pedagogies for the Middle Years

Recognising the intersection of curriculum and pedagogy, this chapter looks particularly at why it is essential that changing a curriculum requires changing approaches to teaching and learning. A range of models for thinking about transformative and engaging teaching and learning practices in the Middle Years is provided.

The case study focuses on making classrooms engaging places to be. Much research discusses student disengagement in the Middle Years. This case study examines the transformational pedagogical practices set up in one classroom to build and extend student engagement: intellectual, behavioural and affective.

Chapter 5   Assessing learning

The case is made for developing new and different approaches to assessment in middle school in the absence of high-stakes assessment. These approaches require assessment to be considered at the front-end of educational planning and decision-making, such that it contributes to enhanced learning outcomes.

An example of a 'rich task' is provided in the case study, along with an assessment rubric. The case materials give you an opportunity to consider how assessment tasks are developed to support student learning. Questions are posed about using a range of assessment methods and providing feedback on student work, and how assessment can be used to inform planning.

Part II – Teaching in the Middle Years

Chapter 6   *Beginning to teach*

This chapter looks specifically at the preparation of Middle Years teachers in initial teacher education, how they can be assisted through coursework and their professional experience. We examine the extent to which employers recognise the requisite skills of beginning teachers in this area and how they mentor and support them.

The case study comprises reflections of a pre-service teacher during the field-based component of a teacher-education program. It provides an authentic insights into the teacher's emerging understanding of the concept 'Middle Years' and 'middle schooling', and what this means for teaching, working with colleagues and connections to campus-based study.

Chapter 7   *Continuing to teach*

Recognising that most teachers of students in the Middle Years are experienced, we examine how current practices can be modified and/or sustained.

The case study is concerned with the formation of a professional learning community. Teaching teams are considered to be an important part of middle schooling. It explores the development of a learning team, the conditions that support professional learning and how the work of the team impacts upon classroom practice.

Chapter 8   *Beyond compliance: leading teaching and learning*

This chapter is concerned with how school leadership can contribute to teachers' professional growth in this area. It looks at the necessary factors and conditions for the growth of schools as learning communities and explores some ways that educational leaders can cultivate these factors. We recognise that leadership may well come from less-experienced teachers who have had some exposure to such ideas and can support their more-experienced colleagues.

The case study draws readers to examine two different approaches to leading innovation in the Middle Years and consider the implications of these approaches for the school as learning community.

Chapter 9   *Evaluating teaching and learning*

This chapter concludes the second part, so the effectiveness of new approaches to teaching and learning are discussed in the context of action research and with a particular focus on action learning. A number of inquiry strategies are discussed, with attention paid to the student voice in the process.

The case study portrays action learning in practice: how teachers have used the student voice to inform change and evaluate its impact in a curriculum-reform project in the middle school.

Chapter 10   *The Middle Years – more than a transition*

The conclusion to the book returns us to the notion of a transformational pedagogy in context and argues for why we believe this work has met that goal. The chapter summarises key components of reform in the Middle Years in Australia and charts some directions and challenges for the future.

In conclusion, we emphasise that:

- Our writing shifts back and forth between the general and the specific, as we need to establish broad claims while, at the same time, indicate that they vary from context to context.
- Our current focus on transformation in the Middle Years is twofold. First, it is a response to the changes that adolescents are going through and, second, it is a response to the rapidly changing and complex contexts adolescents live in now and will live in in the future.
- This book poses rather than solves problems. In effect, it is a form of problem-based education that requires you, the reader, to engage with issues and consider their implications for learning and teaching in the Middle Years.
- Our concern is for you to more fully apprehend the circumstances of young people's learning rather than to fix the 'problem' of adolescence – for it may not prove to be a problem at all, but rather a fascinating challenge.

Each chapter contains a case study that acts as a touchstone for discussion around the challenges, problems and dilemmas faced by those engaged in Middle Years education. Chapters also include provocations – points that we want you to reflect upon.

Finally, we set a task as a means of documenting your own learning as you progress towards becoming a teacher in the Middle Years of schooling. A way to begin is to develop a concept map showing what you see to be the elements contributing to planning for the Middle Years. This map could be used not only as a basis for discussion with your peers, but also as a means to trace the development of your thinking. You could, at the end of this book, develop a second concept map using the same terms. Tracing conceptual change using such maps has great power as an evaluative and developmental tool (Morine-Dershimer 1993).

Comparing the concept maps would not only be a useful guide to your learning, but also one that could be helpful to course designers and to us, authors of this book. Should you do so, we hope that you will send us some examples that might be incorporated in a later edition of this book.

References

Barratt, R. (1998) *Shaping Middle Schooling in Australia – A report of the National Middle Schooling Project.* Canberra: Australian Curriculum Studies Association.

Carrington, V. (2004) 'Mid-year review of the middle years of schooling'. *Curriculum Perspectives*, 24(1), 30–62.

Chadbourne, R. (2003) 'What makes middle schools and middle schooling distinctive, if anything?' *Queensland Journal of Educational Research*, 19(1), 3–12.

Freire, P. (1972) *Pedagogy of the Oppressed.* Harmondsworth, UK: Penguin.

Morine-Dershimer, G. (1993) 'Tracing conceptual change in preservice teachers'. *Teaching and Teacher Education*, 9(1), 15–26.

Shore, I. (1980) *Critical Teaching and Everyday Life.* Chicago, IL: University of Chicago Press.

ACKNOWLEDGEMENTS

This book is the product of the many privileged conversations and interactions we have had with teachers, teacher educators, student teachers, school students and educational researchers over the years. Sincere thanks are due to those many people who have helped us to continually expand our ideas of what education might be, as well as bring authenticity and authority to this text.

In addition, we wish to acknowledge the contribution of a number of individuals and institutions.

We thank the Coalition of Knowledge Building Schools, connected to the Centre for Practitioner Research in the Faculty of Education and Social Work at the University of Sydney. A number of the schools in the coalition have specific programs for the Middle Years and generously allowed us to use case study material to illustrate and illuminate issues in various chapters of the book.

Jane acknowledges the following people for their generosity with ideas, support and encouragement: Tracey Borg; Jodie Mason; Gaye Hoskins; Melanie Meers; Paula Shaw; George Lovecek; John Mitchell; Margaret Mitchell; colleagues, students and friends in the Faculty of Education at Monash University; and the School of Education at the University of Queensland.

From Nicole, thanks are due to the cheer squad – Elenie Poulos, Serena Vecchiet, Joanne Hack and Sharon Brien – who variously provided critical reading (and photographic) skills, support, encouragement and the occasional debate.

We also thank the staff at Thomson for their support and advice through all stages of the preparation of this book. In particular, we thank Elizabeth Vella for her encouragement for the project and her insights throughout the writing process and Gill Smith for her exacting editorial work. Likewise, our thanks are extended to those who reviewed the book at various stages in its production.

The authors and publishers would like to gratefully credit or acknowledge the following for permission to reproduce copyright material:

Association for Supervision and Curriculum Development for extract from Understand by Design by Wiggins, G. & Tighe J, Pg.14 Fig 1.4 Publ. Alexandria VA: ASCD; DEST for *Plain English Report Card* found at http://.dest.gov.ministers/nelson/may05/reportcard_001_a4.pdf Author DEST, Publ. 2005; Dr. Kevin Donnelly, Director Education Strategies, for extracts: Why our greatest story is just not being told, *The Australian* 28 January 2006 and Lets go back to basics beginning with the Three R's, *The Australian* 31 January 2006, Author, K. Donnelly; Harper Collins for extract from Dr. Seuss *Hooray for Deffndoofer Day!* By Geisel, T.S. Prelutkys, J & Smith, L, Published, London, Harper Collins; Ministerial Council on Education, Employment, Training and Youth Affairs (MCEETYA) for extract from 1999 Adelaide declaration on National goals for schooling in the twenty-first century pp.1-5, available at http://www.mceetya.edu.au/nationalgoals/; Phi Delta Kappa International, for extract from *Inside the Black Box* by Paul Black, Dylan William, Phi Delta Kappa Bloomington, Oct 1998 Vol. 80. Iss2, pg 139.

Every attempt has been made to trace and acknowledge copyright holders. Where the attempt has been unsuccessful, the publisher welcomes information that would redress the situation.

ABOUT THE AUTHORS

Susan Groundwater-Smith is currently an Honorary Professor at the University of Sydney, where she co-directs the Centre for Practitioner Research. She is also an Adjunct Professor of Education at the University of Technology, Sydney and at the Liverpool Hope University in the United Kingdom. Her professional background includes 15 years of classroom practice, working in both Victoria and New South Wales. Susan has taught in schools for intellectually disabled children, in a school for young female offenders, mainstream primary classes and classes for gifted and talented students. She has worked in socioeconomically disadvantaged schools as well as those catering for economically privileged families. Each appointment presented its own challenges and was enormously rewarding.

In her work over the past 25 years at various universities, Susan has strongly encouraged teachers to act as researchers of their own practice. She has supported this work in primary and secondary schools in a number of Australian states and territories. Susan is a member of the Coalition of Knowledge Building Schools, established in Sydney, whose purpose is to share school-based research practices. Susan's aspiration for teachers is that they 'walk tall', proud to be members of a profession that has such a profound impact upon all of our lives.

Jane Mitchell is a senior lecturer in the Faculty of Education at Monash University. She began her teaching career as a history teacher in Years 7–10 high schools. This initial experience sparked a longstanding interest in developing pedagogical practices that engage young adolescents. For the past 15 years, Jane has worked as a teacher educator in universities in New South Wales, Queensland, Victoria and the Australian Capital Territory. She has worked in teacher-education programs that specifically focus on the Middle Years and has a keen interest in aligning school reform and teacher-education reform in the Middle Years.

Nicole Mockler is an education consultant with over 10 years' experience leading learning in schools. From 1999 to 2004, Nicole worked at Loreto Normanhurst, where she contributed to the conceptualisation and implementation of major reform in the Middle Years. Nicole now works with teachers and schools across the government, Catholic and independent sectors, predominantly in the areas of pedagogy and curriculum reform, educational change and leadership, and professional learning and development.

Nicole is undertaking a PhD in Education at the University of Sydney, where she also works with Susan Groundwater-Smith in the Centre for Practitioner Research.

LEARNING IN THE MIDDLE YEARS

Pt 1

1

ADOLESCENT LEARNERS: SOCIAL AND PSYCHOLOGICAL CONTEXTS OF SCHOOLING

Education either functions as an instrument that is used to facilitate integration of the younger generation into the logic of the present system and bring about conformity to it, *or* it becomes 'the practice of freedom', the means by which men and women deal critically and creatively with reality and discover how to participate in the transformation of their world (Shaull 1970: 16).

INTRODUCTION

When we write of the Middle Years of schooling – whether about curriculum, structures, student achievement or teaching standards – we do so within a sociopolitical context. We ask you to think about the issues and how these influence what is happening in our schools. This chapter opens with what we have called the 'problem field' in that it sets out matters associated more generally with the sociopolitical context of education and then progresses to the cultural context of schooling and the implications of social geography. It opens up the various issues associated specifically with adolescence and how middle school arrangements have been made to address such issues. It concludes with two case studies that give you scope to debate these issues within the policies and practices of your particular state or territory.

Key questions guiding this chapter are:

1   What contextual issues are focusing interest on the Middle Years?
2   How can we understand adolescent learners in current social contexts?
3   How can schools engage adolescent learners?

THE PROBLEM FIELD

THE SOCIOPOLITICAL CONTEXT OF EDUCATION

While we cannot hope to do justice to the complex educational arrangements in Australia's states and territories, we have selected this example as an illustration of the various social and political forces at work in education. On the eve of Australia Day 2006, the prime minister, John Howard (2006), gave a speech to the National Press Club entitled 'A sense of balance: the Australian achievement in 2006'. Among other things, the prime minister called for 'a root and branch renewal of the teaching of Australian history in our schools'. Turning to the lower secondary and primary school curriculum, Howard asserted that history is taught 'without any sense of structured narrative, replaced by a fragmented stew of "themes" and "issues"'. Curiously, he placed the arrival of the First Fleet in the 19th century, which might suggest that 'accuracy' should also be given credence! Only days before the prime minister's speech, the premier of New South Wales announced the creation of 'Australian values' units in public primary schools that would promote the teaching of 'respect and responsibility' to the state's youth. He went on to tell a gathering at government house that he saw the five 'Rs' – reading, writing, arithmetic, respect and responsibility – as pillars of school policy (Clennell 2006). Both the prime minister's and the premier's pronouncements were made in response to the Cronulla beach riots and their aftermath. The riots suggested that serious racism lies beneath a veneer of espoused multiculturalism.

There are many forces at work when it comes to determining what should go into the school curriculum. Of course, examples such as those above lose their currency over time. You may identify a relevant sociopolitical issue of the day and discuss its impact on education practices.

Each Australian state and territory has independent statutory boards and/or authorities that set out the knowledge, understanding, skills, values and attitudes that students are expected to acquire. For example, the Boards of Studies in NSW and in the Northern Territory set out what is required for all K–12 students, as does the Curriculum Council of Western Australia, the Office of Curriculum, Leadership and Learning in Tasmania and the Queensland Studies Authority. These bodies are independent of government, which, of course, has representation; however, they cannot be said to be entirely free from government influence and pressure. In the examples cited above, the concern was to create social cohesion whether through teaching history in a particular way or singing the national anthem at school assemblies. In other contexts, and on other occasions, governments have sought to influence decisions on assessment and reporting, school management and staffing, equity funding arrangements, de-zoning schools, providing services to special needs students, and so on.

In turn governments are influenced by how popular opinion is swinging about such matters. It is not only the case that they are accountable to the electorate, but also it is a concern to them that the electorate approves of their policies and practices. It is not unusual following an event such as a dog attack, or trends in obesity or road accidents, for the media to call upon governments to amplify the school curriculum in order to address the particular challenge.

PROVOCATION: HOW MANY STAKEHOLDERS?

Think about the range of stakeholders and opinion-makers in Australian education.
1   Who are the principal stakeholders?

2   What are their interests?

3   Where are their opinions about what should be studied and how it should be studied coming from?

4   Is there a hierarchy of stakeholders? Who is at the top and who is at the bottom and why?

THE CULTURAL CONTEXT OF SCHOOLING

Such social and political influences, as previously discussed, take place in a cultural context. Australian culture is complex and continually evolving. Culture is created by the times in which it exists. As Dennett put it in his lecture 'The evolution of culture': 'Consider a cultural inventory of some culture at some time, say 1900AD. It should include all the languages, practices, ceremonies, edifices, methods, tools, myths, music, art, and so forth, that compose that culture. Over time, that inventory changes' (1999: 1).

Imagine Australia in 1901 when it became a Commonwealth. How were Indigenous people regarded? What were the relations between Catholics and Protestants? What kind of architecture dominated the landscape? How was communication handled, internally and internationally? What were the major secondary industries and the processes used in manufacturing? What legal punishments were meted out to the guilty? If you looked at newspaper archives of the day, you would have a sense of a very different Australia to the one today.

Schooling happens within cultural contexts. Importantly, culture also contributes to the ways that we know and understand our students. An ongoing debate relates to the interaction between the environment, both physical and cultural, and what is inherited – the 'nature versus nurture' debate. In an often-quoted discussion of human nature, Wilson proposed that 'genes hold culture on a leash. The leash is very long, but inevitably values will be constrained in accordance with their effects on the human gene pool' (1978: 167). Today, the discussion is far more fluid – the interactions between environment and inheritance are so complex and recursive that it makes for great difficulty to separate the two. Nonetheless, it is important that we understand that the young people with whom we work are shaped by these complex interactions. Later in this chapter, we discuss how the nature of adolescent learning rests upon how we construct and understand adolescence.

A range of theories regarding the definition of adolescence, and indeed childhood itself as a distinct developmental phase, have been proposed over the past century. Some consider adolescence in relation to psychological and physical development and we discuss this further; others have taken an anthropological view and argued that different societies create very different cultural contexts in which childhood and adolescence emerge. This is somewhat controversial. Margaret Mead's *Coming of Age in Samoa* (1928), a classic text in its day, suggested that in a less materialistic and more relaxed society adolescence was a period of continuity and smooth transition to adulthood. Her view has not gone unchallenged and it is important to be aware that theories are most often in a state of change – they are not fixed and immutable. Mead's anthropological thesis has been significantly criticised by such Australian anthropologists as Derek Freeman (1983, 1999), who argued that basic human development transcends culture. Yet other theorists argued that the life stages of childhood and adolescence emerged as distinctive with the advent of industrialisation.

A somewhat divergent view was that of cultural theorist Neil Postman (1982). The invention of the printing press in the Middle Ages, according to Postman, was the beginning of the establishment of childhood in that it created a new symbolic world that required a new conception of adulthood – which excluded children, as reading skills were not easily attained by children. Paradoxically, more recently, Postman saw childhood again being erased, as young people became the subjects of remorseless advertising and consumerism. Now emerging is a new generation with access to multiple and converging technologies that allow for individuation and self-definition and the formation of private relationships with peer groups via electronic communication largely invisible to adults (Larson 1995). Think about how young people use their mobile phones to understand this relationship-building in action.

Whatever the nature of interaction between culture and inheritance there is no question that it is complex and teachers of students in the Middle Years need to be cognisant of it. You need to be highly attuned to diversity within and between groups of young people. All too often, issues related to the major three prongs of schooling – curriculum, pedagogy and assessment – are undifferentiated. It is as if the needs of Australian schoolchildren do not vary across the states and territories that provide their education.

Throughout this book we contextualise the various case studies presented to you. We recognise that a number of our case studies are drawn from the eastern states and territories, because we wished to use studies that had been a part of our own research. They are not manufactured but have been drawn from our own experiences with all of their attendant challenges and dilemmas. With this in mind, we argue that it is increasingly recognised that social geography deserves serious attention.

THE IMPLICATIONS OF SOCIAL GEOGRAPHY

Our being and becoming rests, in part, on where we have been and what made that place and space. Our social histories and our social geographies are inextricably linked. Tuan describes place as 'humanized space' (2002: xii). He sees people as having an emotional bond to the space that they occupy and then transform into place. Place can be seen as a container of relationships. It is organic and dynamic, constantly building. Living in Broome or Port Pirie is not the same as living in Hobart; going to school in a Northern Territory outstation in the wet is not the same experience as attending a junior high school in Canberra in the middle of winter.

While not arguing for determinism, it is clear that place is a critical element in our lives, our development, our values and our experiences. So why does there seem to be a silence about place when discussing policies and practices in education? And why in studies of education is place given little attention other than in references to context, which tends to be local and particular?

When we read or talk about schooling all too often we create an image of sameness. Schools seem not to vary from suburb to suburb, city to city, region to region, state to state. We appear not to attend to the differences. Queensland introduces *Productive Pedagogies*; New South Wales disseminates its *Quality Teaching Discussion Paper*. Mount Isa and Cairns, Broken Hill and Rose Bay – each is assumed to fit the mould. Furthermore, large policy drivers such as skills acquisition in literacy, numeracy and ICT, and compliance training in occupational health and safety and child protection, contribute to the notion of 'one size fits all'.

PROVOCATION: PLACE AND POLICY

1   Thinking about your experience in schools so far, what do you see are some implications of 'one size fits all' educational policy?

2   What are the strengths and weaknesses of this approach?

3   Is it better to have differentiated expectations based on sociocultural factors? Who might 'win' and who might 'lose'? What would be the counterargument?

Much of this policy development arises from a view that it is more equitable and just to provide the same learning opportunities irrespective of geography, aside from some minor modifications such as to term dates for schools in harsher climates. However, there is a compelling argument to the contrary. Thomson, in drawing attention to the skewed distribution of schooling credentials as an outcome of the varying distribution of social resources through different places, notes: 'Despite a variety of different policy approaches [but not differentiated policy approaches][1] and interventions, there is compelling evidence that there has been little shift in post war Australia in the hierarchies of culture and power that produce spatially and socially distributed educational outcomes' (2000: 3).

In discussing the distribution of disadvantage in Australia, Vinson argues:

> neighbourhood effects are stronger at certain times in people's development. In particular, it seems that neighbourhoods affect life chances during early childhood and late adolescence; the very times when a just society would be most anxious to open up life opportunities to children and young people (2003a: 6).

Vinson continues on that social geography can and does contribute to intergenerational reproduction, with concentrations of joblessness and raised rates of crime and incarceration (2003a: 9). In his report *Community Adversity and Resilience*, Vinson (2003b) provides compelling data to indicate that disadvantage is cumulative and intergenerational within specific geographic locations. While he recognises that macro-level policies can and should be developed, they should be sufficiently flexible to respond, at the same time, to significant micro-level differentiation. Comparing this study to one that he undertook many years earlier, he found that there was a 0.86 correlation between the earlier and later occasions, suggesting that little had changed in the interim. Clearly, then, place is an important determinant of access to life chances.

---

1. Our insertion.

To make our case, we turn briefly to two very different communities with bleak stories: Indigenous young people in remote Australia and refugee children and adolescents. Historically, Indigenous people in rural and remote communities have had limited access to a number of different services, particularly with respect to mental health (Mitchell 2000). This is at a time when it is increasingly clear that there is a great need for such services for young people who see themselves to be isolated and removed from the experiences and benefits that are commonplace to their city counterparts. Often lacking literacy skills and living in extremely difficult circumstances, young people experiment with drugs and alcohol, and substance abuse is a commonplace response to the stressors in their lives. There may be few possibilities for local or meaningful employment in the years beyond school, which is often seen as irrelevant to their needs.

Colin Tatz (2001), an academic who has long been concerned with the educational needs of Indigenous people, argues that social disorder leads to health disorders among young people in remote communities. After looking at 43 youth suicides over a 30-month period, he believes that historical and geographic conditions have led to a fatalistic 'up you' reaction by those whose only possession is their lives. In some horrible way it is a rational response to the dilemmas that overwhelm them.

Less dramatic, but equally damaging, is the experience of refugee children and adolescents who have experienced long-term detention (Mares et al. 2002). It is reported that young people's emotional and social development are adversely affected if they are living with parents who are themselves functionally impaired as a result of depression and anxiety related to the stresses and uncertainties of being in detention.

It is clear that the experiences of these young people vary greatly from those living in affluent beachside suburbs in Sydney or in the leafy suburbs of Melbourne or Adelaide. It is true that a number of programs are funded to support communities in difficulty such as the Priority Schools Funding Program or the Indigenous Education Strategic Initiatives Program. However, because of the many ties associated with such programs, they do not accommodate the complexity of social geography. For example, if the number of socioeconomically disadvantaged or Indigenous students in a particular school falls below the designated mark, then assistance for the students is denied. Paradoxically, the community expects fairness in the distribution of funds, which many take to mean that everyone should be entitled to the same allocation. Mark Latham (1998), in an earlier guise as a public intellectual, wrote of 'downward envy': the condition whereby those who already have material and cultural assets are resentful of additional funding being allocated to those with special needs. This discussion is advanced in Chapter 2, which addresses issues of equity and diversity.

Even so, we have to also find the commonalities otherwise education systems would become paralysed in attempting to tailor policies to fit every exigency. Our intention is to recognise these commonalities while challenging you to consider contexts and their implications for the young people attending schools.

THE ADOLESCENT LEARNER

What is common to and what is different about adolescent learners? What are their needs and how do we cater for them?

> I keep picturing … Thousands of little kids, and nobody's around –
> nobody big, I mean – except me. And I'm standing on the edge of
> some crazy cliff. What I have to do, I have to catch everybody if
> they start to go over the cliff (Salinger 1951: 205–6).

Holden Caulfield, the archetypal adolescent, thus describes to Phoebe, his little sister, the picture in his mind of rescuing small children racing through a field of rye, potentially hurtling to their death. What makes the image so powerful and why is *The Catcher in the Rye* such a classic depiction of the chaotic nature of youth, not only in the United States where it is set but also across the Western world? In common with many of his peers, Holden experiences a massive growth spurt, growing six and a half inches in one year. He is noisy; he is perpetually hungry; he takes huge risks without wondering about the consequences; he is on an emotional roller-coaster; he is sexually awakening. He believes himself to be rejected; he sees himself as the ultimate diviner of phoniness; he is simultaneously compassionate and sentimental; he lives in a real and imaginary world. He is a teenager – admittedly an urban, white, middle-class male, but a teenager nonetheless.

Lest we think this a parody or an exaggeration, consider developmental psychologist Michael Carr-Gregg's analysis of the issues facing adolescents. He argues that, from the epidemiological evidence, the rates of drug use, depression, eating disorders, early onset puberty, teenage pregnancy and sexually transmitted diseases are sharply increasing. He partly attributes this to the increased cultural pressures via the mass media that have reduced the period of *latency* that previously allowed young people a kind of breathing space – or as Marcia puts it, a 'moratorium' (1980: 161) – as they make the transition from childhood to early adulthood. All this means that the psychological justification for middle schooling 'has never been stronger' (Carr-Gregg 2001: 1).

Reality shows such as *Big Brother*; large, explicit hoardings along our highways; uncensored previews of R-rated films; and pre-teen clothing for girls that emphasise their sexuality, are all facts of daily life for today's young people in Australia. Girls, and increasingly boys, in early adolescence are vulnerable to messages about their body image and whether their body is acceptable to their peers. Television-watching is a major activity for Australian youth. Becker et al. (2002) found that there is a marked link between watching television and holding a negative body image, leading ultimately to eating disorders such as anorexia nervosa or bulimia. In two South Australian studies, Hargreaves (2002) found that television advertising featured idealised thinness that negatively affected how adolescent girls see themselves. Carrington (2003) also argued that the new technologies, mass media and consumer culture are contributing to how students in the Middle Years see themselves.

DEVELOPING IDENTITY

What then is latency and what does it mean for Middle Years education? Originally a Freudian term, and later taken up by Erik Erikson, it was coined to cover the period of development when the individual develops a balance between the id (the primitive drive for food and comfort) and the ego (which assists in setting boundaries and the growth of identity). The development of identity – that is 'who one is' – is critical in this phase of development. There is a struggle to develop a sense of self and there is a preoccupation with such things as appearance and finding heroes to worship and model oneself upon. At the same time, there is a pressure to establish group identity, with some of the resulting confusion that arises from deciding where one belongs. Krause, Bochner and Duchesne (2003) see identity formation as dynamic and ongoing, but a process that is at its most intense during the adolescent years. This is in spite of the many changes that are occurring in the world in which adolescents live: 'despite sociocultural and technological change the primary task of identity formation remains central for adolescents in this millennium' (Krause, Bochner & Duchesne 2003: 81).

Erikson's theories are psychosocial: that is, they attend to the relationship between psychological development and how individuals interact with each other and their environment. His beliefs are not unchallenged: Krause, Bochner and Duchesne (2003: 77–86) suggest that the theory has its limitations, as do other such theories about life stages, with their notion of an invariant sequence of development. Some have suggested that Erikson's view of latency is implicitly gender-biased with its goals of autonomy, independence and industry, paying little attention to the positive development of relationships. Others have suggested that it is ethnocentric in its focus on individualism, not recognising the impact on identity formation of collectivist cultures such as that found among many Australian Indigenous communities (Purdie et al. 2000). We shall return to this in Chapter 2. Nonetheless, understanding latency is critical to having insight into adolescent behaviour, varied as it might be.

Latency is seen then as a time in which social and physical interaction with the environment allows young people to gather the physical and psychological resources to enable them to cope with the *Sturm und Drang* (turbulence) of adolescence. Typically, boys and girls in the last years of primary school and into the first years of secondary school are seen as more likely to form close same-sex relationships than to be interested in and distracted by the opposite sex. If, as Carr-Gregg asserts (2001, 2004), this period, which typically spanned ages seven to 11, is now being truncated, with puberty also happening earlier, it is clear that this will have a very real impact upon schools and the provisions that they make for learners in the Middle Years.

Of course, the experience of adolescence is not the same for all young people. We should be careful that we do not subscribe to a stereotype of adolescence that suggests that there is very little difference between adolescents. In a study in America, Offer, Kaiz and Albert (2002) suggested that young people raised in 'traditional' families are less likely to have a tumultuous or troubled adolescence. In this context, 'traditional' was taken to mean intact families, who were well grounded in their communities. However, some Australian families are time-poor, lacking ritual and tradition, and having high expectations of material success. A substantial number have only one live-in parent. It may be difficult to find the 'traditional' family, whether in urban areas or rural and remote communities.

As well, Krause, Bochner and Duchesne (2003) remind us that the onset of puberty itself varies. The timing of puberty affects how young people will cope with the rapid changes that are occurring in their bodies. They argue that 'early maturing boys and later maturing girls tend to fare the best' (2003: 8), since the changes manifest themselves in ways that fit the cultural definitions of what it is to look good. Early-maturing boys are seen as muscular and self-confident; late-maturing girls as slim and composed. Late-maturing boys are perceived as less masculine, while early-maturing girls are perceived as more likely to engage in sexually risky behaviour.

Responding to identity issues

None of this information is intended to generate panic. We are mindful that, on the whole, young people in Australia are in good health (with the exception of young Aboriginal and Torres Strait Islander people), although we have well-founded concerns about alcohol and drug dependence, particularly among youth living in rural and remote areas (Australian Institute of Health and Welfare 2003). Rather, this information justifies us in taking the particular needs of the adolescent learner seriously.

Indeed, the significant investment made by Australian states and territories in such initiatives as Mind Matters, a wellbeing program for school development, indicates that this is clearly the case. The program encourages schools to consider mental health issues in adolescent learners and develop an awareness of and empathy towards the social and emotional concerns that trouble young people. With its emphasis on cultural inclusiveness, and its recognition of the range of lifestyles and experiences of young people across the country, the program has had a significant impact upon participating schools (Hazell et al. 2005).

In their recent evaluation of this widely adopted program, Hazell et al. (2005) have noted that school structures and systems should be reconsidered to create an environment that is sympathetic to the needs of today's adolescents. Among the many suggested improvements are the following:

- specific periods to be set aside for pastoral care (or 'academic care')
- sound and clear behaviour management strategies
- horizontal pastoral care structures rather than vertical ones
- timetable reorganisation to reduce stress
- student counselling arrangements that respect confidentiality and privacy
- improvements in the physical environment to build a sense of safety and positive feelings about the school
- continuing development of sound peer-support programs
- increase in possibilities for student participation in leadership and decision-making in the school.

ACADEMIC CARE

We have already referred to some of the literature that discusses the particular personal and social demands on learners during adolescence. It is overwhelmingly agreed that no matter how adolescence is defined and studied, establishing identity and searching for autonomy are the central developmental tasks for the adolescent years – an autonomy that requires resilience and self-reliance. Thus we now turn to the ways that a supportive environment can assist young people to develop resilience, paying attention to gender differences and their implications.

DEVELOPING RESILIENCE IN STUDENTS

Claxton (1999) writes of resilient students as those who are characterised by a view that their learning is 'expandable', whereas 'fragile' students see ability as fixed and immutable. Schools play an important part in providing a safe and caring environment for young people as they progress through adolescence. Brown, D'Emidio-Caston and Benard (2001) believe that schools best do this by:

- having positive expectations
- providing opportunities for participation in the corporate life of the school and its governance
- developing social competence
- providing conditions for real problem-posing and problem-solving
- placing a positive value on young people
- having negotiated boundaries.

This position is echoed by McLaughlin and Byers (2001: 7), who argue that the positive development of a sense of self in the school community depends upon:

- the extent to which students are encouraged and enabled to become active participants in teaching and learning
- the inclusivity of schools

- the relationships that are fostered between staff and learners in and out of the classroom and throughout the course of the teaching and learning day.

Similarly, Nadge has indicated that pastoral care and academic progress are inextricably linked. She argues that in the enhancement of the conditions for student learning, attention needs to be paid to

> developmental, situational and organisational mechanisms in and beyond the classroom in order to assist adolescents to develop positive self esteem and feelings of well being and self efficacy through the school's academic and organisational structures and through adults' relationships with students (2005: 30).

This view has particular cogency for the Middle Years, with its focus upon learner-centredness that requires of learners that they are flexible in their thinking, are confident and are prepared to take risks with their learning.

DEALING WITH GENDER DIFFERENCES

As we have already pointed out, generalisations can be dangerous. The experiences of young people can vary greatly – much depends upon such differences as social class, ethnicity, family structures, geography and so on. As well, we must take account of gender, a proposition we have already raised in relation to body image and puberty and how adolescence is characterised. Lillico (2005) points out that boys often disengage in the critical Middle Years and the gap between them and girls can be quite marked. Quoting Steve Biddulph, who has written extensively on masculinity, he argues that 'boys learn teachers not subjects', and that for some adolescent boys school is a foreign and alien place. Research findings show that boys' literacy achievements take something of a tumble during these years (see, for example, Department of Education, Employment and Training Victoria 1999).

Studies of boys and their achievements during early adolescence tend to emphasise deficits. However, Robert Smith (2003), a music-in-schools advisor in the Northern Territory, suggests that boys bring to school many assets that are not sufficiently recognised. He writes of their prowess in playing sports and electronic games, and in roller-blading and skateboarding, and their remarkable capacities for learning and performing music. He argues that their assertiveness and risk-taking should be capitalised upon rather than countered. Describing Boys' Business, a program initiated by the Northern Territory Music School, he says that 'rather than attempting to constrain an attribute that makes males masculine, it invites boys to engage with activities that allow aggression full play in safe and affirming settings' (Smith 2003).

In addition to the concern for boys, particular attention is being paid to the needs of girls in relation to pastoral care and the social and emotional demands that adolescent girls place on each other through hidden aggression. Simmons (2004) argues on a case-by-case basis that the secret world of girls' aggression is just as harmful to peers as the aggression of boys, but is much harder to recognise. She suggests that naming the problem is an important step in addressing it. Because girls' aggression is difficult to detect, it requires a relatively high level of connectedness between those responsible for their care and the students themselves. Where there is a chasm between the two, it is likely that not only will it continue but also will develop further. It is not just an individual matter but one that is interpersonal and can be woven into the very fabric of the school.

As well, there is the ongoing phenomenon of 'downward behavioural expectations'. Younger and younger girls are expected to become increasingly aware of body shape, cosmetics, relationships with boys and the like. They are the targets of marketing campaigns, whether for clothes, mobile phones, music or films.

DEVELOPING A SUPPORTIVE ENVIRONMENT

All of this points to the need for a pastoral care policy that is embedded in the moment-to-moment transactions of the school day, rather than exclusively in allocated times involving staff with whom students have little connection. It is also important to recognise that a whole-school approach to pastoral care and the emotional and social development of students is essential. The Qualifications and Curriculum Authority (QCA 2001) in the United Kingdom suggests ten key elements for a whole-of-school approach:
- leadership, management and managing change
- policy development
- curriculum planning and resourcing
- teaching and learning
- school culture and environment
- giving students a voice
- providing student support services
- staff professional development, health and welfare
- partnerships with parents/carers and local communities
- assessing, recording and reporting students' achievements.

Later in this chapter we look at two case studies in which schools have considered ways to offer better academic care for students in the critical Middle Years through various transition strategies and emphasising the student voice in a way that is illustrative of student participation and some of the other arrangements previously discussed by Hazell et al. (2005).

We now turn to how adolescent learners engage with school. After all, it is a principal objective of schooling that students be deeply engaged in their learning so that they remain at school and continue to learn beyond school. Disengagement in secondary schooling can lead to early departure, which in turn leads to higher risk of unemployment, poverty and social exclusion (Prime Minister's Youth Pathways Action Plan Task Force 2001). Positive habits of mind that have been well established in the primary years can be derailed during the early years of secondary schooling because insufficient account has been taken of the many issues around middle schooling, as we have raised thus far.

ENGAGING STUDENTS

What is it to be engaged in one's learning? It may not go beyond procedural engagement: that is, undertaking whatever task has been assigned and not 'disturbing the waters'. It is a superficial form of engagement. We have all experienced this in some measure. Think of a time when you have been poorly motivated to undertake an assignment but know that it is required. We generally approach such work in a desultory way; we procrastinate and barely meet our own or anyone else's expectations. As someone studying teaching, this may be the exception rather than the rule but for some students this is the norm – they can see little point in school as it barely connects with their lives.

Munns calls for what he calls big 'E' engagement: that is, the kind of substantive engagement that takes students deep into their learning, giving them 'an emotional attachment to and a commitment to education: the belief that "school is for me"' (2004: 3). He discusses such engagement in terms of students facing significant challenges as a result of low socioeconomic status whereby they 'have historically not had the same emotional attachment and commitment to education as students from more privileged backgrounds' (2004: 2). He suggests that what is required is a significant interruption to the discourses of power so prevalent in today's classrooms. Students can come to understand the nature of powerful knowledge and how it is transacted, transcend the debilitating consequences of resistance and develop a positive sense of their own place and voice. Often it is the case that marginalised and alienated students use their energies and intelligence to oppose and resist, even when it is not in their own best interest. Clearly, Munns is concerned with students coming from more difficult material and social circumstances, but it is also true that these ideas of student engagement apply, albeit somewhat differently, among adolescent learners.

Student engagement can be defined as involving three interrelated dimensions: behavioural, affective and cognitive. In a review of literature on student engagement, Fredricks, Blumenfeld and Paris (2004) define these dimensions as behavioural, emotional and cognitive.

Behavioural engagement draws on the idea of participation, including involvement in academic and social or extracurricular activities, and is considered crucial for achieving positive academic outcomes and preventing dropping out. *Emotional* (or affective) *engagement* encompasses positive and negative reactions to teachers, classmates, academics and school, and is presumed to create ties to an institution and influence willingness to do the work. Finally, *cognitive engagement* draws on the idea of investment, incorporating thoughtfulness and willingness to exert the effort necessary to comprehend complex ideas and master difficult skills (Fredricks, Blumenfeld & Paris 2004: 60).

In their analysis of this multidimensional approach to engagement, Murray et al., focusing on the primary and middle secondary school years, see behavioural engagement as leading to visible outcomes such as completing tasks and acquiring skills; affective or emotional engagement as that whereby an individual's emotions, values and beliefs, such as enthusiasm, optimism and confidence, inform actions; and cognitive engagement as that whereby thought processes and intellectual activity, such as analysis, synthesis and persistence, contribute to meaning-making and interest (2004: 4). Murray et al. concentrate upon factors that lead to student disengagement. They report on studies about middle schooling that document how 'student achievement plateaus or actually declines during the Middle Years and that there is a decline in students' enjoyment of school' (2004: 19). They note that this pattern is consistently stronger for boys. The study suggests that this loss of momentum in academic achievement can be attributed to the lack of recognition of the developmental needs of young adolescents, the kinds of needs previously outlined. Most particularly they note that there is a failure to understand the complexity and depth of the social needs of young people in this phase of their lives.

For this reason, we have chosen to present two cases in which concern about the intersection between social needs and academic performance in the Middle Years is at the fore. The schools have sought to better understand the needs of their adolescent students in relation to their academic care and their adjustment to secondary school[2].

2. Both schools are members of the Coalition of Knowledge Building Schools. To read more about the work of the coalition and the commitment of its members to school-based inquiry and evidence-based practice, see Groundwater-Smith and Mockler (2003).

CASE STUDY 1
Rethinking academic care

Context

Independent Girls' School (IGS) is a well-established comprehensive school catering for K–12 students in metropolitan Sydney. Middle school organisation at IGS (Years 6–8), which has been developing over the past four years, has been flexible and responsive to student needs and concerns. Its current arrangements include home teachers for Year 6 students, a core team in Year 7 whose members cover two to three key learning areas (KLAs) with the same class, and a dedicated team in Year 8 for Maths, English, Science and Human Society and its Environment (HSIE).

Increasingly, students are demonstrating a sense of belonging to and identifying with the middle school as a key transition phase in their development as a student and as a young person.

As a result of a student survey, conducted in the context of a wider benchmark survey, it was found, among other things, that students were not greatly engaged by time spent in houses and in tutor groups, which were designed to provide a bridge between pastoral care and academic achievement. Nor were the students' problems sufficiently acknowledged or attended to. A series of focus groups revealed that the 'house system is neither thought to be of much relevance beyond perhaps sport, nor was the content of house time or commitment by leaders, both student and teachers, consistent across houses'. It was clear that houses were not seen as a medium for solving the girls' concerns, 'because of a lack of connection, knowledge and therefore trust'.

As well, some anxiety was expressed about the vertical arrangement of tutor groups. The original impetus for this organisational feature was that students would be assigned to one tutor with whom they could build an enduring relationship for their secondary school years, 6–12, including those spent in middle school. Staff changes, however, often meant that the desired continuity was not possible, but the vertical grouping was maintained. Many Year 6 students felt excluded by this arrangement, while some students from all middle school year groups felt less than enthusiastic about their encounters with older students – in particular those in Year 9: 'Forcing girls together arbitrarily who have little in common (including age) is clearly not working.'

In recommendations following the survey and focus groups, and in discussion with the director of pastoral care, it was determined that the pastoral care programs for middle school be revised and their implementation evaluated. In her proposal for a middle school pastoral care framework, the head of middle school indicated that it should:

- build belonging
- nurture resilience
- make connections
- enable safe risk-taking
- value individuals as well as community.

  The proposed structure was to be as follows:
- Year 6 – four home-room teachers who would be mentors for the students in their class
- Year 7 – six core teachers who would be mentors for the students in their class
- Year 8 – seven core subject teachers who teach only Year 8 and would be mentors for one of their Year 8 classes.

  One leading teacher would be appointed for each year with the responsibility for supporting mentors in the implementation of the program. There also would be a middle school pastoral care coordinator who would be a member of the middle-school team and liaise with the director of pastoral care and the head of the middle school. Mentors would take responsibility for pastoral care by meeting students at the beginning of each day and for one full period per week. House time would be halved.

The proposed framework was implemented for the first time in 2004. While it was premature to evaluate its effectiveness after only a short period of time, it was seen as important that attention should be paid to initial concerns in order that the program go forward in an orderly and well-informed fashion. Consequently a formative evaluation was planned.

Formative evaluation

In order to investigate the planning, motivation, resourcing, monitoring and supporting learning within a pastoral care context, all key stakeholders were consulted. The following strategies were employed.

- *Students*: A student research advisory group was convened comprising students from each year group. They undertook a research workshop with the evaluator and contributed questions to a questionnaire to be delivered to all middle school students. Subsequently they met to consider the student responses and to illuminate them.
- *Teachers*: All teachers undertook a taped 'self-interview' addressing key questions: How are things now? How might things be? How should things become? They were given no longer than ten minutes to respond. The evaluator abstracted key issues and treated them anonymously.
- *Parents and caregivers*: In consultation with leading teachers, scenarios were developed for discussion and debate. Eight parents met to discuss the scenarios and were provided with a narrative account of the meeting that they endorsed as a form of membership check.
- *Executive*: Interviews were conducted with the director of pastoral care and the school principal. The head of middle school and the pastoral care team of the middle school were consulted throughout the evaluation.

A question common to all groups was that posed by Hamblin: 'How would the school be different if pastoral care were taken away?' (1989: 35)

Results

A number of common themes emerged from the full data set. Each of these was discussed with the pastoral care team, who ratified the interpretations made by the evaluator. The themes covered were connectedness, communication, accessibility, transition, reporting to parents, mentor training, relationship to house system, Big Sister program, school organisation, curriculum improvement and a school without pastoral care. This extract from the larger report, which ran to over 100 pages, only focuses on the first two and the last of these themes.

Connectedness

A major benefit perceived by teachers and students alike was that of the possibility of connecting learning in the key learning areas to academic and pastoral care.

In their self-interviews, mentor teachers saw the program to be working well, in particular for younger girls who were accustoming themselves to a new system and environment. Mentors suggested that a greater rapport was being developed and that increased contact with students allowed for issues to be quickly identified and dealt with.

All student groups also identified connectedness as a benefit. The new system allowed them to know their mentor better and, in turn, the mentor to know the students: 'We can talk to her about anything, she helps if we need help', 'You can bond with your mentor and she can get to know you'. Several girls referred to their mentor being their core teacher and that this ensured that they did not have a homework overload: 'They know what homework and assignments you have and don't give you too much.'

All stakeholders were sensitive to the need for strong links between teaching and learning, the curriculum, and academic and pastoral care. It was seen that these links were best provided through the mentoring process in which mentors were those who taught the students in key learning areas. Nonetheless, it was clear that it was not possible at that time to staff the mentoring program with middle school core subject teachers. This was keenly felt by the students whose mentors were not their core subject teachers. Equally, teachers perceived that such a link was highly desirable.

This connectedness anchored students and gave them opportunities to bond effectively with their middle school teachers and their peers. The environment was seen as one that nurtured and reinforced students' sense of belonging and identity. However, the notion of connectedness did not refer exclusively to the middle school, but also to being a member of the whole IGS family. The student advisory group suggested that the best solution was to have a network of people 'ready to help', including core teachers, mentor teachers (when they were not the same) and house tutors.

Communication

All groups saw the possibilities for enhanced communication with the newly evolving mentor system. Year 8 students' comments were helpful as students from this cohort had the experience of the former pastoral care arrangements: 'Everyone gets a SAY about what they want compared to house time when all we do is talk about house stuff', 'It allows us to be up to date with notices etc. I've also found personally it has helped me to be more organised'.

For some parents, however, there was still confusion resulting from them also having to make the transition. Parents were not entirely clear about the mentors who were not teaching in core areas and whether there were still points of contact beyond the daily roll call and assigned mentor time. Generally, they were affirming of the intended relationship between mentors and students and the fact that, as a one-year relationship, it was possible to deal with clashes if and when they occurred.

They believed the new program was a further demonstration of the school's commitment to its younger students in the early years of secondary schooling. They felt that there was a *bona fide* curriculum in human skills and that 'if a child is having a problem there is someone who can be found and can help'. Finding the mentor was quite critical in that, in the past, tutors were not always easily available to students in times of need.

A school without pastoral care

In responding to the question what would IGS be like if pastoral care were taken away, teachers, students, parents and the executive were all firm that it was the very core of the school's business: 'I would hate to see it taken away. I have worked in schools where there was no clearly structured program. While class teachers do address human skills and values it needs a whole school approach. If the school is saying that "we are looking at the whole person as part of the philosophy of transforming learning" then we need to address not just the academic needs but the social and emotional needs across the board. It needs explicit teaching and integration at one and the same time.'

These views were echoed by the director of pastoral care and the school principal. For example, the director of pastoral care responded, 'I'd hate to think!' She indicated that the program as it had existed 'has generally turned out confident young women; now it has to develop confident and *resilient* young women'.

DISCUSSION STARTERS

This case study is a digest of some of the strategies used to inquire into academic care in the Middle Years at IGS and the results. If you were to generate four to five recommendations for the next steps to be taken by the school, what would they be and on what grounds would you argue for these recommendations?

CASE STUDY 2
Learning in teams

Context

Inner West Girls' High School (IWGHS) is a comprehensive secondary school, located in Sydney's inner west, meeting the needs of students from a diverse range of cultural and language backgrounds with the majority of Muslim Lebanese extraction, some of Turkish origin, and a number from the Pacific islands and South-East Asia. Many of the students are the second or third generation born in Australia.

Following an executive conference held in August 1994, the school determined to focus upon the transition experiences of girls coming into Year 7. It was perceived that this was a time when students were required to adjust to the changing environment of a secondary school where they often knew few of their peers and no longer were in the care of a home teacher who knew them well. It was also a period, educationally, when there was a growing focus upon the Middle Years and the attendant demands made on young people.

In the early 1990s there was also increased attention paid to the 'key competencies' that learners needed to take from school into the workforce. While the focus was on the later years of schooling, it was seen that the generic competencies could form the foundation for teaching and learning in the Middle Years. The competencies were:

1   collecting, analysing and organising information
2   communicating ideas and information
3   planning and organising activities
4   working with others and in teams
5   using mathematical ideas and techniques
6   solving problems
7   using technology (Mayer 1992: 5).

The competencies were thought to have value for all young people regardless of the post-compulsory pathway that they might take in later years. They applied across the range of key learning areas and were able to be developed in a wide variety of settings. Essentially they applied to the capacity to complete a task and were significant for student engagement.

In the context of discussions regarding middle schooling and the generation of key competencies, the decision was made to adopt a 'teams approach' to both teaching and learning in the Middle Years at the school. In its first year, 1995, the approach applied to Year 7 only, but following an extensive evaluation, it was decided to extend it to Year 8.

The original proposal embodied both students and their teachers working in teams. In the latter case, teaching teams were expected to link with the welfare team and to have an overall grasp of student wellbeing. Student teams were formed to embody cultural diversity, a variety of primary school backgrounds and a range of intellectual ability. Teaching teams were developed for each class in Year 7 and Year 8 with the teachers of English, Maths, Science and HSIE having one timetabled period each week for a team meeting.

In 2005 it was ten years since the initial innovation was implemented. Many teachers currently working at IWGHS have joined the staff in recent years and, while they may have had some induction into the teams approach and its underpinning philosophy, they are not entirely clear as to the approach's purpose or value. It was decided that it was timely to revisit the structure and function of both student and teaching teams.

Evaluation design

A 'layered' approach to the evaluation was decided upon. Qualitative responses would be obtained through focus group discussions, the results of which would be 'tested' via a questionnaire. Both students' and teachers' voices would be included.

Students

Twenty-four Year 10 students met with the research consultant, with two members of IWGHS staff acting as observers. The students were trained in conducting focus groups, following the same 'question route' that would be taken with younger girls. Working in teams of three, the Year 10 students conducted focus groups with Years 7 and 8. Altogether, they presented 19 reports representing the views of 100 students to the research consultant. At the conclusion to the focus groups, each participant completed a follow-up questionnaire that indicated the extent to which they believed that their views had been heard. They also, individually, were able to suggest any further questions that they might have been asked and to provide a 'message to their teachers'.

Following an analysis of the student responses, a 20-item questionnaire followed by three scenarios were completed by all Years 7, 8 and 10 students. The questionnaire was analysed by a Year 10 Business Studies class; the scenarios were dealt with by the research consultant.

Staff

The research consultant conducted focus group interviews with all available teachers and ancillary staff [3] over a three-day period. A consolidated report was prepared for each of these days and returned to participants for a membership check. A 20-item questionnaire was subsequently developed and distributed to staff. Twenty-nine members of staff completed the survey.

Results

Students

Overall, students could see the merits of working in teams, particularly in Year 7. The structure provided opportunities for them to make friends and adjust to the new environment: 'When I first came I thought I would be all by myself but then when I was put into a team, the students in my team helped me with my work, showed me around the school and even let me sit with them. Now my team mates are my best friends' (or as another student put it, 'my best, best, best friends'). All the same, a minority of Year 7 students strongly disagreed that the teams assisted in their adjustment: 'When I first came to this school I was a little embarrassed, but I found a lot of friends than the team I was sitting next to. So what I'm trying to say is teams suck. TEAMS ARE NOTHING BUT TROUBLE.'

---

3. Ancillary staff included teachers' aides (special needs) and community liaison officers.

While a majority, by a narrow margin, of Year 8 students still agreed that teams assisted them to meet others and work with them, there was an increase in those who preferred change: 'I felt it was boring, putting us in team. I like it when I am not in a team because you learn more better without a team. Please do not put me in a team again. Thankyou for your understanding.'

Year 10 students looked back on their team experience in positive terms, particularly when it came to forming friendships: 'I felt nervous and I needed a friend to help me settle in. Being in teams definitely helps to gain long term friendships.' Again, for a small minority it was not such a good experience: 'Yes, I did meet a friend but did not like the others. They were rude, loud and didn't care about anyone but themselves. Sometimes they would make the group leave you out.'

Most students could articulate how their peers assisted in their learning but recognised that undoubtedly there were stresses associated with working in teams. Some of these arose from groups in which a particular member was disruptive and uncooperative. There were concerns that teams were held accountable for what was the behaviour of only one member. There also was a concern that, at times, students were too reliant on one team member – '[you're] expecting someone else to come up with the answer' – and that some did not make a fair contribution to the team's effort.

The matter of reliance became particularly evident when it came to undertaking individual tests and the students were expected to work independently: 'I mostly rely on my team to help me but when we do have tests I sit clueless because I'm used to asking my team' (Year 8). Moving up through the school, there was an increasing trend for students to see this as a problem: 'I found that when a teacher is teaching and I didn't understand, so I turned to my team and they helped me heaps, but when it came to an exam I couldn't work on my own because I couldn't understand the question' (Year 10). In some cases there was some pressure for more-able students to provide answers to others: 'Some team members get very angry if when you are doing a tests and you don't give them answers.'

There was a great deal of agreement that, even given the benefits of teams, two years was too long for the teams to work together. Students indicated that they would like more flexibility in the arrangements, with opportunities to work in pairs or alone or even have the teams re-formed after a period of time.

The results of the questionnaires were quite mixed. On one hand, it was clear that students felt that teams gave them a chance to work with others, share ideas, assist with communication, learn about other cultures, provide understandable explanations, and be a source of motivation. On the other hand, they found that teams could be distracting and disturb their concentration, and that they wanted to work alone sometimes. There was a tendency to become too dependent on each other. They wanted a chance to get to know each other before being put into a team, and to be able to change teams and get assistance in dealing with difficulties within the team.

It was strongly agreed that there was too much competition between teams. In terms of teaching and learning students wanted to have more fun, more hands-on activities in class and clearer explanations from their teachers. Finally, overall, they wished to continue with teams.

Staff

Focus groups: Like the students, the staff could see both the merits and the difficulties of a teams approach. For many, especially those relatively new to the school, the rationale for the approach was unclear, although they could see its potential contribution to supporting student learning through cooperation and communication. If the approach was to continue then it would be important to revisit the basis of the innovation and provide sustained induction and professional development.

Teachers who were involved in developing the approach over a number of years commented upon it as an effective behaviour management strategy in that, following its implementation, there was a reduction in conflict among and between students. A key staff member who assisted in student conflict resolution contributed to the effective implementation of the approach in its early days. This specific support had not been available for some time.

There was a view that there should be greater flexibility in applying the approach, either in response to the demands of a particular key learning area or the abilities of the given students.

Some teachers were concerned that when applying the teams approach to professional learning there was a lack of clarity about what was intended. As well, there was a question of equity in that the resources invested in release time for teams privileged some teachers and marginalised others. For some, team business had become 'secret business'. While there was some ambivalence and uncertainty, it did seem that the merits of the approach outweighed its disadvantages, but that it was time to renew and refresh the approach.

Survey: From the focus group discussions, a 20-item survey was distributed to all staff. Twenty-nine members of staff returned the survey. The results were quite mixed with responses equally distributed across the range. However, there was clear agreement that:

- The school must renew the teams approach if it is to continue.
- Teachers needed more flexibility in applying the teams approach.
- The teams approach was too inconsistently applied to make it a worthwhile strategy.
- Students needed better preparation in working in teams effectively.
- Teachers needed support in developing sound strategies for teaching teams rather than individual students.
- The best thing would be to keep teams but rethink the approach.

Recommendations

The overall recommendations were:

1 The teams approach should be implemented in Year 7 as a comprehensive and appropriately supported school policy.
2 Skills development, with respect to working effectively in teams for both teachers and students in Year 7, should be systematically provided such that the approach can be implemented with a high degree of fidelity.
3 Teacher teams should be inclusive of teachers of the core units in Year 7, as well as ancillary staff who contribute to student learning in Year 7.
4 Minutes of team meetings should continue to be posted on the school intranet for purposes of transparency and as a contribution to overall professional learning for teachers.
5 There should be two teacher-team meetings per year in which all Year 7 teacher teams come together to analyse the effectiveness of the adopted strategies.
6 Teachers new to the school should be inducted into the teams approach, its purpose and its development.
7 A staffing arrangement should allow for the mentoring and support of Year 7 teachers in developing quality learning in the context of teams, with some thought given to appointing teachers with primary teaching experience.
8 Consideration should be given to a program of transition for students moving from Year 7 to Year 8.
9 All staff should be committed to supporting the Year 7 program.
10 Students and teachers should produce a charter for teaching and learning to which all are committed to be displayed in every classroom.

DISCUSSION STARTERS

Here is very different case of how a school designed conditions of student learning in the Middle Years. Many of the recommendations cited above are structural; however, referring to Recommendations 1, 2, 6 and 10, what do you consider the most difficult constraints the school will face in implementing them? (In the case of Recommendation 6 you could consider how you would want the induction program to run if you were a teacher-education student in a professional placement at the school, or a teacher new to the school.)

CONCLUSION

In this chapter we have focused primarily upon the needs of the adolescent learner in terms of what it is to be a young person growing up in a rapidly changing world mediated by cultural practices that make more and more demands of them. We have discussed the concerns for students during this stage of their lives and how they can remain substantively engaged in their schooling. We have recognised that adolescence is itself a contested term. We have considered some of the issues surrounding resilience and how schools can provide for, stimulate and nurture students as they transit early adolescence and learn about themselves.

Holden Caulfield, JD Salinger's teenager growing up in 1950s New York, embodies the very core of adolescence through his odd and erratic behaviour. In *The Catcher in the Rye* we are taxed to think about society's attitude and response to young people and how they understand their experiences. In particular, the book draws our attention to the capacity of young people to detect what is 'phony' in an increasingly materialistic and corrupting world. Now, over half a century later, the journey of Holden still rings true. What is different is the desire for schools and the broader community to place a greater value on the adolescent experience and to develop structures and strategies that will honour young people while still also challenging them.

If the pedagogy of the Middle Years is to be of the transformative kind referred to in the preface to this book, it will need not only to focus upon transforming teaching and learning but also upon assisting us to rethink what it is to be an adolescent. It needs to connect teaching and learning to the many and diverse biographies of the students who are occupying a world very different to those that their teachers grew up in. An adolescent Indigenous student living in a remote community in the Northern Territory will experience growth and change very differently to a 14-year-old girl living in one of Perth's leafier suburbs. She, in turn, may share much with her gender and age group living in a small Tasmanian community or a mining town in New South Wales, but features of her life will be hers and hers alone. In the next chapter we shall be particularly concerned with how curriculum reform can contribute to these multiple foci.

References

Australian Institute of Health and Welfare (2003) *Young People: Their Health and Wellbeing 2003.* AIHW cat. no. PHE 50. Canberra: Australian Institute of Health and Welfare.

Becker, A. et al. (2002) 'Eating behaviours and attitudes following prolonged exposure to TV'. *British Journal of Psychiatry,* 180 (June), 509–14.

Brown, J., D'Emidio-Caston, M. & Benard, B. (2001) *Resilience Education.* Thousand Oaks, CA: Corwin Press.

Carr-Gregg, M. (2001) Keynote address to the Middle Years of Schooling Association annual conference, Brisbane, 26 May.

Carr-Gregg, M. (2004) 'The new adolescent'. *The Age,* 30 April.

Carrington, V. (2003) 'Mid-term review: the Middle Years of schooling'. *Curriculum Perspectives,* 24, 30–41.

Claxton, G. (1999) *Wise Up.* London, UK: Bloomsbury.

Clennell, A. (2006) 'Teachers scorn anthem idea of schools'. *Sydney Morning Herald,* 23 January. Accessed 27 January 2006 from www.smh.com.au/news/national/teachers-scorn-anthem-idea-for-schools/2006/01/22/1137864809572.html.

Dennett, D. (1999) The evolution of culture. The Charles Simonyi Lecture, Oxford University, Oxford, UK, 17 February.

Department of Education, Employment and Training Victoria (1999) *The Middle Years: A Guide for Strategic Action.* Melbourne: Department of Education, Employment and Training.

Fredricks, J., Blumenfeld, P. & Paris, A. (2004) 'School engagement: Potential of the concept, state of the evidence'. *Review of Educational Research,* 74(1), 59–109, American Educational Research Association.

Freeman, D. (1983) *Margaret Mead and Samoa: The Making and Unmaking of an Anthropological Myth.* Cambridge, MA: Harvard University Press.

Freeman, D. (1999) *The Fateful Hoaxing of Margaret Mead: A Historical Analysis of Her Samoan Research.* Boulder, CO: Westview Press.

Groundwater-Smith, S. & Mockler, N. (2003) Holding a mirror to professional learning. Paper presented to the Annual Conference of the Australian Association for Research in Education and the New Zealand Association for Research in Education, Auckland, 29 November – 3 December.

Hamblin D. (1989) *Staff Development for Pastoral Care.* Oxford, UK: Blackwells.

Hargreaves, D. (2002) 'Adolescent body image suffers from media images of the impossibly thin'. *Flinders Journal,* 13(9), 10–23, Flinders University, SA.

Hazell, R., Vincent, K., Greenhalgh, S., Robson, T. & O'Neill, D. (2005) *Evaluation of Mind Matters. 8th Interim Report 1/7/2004–31/1/2005.* Report to the Australian Principals Association's Professional Development Council and the Evaluation Reference Group. Newcastle: Hunter Institute of Mental Health.

Howard, J. (2006) 'A sense of balance: the Australian achievement in 2006'. Address to the National Press Club, Great Hall, Parliament House, Canberra. Accessed 27 January 2006 from www.pm.gov.au/news/speeches/speech1754.html.

Krause, K., Bochner, S. & Duchesne, S. (2003) *Educational Psychology for Learning and Teaching.* Melbourne: Thomson.

Larson, R. (1995) 'Secrets in the bedroom: Adolescents' private use of media'. *Journal of Youth and Adolescence,* 24(5), 535–50.

Latham, M. (1998) *Civilising Global Capital.* Sydney: Allen & Unwin.

Lillico, I. (2005) Learning in the Middle Years. Keynote address. *Middle Years Conference, 2005 – Resilience, Engagement, Success,* 5–6 October, Sydney.

McLaughlin, C. & Byers, R. (2001) *Personal and Social Development for All.* London, UK: David Fulton.

Marcia, J. (1980) 'Identity in adolescence', in J. Adelson (ed.) *Handbook of Adolescent Psychology,* 5th edn. New York, NY: Wiley, 159–87.

Mares, S., Newman, L., Dudley, M. & Gale, F. (2002) 'Seeking refuge, losing hope: parents and children in immigration detention'. *Australas Psychiatry,* 10, 91–6.

Mayer, E. (chair) (1992) *Report of the Committee to Advise the Australian*

Education Council and Ministers of Vocational Education, Employment and Training on Employment-Related Key Competencies for Post Compulsory Education and Training, September, Carlton South: Australian Education Council.

Mead, M. (1928) *Coming of Age in Samoa: A Psychological Study of Primitive Youth for Western Civilisation*. New York, NY: William Morrow.

Mitchell, J. (2000) *Evaluation report on the second year of bringing child and adolescent health services to rural communities 1998–1999*. A Rural Health Support, Education and Training (RHSET) funded project, grant no. 394, North Sydney: NSW Health Department.

Munns, G. (2004) A sense of wonder: student engagement in low SES school communities. Paper presented at the Australian Association for Research in Education Annual Conference, Melbourne, 28 November – 2 December.

Murray, S., Mitchell, J., Gale, T., Edwards, J. & Zyngier, D. (2004) *Student Disengagement from Primary Schooling: A Review of Research and Practice*. Report to the CASS Foundation. Melbourne: Centre for Childhood Studies, Faculty of Education, Monash University.

Nadge, A. (2005) 'Academic care: building resilience, building futures'. *Journal of Pastoral Care in Education*, 23(1), 28–33. The National Association for Pastoral Care in Education.

Offer, D., Kaiz, M. & Albert, D. (2002) 'Northwest study refutes "sturm und drang" theory of adolescence'. 2 December. Northwestern University, Illinois. Accessed on 12 January 2006 from www.eurekalert.org/pub_releases/2002-12/nu-nsr120202.php.

Postman, N. (1982) *The Disappearance of Childhood*. New York, NY: Delacorte Press.

Prime Minister's Youth Pathways Action Plan Task Force (2001) *Footprints to the Future*. Canberra: AusInfo.

Purdie, N., Tripcony, P., Boulton-Lewis, G., Fanshawe, J. & Gunstone, A. (2000) Positive self-identity for Indigenous students and its relationship to school outcomes. Report prepared for the Department of Education, Science and Training, Canberra. Report 7/2000.

QCA (2001) *Personal, Social and Health Education and Citizenship*. London: Qualifications and Curriculum Authority, Department for Education and Skills.

Salinger, J.D. (1951) *The Catcher in the Rye*. London, UK: Hamish Hamilton.

Shaull, R. (1970) Foreword in P. Freire, *Pedagogy of the Oppressed*. London, UK: Penguin.

Simmons, R. (2004) *Odd Girl Out: The Hidden Culture of Aggression in Girls*. Melbourne: Schwartz.

Smith, R. (2003) 'Boys are okay'. *EQ Australia*, Winter, Curriculum Corporation. Accessed 14 October 2006 from www.curriculum.edu.au/eq/archive/winter2003/html/article_02.shtml.

Tatz, C. (2001) 'Aboriginal youth suicide'. *The Health Report*. Monday 6 August. Radio National, ABC.

Thomson, P. (2000) Young people: risks and/or assets. Paper presented to the NSW Full Service Schools Expo, *Working Together, Reducing the Risk*, Sydney University, 3–6 December.

Tuan, Yi-Fu (2002) 'Foreword', in K. Olwig, *Landscape, Nature and the Body Politic*. Madison, WI: University of Wisconsin Press.

Vinson, T. (2003a) *Black Holes of Entrenched Disadvantage in Australia*. 10 November. International Social Service – Australian Branch. Accessed on 20 January 2006 from www.iss.org.au/media/pdfs/black_hole_address.pdf.

Vinson, T. (2003b) *Community Adversity and Resilience*. Melbourne: The Ignatius Centre for Social Policy and Research.

Wilson, E. (1978) *On Human Nature*. Cambridge, MA: Harvard University Press.

2

YOUNG PEOPLE: IDENTITY, DIVERSITY AND INCLUSION

How do they as adolescents reconcile who they are within a culture of a school where sameness is assumed yet great differences also exist? (Tsolidis 2006: 56)

INTRODUCTION

This chapter is about differences between young people and how differences relate to schooling. Discussion concerned with the Middle Years, middle schools and middle schooling often focuses on the similarities between young people. Age and stages of social, psychological and physical development underpin these similarities. However, as we discussed in Chapter 1, age and stage of development intersect with other aspects of background, culture and identity to create considerable differences between young people both as individuals and as members of groups. Think, for example, about the differences between young male students and young female students, between young people from the city and from the country, between young people from diverse cultural backgrounds. Go one step further and think of the differences between young females in rural areas and young females in urban areas, or young male 'computer geeks' and young male 'sports jocks'. In each case we are creating and refining identity categories. What do these identities and differences mean in the context of schooling? What do they mean for students' access to, experience of and outcomes from schooling? What do they mean within particular school and classroom cultures? The way that similarities and differences between students are constructed and understood has significant ramifications for school organisation, pedagogical practices and students' engagement with school.

Within school contexts some differences between students matter more than others. They matter because the differences can underpin school and classroom practices that include some and exclude others, engage some and disengage others and advantage some and disadvantage others. Here, we cannot examine in detail all aspects of how these differences are constructed and played out in schools. Instead we focus on student differences pertaining to gender, social class, Aboriginality, ethnicity and location. Understanding these important differences is crucial for educators, particularly given the rapidly changing, diverse and complex social geography, as described in Chapter 1 and elaborated on in this chapter.

Key questions guiding this chapter are:

1   What are key social patterns underpinning similarities and differences between young people?
2   What role does school play in creating similarities and differences between young people?
3   How can school and teaching practices be inclusive of student diversity and difference?

YOUR EXPERIENCE OF SCHOOLING

PROVOCATION: PATTERNS IN YOUR EXPERIENCE OF SCHOOL

As a starting point for thinking about patterns of similarity and difference between young people, and categorisation, think about your experiences as a young adolescent in the Middle Years and the various factors that influenced your sense of yourself as a teenager and as a student. Think also about your experience of school.

1   What was your sense of yourself as a student? Were you 'good', smart, sporty, tough, well behaved, popular, 'nerdy', 'geeky', rebellious, engaged, disengaged, conscientious, self-conscious or 'cool'? Were you none of these or a combination of some of them? What terms would you use to describe yourself? What terms did others use to describe you? What was the basis for these descriptions?

Think back to the peer and friendship groups you had.

2   What fashion codes, ways of communicating, attitudes to school, behaviours in class, activities ▼
inside and outside school characterised the different groups of students? Name the different ▼

▶ ▶ ▶

groups that formed in your school. What common ground held groups together – was it, for example, interests, background, gender, ethnicity? How strong an influence did peer groups have on your sense of yourself as a student and your attitude to school?

Think about the influence of your family on your attitude to school.

3   What influence did your family have on your attitude towards schooling? What expectations and aspirations did your family have for you as a student? How did the expectations of your family align with or differ from other families? What school experience did your parents have? What schooling options were available to your family? What links can you see between your family expectations, the type of school you attended and your gender, ethnicity, social class or where you lived?

Reflect on how your schooling affected you.

4   In what ways did your schooling influence your sense of yourself, your peer groups and the opportunities available to you? Think, for example, about the school location (city, regional, rural, remote); school type (comprehensive or selective, coeducational or single-sex, government or non-government, religious or non-religious); school size; school environment, resources and curriculum; school ethos and rules; and school structure and organisation.

5   How would you describe the school culture? How did individuals and groups fit into that culture? Think of the influence of particular teachers. In what ways did teachers' expectations and attitudes influence your educational experience? How important was your experience of school to the pathways that you have since followed?

In responding to these questions we hope you have been able to build a picture of the complex array of factors that influenced who you were as a student and the pathways you have since taken. In particular we hope you have connected some broad social factors with the 'nitty gritty' of school and classroom practice. You could compare your experiences with that of others to ascertain some ways that patterns of similarity and difference between students are constructed.

Examining your own experiences is useful for a couple of reasons. First, it is a starting point for understanding the complexity of contextual factors that influence the experiences of students in schools. Second, it is a starting point for thinking about how your experiences influence the assumptions and values that you have about teaching and schooling. Being able to critically examine your own experiences and assumptions is extremely important when working with students whose backgrounds, cultures, values, experiences and assumptions are different from your own. Indeed, given the great diversity of Australia's school-age population, it is highly likely that you will be teaching young people whose cultures and backgrounds differ from your own.

We hope that you thought about how individual, family and peer groups intersected with broad social factors such as gender, ethnicity, social class and location to underpin your educational experiences and how you constructed your identity as a student. These intersections are complex and play out for different people in different ways. Think of the great diversity in Australia in cultural, linguistic and ethnic backgrounds and what this means for students' educational experiences. Consider, for example, a Year 8 student recently arrived from Hong Kong who speaks both Chinese and English, a refugee student recently arrived from war-torn Sudan who has had severely interrupted schooling and speaks little English, and a fourth-generation Anglo-Australian student. Each will have different experiences of education because of their backgrounds, different cultural assumptions about schooling and different educational needs. The picture becomes more complex if we consider cultural background alongside factors such as social class, gender and family expectations.

To compare with your own experience, as well as to illustrate this complexity, recent research by Tsolidis (2006) is useful. She asked young people in one Melbourne high school to describe the student subcultures. They identified popular kids, cool kids, nerds, geeks, wogs, musos, Goths, Asians, Russians, hardcores, blonde girls and jocks. Tsolidis describes how membership of subcultures could be based on ethnic background, social class, gender, physical appearance, attitude or hard work at school. She goes on to suggest that students' aspirations and achievements were mediated by these student subcultures and the broader culture of the school.

EXPERIENCES OF YOUNG PEOPLE AND SCHOOLING

We draw on some of the ideas considered above to develop a conceptual framework for the key dimensions of social difference and its relationship to schooling. From analysing your experience you know that varied and overlapping factors influence the experiences and identities of young people. Figure 2.1 illustrates some of these critical factors and their interrelationship. Schooling and classroom practices are one part of the complex set of relations described in this diagram.

Social factors such as class, gender, ethnicity and culture, indigeneity, abilities and location are consistently mentioned in educational contexts because of their relationship to educational opportunities, experiences and learning outcomes. In more recent times, and given processes of rapid social change associated with globalisation, factors such as new technologies, new forms of

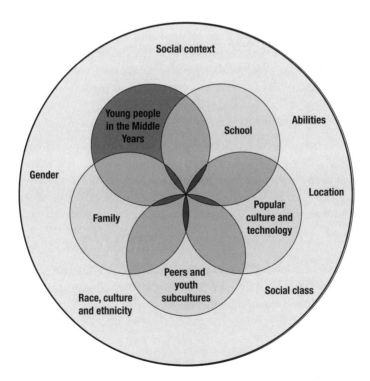

Figure 2.1 Social factors influencing the experiences of young people

consumer culture and shifting patterns of family relationships are likewise considered important to understanding young people's identities and experiences of schooling. These relationships are both complex and varied. Indeed much recent educational research focuses on the relationships and intersections between these social factors and educational experiences of young people. We briefly outline how differences within these social categories are talked about in educational contexts.

THE IMPACT OF SOCIAL FACTORS ON SCHOOLING

Social class

Social class is a key influence on educational access and outcomes. Students from high-income families tend to do better at school than students from low-income families (Connell 1993). This difference is not simply a function of money and income, but of differential access to the social, cultural and material resources that can influence educational opportunities. These resources include access to books and technology in the home, level of parents' education, ability to pay for school tutoring and alignment of values between home and school. Likewise, schools in the poorest communities often have fewer resources and higher rates of teacher turnover than schools in wealthy communities.

Race, culture and ethnicity

Australia is a country of considerable racial, ethnic, linguistic and cultural diversity. Within this diversity are differences in educational provision, experience, expectations and outcomes. For example, and as discussed later in the chapter, there are considerable differences between Indigenous and non-Indigenous Middle Years students in educational outcomes. Recent educational developments have focused on how comparisons, particularly between majority and minority cultures, can be framed in terms of 'difference' rather than 'deficit' and how pedagogical practices can recognise and respond to the cultural and linguistic diversity found in many Australian schools.

Gender

The relationship between gender and school experience has been subject to ongoing debate. Differences between boys and girls can be analysed along many educational planes: opportunities, subject choice, expectations, outcomes and levels of engagement. Schools are recognised as important sites for young people to construct their gender identity, their conceptions of masculinity and femininity and their associated overlap with sexuality. Key ideas related to gender are developed later in the chapter.

Abilities

Within any population and school and classroom grouping are differences between students in relation to their cognitive and physical abilities. A strong focus in educational practice in recent years has been to develop school and classroom practices that are inclusive of students of all abilities.

Location

Differences between students in rural and remote and urban communities often pertain to level of access to educational resources. For example, many students in remote communities do not have easy access to high schools, so the transition from primary school to high school is not necessarily straightforward. In many rural and remote areas, high teacher turnover can affect school stability and the relationships that students build with teachers over time.

New technologies and consumer culture

For many young adolescents, new technologies and forms of consumer culture are critical to their identities, friendship groups and membership of school subcultures. Mobile phones, iPods, Wikipedia, online chat rooms and computer gaming are tools taken for granted by young people in ways quite different to previous generations (Carrington 2006). The implications of new technologies and consumer culture for students' experiences at and knowledge and views of school are only just beginning to be researched and understood.

Families

Family size, structure, parental roles, mobility and values play a critical part in how young adolescents construct their identity and frame their educational experience. Many sociologists note the changes taking place to family structures and roles, with, for example, an increasing number of young people living with one parent (Carrington 2006).

Friendship groups

Peer cultures and friendship groups can be particularly important for young adolescents and critical to their engagement at school. The importance attached by young people to the social and friendship dimensions of schooling is often raised as a concern by teachers because of the ways that it can overshadow the academic dimensions of schooling. How friendship groups align with other social factors such as gender and ethnicity can be central to constructions of identity (Hey 1997).

Individual factors

Interacting with social factors such as those described above are a range of individual psychological, personality and physical factors that underpin identity and participation in schooling, including self-esteem, motivation, academic abilities, physical size, and so on.

While identifying patterns and relationships in the experiences of young people and their schooling is important for educators, there are tensions associated with this task. Keep the following cautions in mind when interpreting descriptions, explanations and practices associated with these patterns:

- Individuals and their experiences take place within multiple and interrelated contexts. There is not a simple cause-and-effect relationship between individual contextual factors and students' school experience (Batten & Russell 1995). Typically, there is considerable intersection between the social factors described above.
- A young person's identity is not necessarily fixed and static, rather it is responsive to context and changeable over time (Tsolidis 2006).
- Using categories of difference that are based on negative stereotypes, that 'over-determine' or that assume a deficit can locate problems at the feet of the group themselves and leave unchallenged the school and other social practices that serve to marginalise (Connell 1993).
- We are in a period of rapid social change – globalisation, new technologies, movement of people across the world and terrorism create new lines of similarity and difference between people that have important ramifications for young adolescents as they construct their identities, and for schools in which new patterns of similarity and difference are played out (Carrington 2006).

Schools and the construction of difference

Students come to school with varied backgrounds, assumptions and aspirations. Schools not only respond to students' different backgrounds and experiences, but also the practices within schools themselves regulate, mediate and influence the patterns of similarity and difference between students. The combined effect of these practices can be critical for students' learning, behaviours, engagement, social relations, choices and sense of self. Below is a brief description of common ways that patterns related to social difference can be understood in relation to the practices of schooling.

1 Patterns in relationships between students' backgrounds and identities, and measures of educational experiences, achievement and engagement – for example, results in standardised literacy tests for students can be correlated with factors such as gender, ethnicity and social class.
2 Formal practices in schools that respond to and regulate differences between students – a number of school practices (conceived in broad and narrow ways) respond to and regulate similarities and differences between students. These practices can have positive and negative effects on student learning and sense of self.
   • School type, philosophy and culture – different types of schools group students in particular ways. Think about government and non-government schools, selective and comprehensive schools, religious and secular schools, single-sex and coeducational schools, mainstream and special schools, and traditional and progressive schools.
   • School organisation – for reasons that are both educational and practical, schools group students in particular categories: age and multi-age groups, mixed ability and streamed classes, home groups, single-sex and mixed-sex groups are examples. There are pros and cons associated with each.
   • Whole-school and targeted initiatives that respond to the needs of different groups – many school-based initiatives are designed to respond to the specific needs of particular groups of students. The development of middle schools is an example. Other strategies have a whole-school focus: for example, making schools engaging for all students.
   • Classroom practice and teacher expectations – teachers can have differential expectations of students. These expectations might be based on, for example, students' gender, social class or ethnicity. Expectations (both positive and negative) can have an impact on student learning outcomes and self-esteem.
3 Informal school practices that regulate differences between students – peer relations and playground interactions play a very important role in students' lives. Schools are important sites where friendships are made, peer group influence is sharply felt and a sense of identity developed. This is particularly so for young adolescents. The subcultures and groups that students identify with reflect complex interrelationships between students' interests, abilities, cultures, gender and class.

The politics and ethics of difference

As you may have noted, there are political and ethical dimensions to the ways some differences between students are constructed both inside and outside school. When differences between individuals and groups are underpinned by systems of power and privilege that include some and exclude others, or that advantage some and disadvantage others, then questions can be raised about the fairness, justice and equity of such systems. Schools feature prominently in discussions of justice and equity because they are sites that can reinforce advantage and disadvantage, and because they are sites in which inequalities and exclusions can be addressed and reduced.

Over the last 40 or so years considerable attention has been paid in Australia to social justice and education, and to the development of practices that are inclusive of and fair for all students. In some cases the social justice focus has been on the ways in which resources are distributed so as to enable equality of access to education; in other cases it has concerned the recognition of difference and diversity. In the 1970s and 1980s, concerns with social and economic equity prompted the development of educational policies and programs to respond to the particular needs and experiences of students who were marginalised from, or disadvantaged by, mainstream educational practices: students from low-income families, Indigenous students, female students, students with disabilities and students from non-English-speaking backgrounds.

Typical concerns with schooling and social justice were enshrined in the 1999 Adelaide Declaration – an agreed agenda for schooling developed by federal, state and territory governments.

The Adelaide Declaration 1999 (Section 3)
→ → →

Schooling should be socially just, so that:

- students' outcomes from schooling are free from the effects of negative forms of discrimination based on sex, language, culture and ethnicity, religion or disability; and of differences arising from students' socio-economic background or geographic location
- the learning outcomes of educationally disadvantaged students improve and, over time, match those of other students
- Aboriginal and Torres Strait Islander students have equitable access to, and opportunities in, schooling so that their learning outcomes improve and, over time, match those of other students
- all students understand and acknowledge the value of Aboriginal and Torres Strait Islander cultures to Australian society and possess the knowledge, skills and understanding to contribute to, and benefit from, reconciliation between Indigenous and non-Indigenous Australians
- all students understand and acknowledge the value of cultural and linguistic diversity, and possess the knowledge, skills and understanding to contribute to, and benefit from, such diversity in the Australian community and internationally
- all students have access to the high quality education necessary to enable the completion of school education to Year 12 or its vocational equivalent and that provides clear and recognised pathways to employment and further education and training.

Ministerial Advisory Council on Education, Employment and Youth Affairs 1999

The Adelaide Declaration is concerned with the equitableness of educational opportunities and outcomes, the fairness with which educational resources are distributed, and the recognition granted to all students irrespective of their culture and background. Documents such as the Adelaide

Declaration are important because they provide broad and agreed-on policy frameworks to guide educational practice.

At the same time, it is important to note that policy emphases in relation to social justice and education shift and change in light of the needs of particular groups, the effects of particular social-justice initiatives and prevailing political values. It could be argued, for example, that over the last ten to 15 years in Australia there has been a shift in emphasis away from educational policy concerned with equity towards that concerned with individual aspiration, choice and competition. How individual schools, as well as educational and social policy makers, balance (or not) the collective good and needs of the whole community, including the most at-risk students, with the rights and aspirations of individuals is subject to heated and considerable debate.

BUILDING INCLUSIVE PRACTICES

The above point notwithstanding, there are wide-ranging initiatives that respond to the educational needs of particular groups of students based on the principles of equity, inclusion and social justice. Some are concerned with government policy (for example, funding programs for students from low-income families). Some are school-based (for example, anti-bullying programs, multicultural harmony days) and some are concerned with classroom practice (for example, around teacher expectations). Some target the needs of particular groups of students (refugees, students with disabilities, students whose first language is not English).

Other programs have been targeted to all students in that they seek to challenge the practices and systems that lead to inequalities and injustice. For example, curricula in the social sciences and health can address racism, sexism and homophobia; classroom practices can be designed to be inclusive of students with diverse abilities; high-quality pedagogy can extend learning outcomes for all students.

In this chapter we cannot do justice to the breadth and depth of debate and initiatives related to student difference, diversity and inclusion. Instead we take two areas that have particular currency in the Middle Years and tease out some of the debates, policies and practices as they pertain to identity, difference, social justice and educational experience. These areas are gender and education (specifically boys' education) and education for Indigenous students. We have chosen these areas because of current concerns about measures of educational achievement and engagement for both Indigenous students and boys in the Middle Years. We emphasise that the experiences of boys and Indigenous students need to be understood in relation to complex sets of social and educational factors that include class, history, public policy, and school organisation and classroom pedagogy. In each case we consider some of the issues underpinning these concerns and some school and classroom practices designed to address concerns.

Do note that these illustrations are intended as an introduction to the issues and we strongly encourage you to extend your reading in these areas to build a fuller appreciation of the debates and strategies.

GENDER DIFFERENCES

Earlier in the chapter we asked you to consider some of the differences between and among boys and girls in your school experience. This section enables you to locate your experiences within some broad and strongly contested debates about gender and education. Explanations for differences between boys' and girls' educational expectations, opportunities, learning outcomes, levels of engagement, patterns of behaviour and forms of socialisation vary considerably. Whether the differences constitute educational advantage for one gender over another is contested. Likewise, strategies advocated by schools to address the specific needs of girls and boys are highly varied. While discussions about gender are evident in all schooling sectors, the Middle Years are particularly important for the following reasons: the physical, social and emotional changes associated with adolescence are considered critical to how young people define their masculinity, femininity and gender relations; and the different ways that males and females mature and socialise during adolescence influences their learning. More specifically, there is current concern about boys' disengagement from schooling in the Middle Years.

Background issues

Significant initiatives related to gender equity in Australia have taken place over the past 40 years. In the 1970s and 1980s the key focus was on the education of girls (Collins, Kenway & McLeod 2000). Major concerns were that girls were under-represented in high-status subjects such as maths and science, school practices reinforced narrow sex-role stereotypes (girls did cooking and sewing while boys did woodwork and metalwork), teachers' classroom expectations were influenced by stereotypes of the capabilities and behaviours of girls and boys, and studies of classroom interactions showed that teachers spent more time with boys than girls. A range of policies and practices were developed to provide more equitable opportunities and outcomes for girls. These included programs to encourage girls into maths, science and technology; girls-only maths and science classes; self-esteem classes for girls; using women who worked in non-traditional areas as role models; and classroom practices that were inclusive of boys and girls (focusing on teacher time and expectations).

During the late 1980s and early 1990s, research directions associated with gender and education shifted, moving away from conceptualising girls as one homogenous group. Focus turned to how gender intersected with class, ethnicity, sexuality and location, for example, to influence girls' experiences of schooling. There was a call for programs that were more specifically targeted to the needs of particular groups of girls. At the same time, research also turned to encompass in more detail how boys experienced schooling, the relations between males and females (and masculinity and femininity) in a range of school contexts and how these relations both enabled and constrained the identities and behaviours of boys and girls.

Current concerns with boys' education

In the late 1990s and early 2000s, concern about gender and education has been more explicitly directed towards policy and practice about boys' learning (Weaver-Hightower 2003; Francis & Skelton 2005). The focus on boys' education can be linked in part to some issues particularly noticeable in the Middle Years: boys' lower achievement in measures of literacy compared to girls; boys' higher rates of suspensions and exclusions compared to girls; and boys' disengagement from school evidenced by disruptive behaviour, poor motivation, negative attitudes and bullying (House of Representatives Standing Committee on Education and Training 2002; Lingard et al. 2002).

Possible and competing arguments put forward to explain concerns about adolescent boys' achievement and engagement include:
- There are not enough male teachers in upper primary to act as role models for boys.
- Many assessment practices now common in schools favour girls over boys (Cresswell, Rowe & Withers 2002). For reasons of nature, maturation or socialisation many young adolescent boys do not do as well as girls on assessment tasks that require extended verbal and written skills.

- Boys' (active) learning styles and development are not adequately catered for in many Middle Years classrooms (West 1999).
- Forms of masculinity that have high status in some adolescent peer groups have embedded within them anti-academic behaviours (Foster, Kimmel & Skelton 2001; Lingard et al. 2002). In other words, it is 'cool' to have negative attitudes towards school and to reject conscientious behaviours associated with schooling, and in particular subjects such as English that are seen as feminine or 'gay'. At the same time, those not conforming to this 'cool' or dominant form of masculinity are criticised for being 'nerdy' or 'gay'. Some researchers suggest that forms of anti-school masculinity and disaffection are more prevalent among boys in low and increasingly middle socioeconomic communities.
- More-nuanced readings of the differences between boys' and girls' achievement and engagement are required. The question 'Which boys and which girls?' has been posed to make the point that a range of other social factors such as social class and culture intersect with gender, or indeed may be more important than gender, in explaining differences between student achievement and engagement (Collins, Kenway & McLeod, 2000; Lingard et al. 2002). Thus, in relation to the research about literacy scores for students in the Middle Years, it is worth noting that boys from high socioeconomic backgrounds tend to score more highly on standardised literacy tests than girls from low socioeconomic backgrounds. Yet boys from low socioeconomic backgrounds tend to score lower on measures of literacy than girls from the same socioeconomic backgrounds.

School practice and policy

One consequence of these varied, and sometimes competing, explanations for boys' educational engagement has been the development of a variety of school and pedagogical practices relevant to both boys and girls.

The Australian government policies 'Boys' Education Lighthouse Schools' and 'Success for Boys' are examples of major initiatives targeted towards boys. Funding is for specific school-based projects designed to enhance aspects of boys' engagement and achievement. The Success for Boys policy has as its focus literacy and assessment, using communications technologies to promote active learning and positive male role models.

Likewise, other states, systems, practitioners and researchers are developing particular programs and strategies. Examples of common strategies and programs are listed in Table 2.1. There is considerable debate about both the assumptions underpinning different strategies and their efficacy. Some argue for strategies focused on boys; some for strategies for both boys and girls.

Complicating the issues

Obviously, varied strategies have been developed as part of boys' education initiatives, yet there are questions regarding their effect. One problem with many of the strategies advocated is that they have not been subject to detailed evaluation (Weaver-Hightower 2003). Thus, while there are many anecdotal reports of useful outcomes associated with strategies, it is difficult to ascertain if the strategies have any sustained effects, particularly in relation to literacy scores, levels of engagement and so on.

A second problem with *some* of the strategies for boys is that they are based on the assumption that all boys are the same. They can set up an unhelpful dichotomy between boys' and girls' learning

Table 2.1   Gender strategies and programs

STRATEGY AND PROGRAM FOCUS	EXAMPLES
Classroom strategies	
targeted to boys' learning styles and needs	• active learning (practical, fast-paced, short-term, high-energy structured activities; use of technologies) • structured teacher-led activities; explicit instructions • curricular relevance to boys • cultural relevance (for example, for Indigenous boys, Pacific Islander boys) • using ICT to engage boys
for both boys and girls	• variety of strategies: individual and group activities; collaborative and competitive activities; assessment tasks that require both short answers and extended responses; practices that enable reflection and action; multiple opportunities for success; varied forms of feedback • listening to students; negotiating outcomes • high expectations for girls and boys • productive pedagogies for both boys and girls
School programs	
targeted to boys' needs	• male mentors and role models for boys • building boys' literacy skills • focus on feelings, confidence, conflict, self-discipline • boys-only classes for English and literacy
targeted towards boys and girls and gender relations	• anti-violence and anti-bullying programs • challenging dominant forms of masculinity • teacher professional development to build knowledge of gender and education • whole-school gender strategy

(West 1999; Mills 2000; Zbar, Bereznicki & Trist 2003; Francis & Skelton 2005)

styles; they can reinforce prevailing stereotypes about boys and girls; and they can overlook how gender is connected to social class, ethnicity, sexuality, location and disability. Indeed, the criticism of many of the strategies targeted towards girls in the 1980s holds true for strategies directed at boys in the 2000s.

As a way forward, Lingard et al. (2002) suggest that models of good teaching such as Productive Pedagogies (discussed in Chapter 4) lead to improved and more-equitable outcomes for all students. What is important about this particular model of pedagogy is that teachers' recognition of difference is central to good teaching. The argument put by Lingard et al. (2002) is that an understanding of the 'which boys and which girls?' question is essential as part of this recognition.

SCHOOLING IN INDIGENOUS COMMUNITIES

In her maiden speech to the New South Wales parliament, Linda Burney (2003) said:

> Education is the pillar, the cornerstone of social justice. It is what equals us out whether you are from Canterbury Boys High School, Penrith High School or the Kings School . . . Many people have said, 'What got you into this place?' It is simple: I could read.

Burney was the first Indigenous person elected to parliament in New South Wales. Her comments about the value of education, and about being able to read, are critical to current discussions about strategies to address the cycle of poverty within many Indigenous communities and the legacy of dispossession, exclusion and racism following British colonisation.

As a starting point, it is important to acknowledge the history and identity shared by Indigenous people, as well as the considerable diversity in clan and community affiliations, languages, locations and cultures. For example, the experiences of Indigenous students in cities may be very different from that of students in remote communities; the experiences of young adolescent girls in a remote community may be different from that of young adolescent boys.

While we focus on educational issues facing Indigenous communities, we note the need to ensure that effort is directed not only to programs for Indigenous students, but also to programs that enable all students to learn about Indigenous history and culture, to support cross-cultural understanding and to build the collective commitment necessary to ensure equitable opportunities and outcomes for *all* young people.

Educational outcomes for Indigenous students

There have been clear improvements in school participation and completion rates for Indigenous students over the last 30 years. Nevertheless, comparisons between Indigenous and non-Indigenous students reveal some stark inequalities in both educational participation and outcomes.

- School attendance – the literature generally acknowledges that school attendance rates for Indigenous students are low compared to non-Indigenous students (Bourke, Rigby & Burden 2000). It is notable that attendance rates and school retention rates continue to drop from Year 7 through to Year 12. School attendance is usually lower in remote areas than other areas. Low attendance means that students find it difficult to build school-based skills and knowledge in a systematic way.
- Standardised test results – English literacy and numeracy tests conducted in each state and territory in Years 3, 5 and 7 reveal noticeable differences in levels of literacy and numeracy between Indigenous and non-Indigenous students. A review of Aboriginal education conducted in New South Wales showed that, in 2003, the reading level for Indigenous students in Year 7 was, on average, three to four years behind the reading level of non-Indigenous students. The same review also noted that 45 per cent of Indigenous students in Year 7 did not meet elementary reading proficiency levels, compared with 17 per cent of non-Indigenous students (New South Wales Department of Education and Training 2003). The consequences of having low levels of English literacy and numeracy are significant. Most schoolwork in the Middle Years assumes a degree of functional literacy; not being able to read and write can lead to lack of achievement, low self-esteem, frustration and disengagement.
- Self-identity – a recent study of the self-identity held by young Indigenous people found that, while many young people had a positive image of themselves as Indigenous, and as good at sport,

they did not necessarily have a positive image of themselves as a student (Purdie et al. 2000). Other reports indicate that Indigenous students are likely to experience racism within their schooling (New South Wales Department of Education and Training 2003).

Educational issues for Indigenous students

In accounting for the educational experiences of many Indigenous students, a complex set of factors should be considered. These factors are located both in the workings of schools as well as in broad historical, political and economic contexts that frame the experiences of Indigenous people. Some of these overlapping factors are detailed below.

School factors

- Curriculum design and relevance – the first issue concerns the limited ways that Indigenous people are represented in curricula; the second concerns the lack of relevance that curricula may have for young Indigenous people.
- Teacher professional learning – many reports question whether teacher-education programs adequately prepare teachers to work with Indigenous students and teach Indigenous studies. There are also few Indigenous teachers working in schools or enrolling in teacher-education programs.
- Teacher expectations and attitudes – low expectations, negative attitudes and a lack of cross-cultural understanding on the part of teachers can affect the participation of Indigenous students.
- Teacher mobility – there is more teacher mobility in many schools with a high proportion of Indigenous students, meaning a lack of ongoing stability for students.
- School access – access to schools, particularly high schools, in remote communities is problematic.
- English language literacy – English is not the first language for many Indigenous students, particularly in remote communities. The degree to which Indigenous students have opportunities to learn in their first language, and the degree to which they have access to specialist ESL teachers, varies.
- Cross-cultural knowledge and understanding – some practices that are taken for granted in schools are at odds with practices in Indigenous communities. For example, publicly praising a student, common in many schools, may in fact be humiliating for some Indigenous students.

Family, social, historical and political factors

The educational experiences of young Indigenous people need to be set into a broad context. In some Indigenous communities, poverty, poor housing, ill-health, poor nutrition, welfare dependency and limited employment opportunities clearly have affected how young people participate in schooling. Likewise, these current problems should be located within the historical context that Indigenous people have suffered the effects of racism, injustice and lack of self-determination over the past two centuries. These problems also should be understood within a public-policy framework that has failed in systematic or coherent ways to address the issues faced by Indigenous Australians.

Policies, programs and practices

Numerous strategies and interventions have been designed to address the needs of young Indigenous students, particularly over the last 30 years. There is increasing acknowledgement of the need for coordinated action across the areas of health, housing, employment, governance and education. This requires major, long-term and coordinated strategies, resourcing and commitment. Notwithstanding this, there are schools and communities in which systematic improvements in learning outcomes for Indigenous students have taken place.

Consistently identified in recent policy documents, as well as in successful schools, is the need for good classroom teaching and school strategies that encourage student participation and engagement. The need for good classroom teaching is shown in the example of the whole-school approach developed by Chris Sarra, then principal of Cherbourg State School in Queensland.

School culture and ethos

Many schools are working to build a school culture that encourages the participation and engagement of Indigenous students. Sarra was the first Aboriginal principal of Cherbourg State School, an Aboriginal community school in Queensland. During his time as principal, he implemented strategies to extend learning outcomes for Indigenous students. For him it was crucial to break the twin problems of teachers blaming the community for students' failure and the community blaming the school and teachers for students' failure. Key programs and strategies implemented in Cherbourg State School included:

- developing a vision, encapsulated in the school motto 'strong and smart', that embraced the expectation that students' learning outcomes would be comparable to those of other students in Queensland, and that students would have a strong sense of their Aboriginal identity
- building a commitment to these ideas in the teaching staff (Indigenous and non-Indigenous) as well as the community
- challenging students to improve school attendance, behaviour and learning, and expecting improvements
- implementing a cross-school Aboriginal studies program to assist students to learn about not only their history but also current issues facing Aboriginal communities. The program was not an 'add on' to the curriculum, but was a central part of the program of study (Sarra 2006).

Sarra's analysis of student data shows that over a period of five years (1999–2004) student absenteeism decreased and scores in Year 7 standardised measures of literacy increased in alignment with age-based averages.

Transforming teaching

What does good teaching in schools with Indigenous students involve? The report by the New South Wales Department of Education and Training provides some useful starting points. Teachers should:

- have high expectations for Indigenous students
- be committed to working with Indigenous students
- build opportunities for student success and confidence
- give explicit and sequenced instruction
- set relevant and meaningful tasks
- have expertise in monitoring and extending literacy skills (2003: 189–90).

We consider what good teaching with Indigenous students involves in the case study below, which documents the experiences of a beginning teacher, Julie, in her first two years at a remote community school and the beliefs and practices that she developed through her work in this school.

CASE STUDY

Challenging the 'taken for granteds' of schooling

Throughout her university degree Julie had taken courses about Indigenous history, culture and politics. She had also pursued these interests through her teacher-education program. In her teaching rounds she taught in schools that had Indigenous studies programs and had built a strong commitment to social justice and schooling. Julie was therefore keen to work in a school in an Indigenous community and sought an appointment in a remote community school. Julie was posted to a K–10 school in a township of about 1000 people.

Before taking up the appointment, Julie participated in a series of workshops for teachers working with Indigenous students in remote schools. This background was crucial in providing Julie with a sense of the context she would be working in, as well as offering some specific teaching strategies that she could develop and employ in ways relevant to her school context.

Living in the community meant that Julie could see how poverty and ill-health experienced by Indigenous people in this community affected students' involvement in school. Students sometimes arrived at school tired and hungry. A large number of students had ongoing health problems, particularly hearing problems. Attendance at school was infrequent for many of the young people in Julie's combined Year 7, 8 and 9 class.

One key thing that was clear to Julie as soon as she started work in the school was that she couldn't take for granted many of the routines and values so often associated with schooling. Assumptions about what teachers should do and what students should do, which she had built up through her experience as a school student and as a pre-service teacher, were suddenly challenged. The communication between teachers and students is an example: Julie couldn't assume that students would simply sit at their desks and listen to her talking from the front of the classroom. In part it was because some students had hearing problems and couldn't hear her clearly. In part it was because English was a second language for most students and the students had varying levels of English language competency. In part it was because students did not have a lot of experience with the routines of the classroom. And in part it was because both Julie and her students held different assumptions about relationships between adults and young people, and between Indigenous and non-Indigenous people.

The difficulties that Julie faced cannot be underestimated. Working in a combined Year 7, 8 and 9 class required her to peel back layers of 'taken for granteds' in what teachers do and what students do. This process of 'peeling back' enabled Julie to identify core practices in her teaching and her beliefs, as outlined below.

- Building positive relationships with students – when Julie first started at the school one of the critical issues was to build positive relationships with the students. Students didn't know her and didn't want to be 'bossed' around by her, and so it took some time to build relationships. Key to what Julie did was being fair, consistent and caring, and 'being there'.

- Dealing with students on an individual basis – linked to the above was the effort that Julie made each day to work with students individually. This was important for a couple of reasons. First, it enabled her to praise students one-on-one in ways that avoided what for many students was the embarrassment caused by being praised in front of the whole class. Second, dealing with students on an individual basis was also an important strategy in responding to the sporadic school attendance of some students. It meant that she could connect with students who attended school regularly, as well as build work options for those who attended infrequently.

- Building routines – during the morning session in particular Julie had a set structure that enabled students to build routines related to learning. This structure included some quiet time, some time for reading and writing, and an expectation that every student would complete some work. This routine was important because it provided a structure for learning and for achievement.
- Changing strategies – not all teaching strategies worked all of the time. Some worked only for a period of time. Julie had to change strategies regularly as a way of motivating and engaging students.
- Building shared understanding about what schooling is for – a key issue that Julie faced was that many students did not have a strong sense of purpose associated with schooling, particularly once they got to Year 8 and 9. For some of the students, school seemed like a ten-year punishment. For other students, it seemed like a long series of activities that kept them busy but had no real purpose. The sorts of knowledge the mandated curriculum required students to acquire seemed very distant to the needs and interests of these young people and their community. At the same time, Julie acknowledged that without access to this knowledge, students and their community were at risk of further marginalisation from the broader Australian society. Julie therefore developed units that linked local cultural knowledge with 'outside' knowledge. A history unit, for instance, provided students with opportunities to connect issues about their own cultural identity to events in Australian history over the past 200 years. This unit opened conversations, not only with the students but also with their families and Indigenous teaching staff at the school.

DISCUSSION STARTERS

1   What are some of the ways that Indigenous students' experience of school could vary across locations – in urban and regional areas for example? What are the implications for the pedagogical practices used by teachers? What strategies could be employed to create inclusive classroom and school cultures in schools where Indigenous students make up a minority of the population?
2   Julie's experiences challenged many of her own assumptions about schooling and teaching. Describe similar experiences in which your own assumptions about schooling and teaching were challenged.
3   Both Julie and Chris Sarra describe efforts to create school and classroom cultures that were responsive to the students. Describe occasions when you have seen a classroom or school culture change to accommodate students, particularly those who may be disenfranchised from mainstream culture.

CONCLUSION

This chapter has considered how similarities and differences between students are constructed in the context of schooling; and how differences within and across groups, and schooling practices themselves, can advantage some and disadvantage others. Also discussed were the issues related to the needs of two groups of Middle Years students at risk of educational disengagement, and possible pedagogical and school responses.

We have examined the complex relationships between social factors such as gender, ethnicity, Aboriginality, social class and location, and educational opportunities, experiences, aspirations and outcomes. These relationships are critical to how educators understand and respond to differences between students and build practices that are fair and equitable.

Myriad policies and practices have been developed to respond to differences between students. A consistent message is the need for school and classroom practices that transform learning for all students. These practices are underpinned by the values held by educators and their understandings of, and sensitivity to, the differences between students (Hayes et al. 2006). Understanding can be deepened through building specific knowledge of students' contexts and cultures, examining our assumptions about difference and critically analysing the often taken-for-granted values in schools and classrooms.

The challenge that we take up in the next three chapters is to consider how curriculum, pedagogy and assessment practices in the Middle Years can be designed to transform learning for *all* students in complex and changing times. We conclude with a thought-provoking comment by sociologist Richard Teese:

> the quality of a school system can be judged by the experience of the most vulnerable children in it . . . real commitment to them is a real commitment to all children everywhere in the system. It must be supported by an intensity of effort, high expectations and solidarity in sharing resources (2006: 159).

References

Batten, M. & Russell, J. (1995) *Students at Risk: A Review of the Australian Literature 1980–1994.* Melbourne: Australian Council for Educational Research.

Bourke, C., Rigby, K. & Burden, J. (2000) *Better Practice in School Attendance: Improving the School Attendance of Indigenous Students.* Canberra: Commonwealth Department of Education, Training and Youth Affairs.

Burney, L. (2003) Inaugural speech. New South Wales Legislative Assembly Hansard.

Carrington, V. (2006) *Rethinking Middle Years: Early Adolescents, Schooling and Digital Culture.* Sydney: Allen & Unwin.

Collins, C., Kenway, J. & McLeod, J. (2000) *Factors Influencing the Educational Performance of Males and Females in School and their Initial Destinations after Leaving School.* Canberra: Commonwealth Department of Education, Training and Youth Affairs.

Connell, R.W. (1993) *Schools and Social Justice.* Philadelphia, PA: Temple University Press.

Cresswell, J., Rowe, K. & Withers, G. (2002) *Boys in School and Society.* Melbourne: Australian Council for Educational Research.

Foster, V., Kimmel, M. & Skelton, C. (2001) 'What about the boys? An overview of the debates', in W. Martino & B. Meyenn (eds), *What About the Boys? Issues of Masculinity in Schools.* Buckingham, UK: Open University Press.

Francis, B. & Skelton, C. (2005) *Reassessing Gender and Achievement: Questioning*

Contemporary Debates. London, UK: Routledge.

Hayes, D., Mills, M., Christie, P. & Lingard, B. (2006) *Teachers and Schooling: Making a Difference*. Sydney: Allen & Unwin.

Hey, V. (1997) *The Company She Keeps: An Ethnography of Girls' Friendship*. Buckingham, UK: Open University Press.

House of Representatives Standing Committee on Education and Training (2002) *Boys: Getting it Right. Report on the Inquiry into the Education of Boys*. Canberra: Commonwealth of Australia.

Lingard, B., Martino, W., Mills, M. & Bahr, M. (2002) *Addressing the Educational Needs of Boys*. Canberra: Department of Education, Science and Training.

Mills, M. (2000) 'Issues in implementing boys' programmes in schools: male teachers and empowerment'. *Gender and Education*, 12(2), 221–38.

Ministerial Advisory Council on Education, Employment and Youth Affairs (1999) *The Adelaide Declaration on National Goals for Schooling in the Twenty-First Century*. Accessed on 26 July 2006 from www. mceetya.edu.au/mceetya/nationalgoals/natgoals.htm.

New South Wales Department of Education and Training (2003) *The Report of the Review of Aboriginal Education, Yanigurra Muya: Ganggurrinyma Yaarri Guurulaw Yirringingurray, Freeing the Spirit: Dreaming an Equal Future*. Sydney: New South Wales Department of Education and Training.

Purdie, N., Tripcony, P., Boulton-Lewis, G., Fanshawe, J. & Gunstone, A. (2000) *Positive Self-Identity for Indigenous Students and its Relationship to School Outcomes*. Canberra: Commonwealth Department of Education, Training and Youth Affairs.

Sarra, C. (2006) 'Armed for success'. *Griffith Review*, Autumn, 185–94.

Teese, R. (2006) 'Condemned to innovate'. *Griffith Review*, Autumn, 151–9.

Tsolidis, G. (2006) *Youthful Imagination: Schooling, Subcultures and Social Justice*. New York, NY: Peter Lang.

Weaver-Hightower, M. (2003) 'The "boy turn" in research on gender and education'. *Review of Educational Research*, 73(4), 471–98.

West, P. (1999) 'Boys' underachievement in school: some persistent problems and some current research'. *Issues in Educational Research*, 9(1), 33–54.

Zbar, V., Bereznicki, B. & Trist, S. (2003) *Meeting the Challenge: Guiding Principles for Success from the Boys' Education Lighthouse Schools Programme Stage I 2003*. Canberra: Australian Government Department of Education, Science and Training.

3

RETHINKING CURRICULUM FOR ADOLESCENT LEARNERS

Our containing systems and structures must be reformed so that schools, both primary and secondary, are allowed to become places of engaged production, more like workshops than lecture rooms, more like the ideal workplaces of the future than the factories of the past. This is not to do away with reflectiveness, civilised conversation, story, wonder and critique.

If, however, issues of control, regulation and safety push aside visions of the ideal society as the new national framing proceeds, we may see a curriculum retro-revolution which will have us fighting for our lives a few years into the twenty-first century (Boomer 1999: 143).

INTRODUCTION

The ideas of Garth Boomer have had a profound effect on the landscape of education in Australia for the past 30 years. While his fears of a 'curriculum retro-revolution' that has us 'fighting for our lives' has not been realised in the first decade of the 21st century, at the same time, neither has his vision for classrooms as places of engaged production come to fruition, as a rule. His assessment in 1991 that the recent history of curriculum in Australia was 'a tale of two epistemologies' could also apply today, whereby a number of different understandings are at work in government policy, curriculum documents and schools themselves. In order for pedagogy and learning to be truly transformative, the curriculum structures within which they sit must be intellectually rigorous and thoughtfully constructed. In this chapter, we provide a broad picture of curriculum for the Middle Years, beginning with the social and political context of Middle Years curriculum. We then examine approaches to Middle Years reform across Australian states and territories, and conclude by examining approaches to curriculum design and models of curriculum integration for the Middle Years.

Key questions guiding this chapter are:

1   What are the big picture debates about curriculum in the Middle Years?
2   What are the key directions and features of Middle Years curriculum development in Australia?
3   What curriculum design principles and models can you draw on to inform your classroom practice?

THE POLITICS OF CURRICULUM DEVELOPMENT

Curriculum is never apolitical. As already suggested, it is always a product of its time and is constructed on ground that is highly contested, has multiple and competing stakeholders and is constantly in a state of movement and transformation. While, on the surface, it might seem that students are the key and primary stakeholders in terms of curriculum, governments, both state and federal (of all political persuasions), use the curriculum as a political tool. It can be a means of exerting control over an unwieldy and, at times, defiant teaching profession and, on a macro level, a method of both casting and reflecting national and state priorities over long periods of time.

Historically, the development of school curriculum in Australia is in many ways a story of struggle for control and power on the part of state and federal governments. The 'new national framing' mentioned by Boomer was undertaken in the early 1990s by the Keating government in preparation for the introduction of a national curriculum, an initiative that was eventually abandoned after it failed to gain endorsement from states and territories. Now, we are once again engaged in discussions about a national curriculum and leaving qualification, this time an extension of the 'standards and accountability' agenda currently favoured by conservative governments in the Western world.

The impact of the agenda of conservative politics on school curriculum is well documented and debated. Apple (2000, 2001, 2002), for example, has devoted a substantial body of work to this discussion in the American context, while in the Australian context, the proliferation of a 'common sense' approach to education, championed by such people as Kevin Donnelly (2004), who are both funded and endorsed by the Howard government, reflects the current policy direction. Donnelly, an ex-chief of staff for a senior Howard government minister, has in the past five years become a self-styled education 'expert', and his particular perspective on education is perhaps best summed up by extracts from two of his recent articles. On the notion that students of the 21st century need to learn critical and higher order thinking skills, he comments:

> As the ACDE (Australian Council of Deans of Education) has argued in *New Learning: A Charter for Australian Education*, old-fashioned ideas about right and wrong answers and teaching the three R's have to be jettisoned in favour of the new basics. The new basics are defined as developing 'self-awareness, problem-solving and intercultural skills' so that learners are equipped with 'multiple strategies for tackling a task and a flexible solutions-orientation to knowledge'.
>
> What's ignored is that high standards and higher order skills depend on rote learning and mastering the basics. Also ignored is that in the real world there are right and wrong answers and that generic skills such as problem solving are subject-specific (Donnelly 2006a).

And on the problems of History in secondary school in Australia and the evils of education aiming to foster social justice:

> Since the 1970s and '80s, as outlined in *Why Our Schools Are Failing*, left-wing academics, education bureaucracies and professional associations have embarked on the long march through the institutions to overthrow more conservative approaches to education.
>
> The so-called traditional academic curriculum, with its emphasis on initiating students into established disciplines such as history and literature, and the belief that education can be impartial, have been attacked as misguided, Eurocentric and socially unjust.
>
> European settlement is described as an invasion, Australia's Anglo-Celtic heritage is either marginalised or ignored, indigenous culture is portrayed as beyond reproach and teachers are told they must give priority to perspectives of gender, multiculturalism and global future.
>
> The 1999 Queensland SOSE curriculum, for one, was also decidedly New Age and one-sided. The values associated with the subject mirror the usual PC suspects, such as social justice, peace and ecological sustainability' (Donnelly 2006b).

As reflected in these extracts, the current political agenda has hijacked a number of rather unhelpful dichotomies in an attempt to simplify complex arguments to a 'common sense' level. In the main, the dichotomies are about:

- *content*, as opposed to lifelong learning skills
- *standards*, as opposed to the allegedly haphazard approaches embraced by the liberal agenda
- *transmission*, as opposed to student-centred learning
- *competitive assessment*, as opposed to outcomes-based education.

It is particularly salient to think about the politics of curriculum development for the Middle Years, as much of the thinking and writing on Middle Years reform has been carried out at the hands of 'progressive' educationists who have embraced constructivist and critical approaches to curriculum and learning, and embedded these in their work on learning in the Middle Years. Notions of negotiated, differentiated and integrated curriculum grow largely out of conceptualisations of education that emphasise such principles as:

- students as active participants and decision-makers in their learning
- students as knowledge creators
- collaborative learning
- critical thinking
- metacognition (the capacity of students to understand the ways that they learn).

These principles respond to the call issued by the Australian Council of Deans of Education in 2001 to develop new understandings of learning that are about:

> *creating a kind of person*, with kinds of dispositions and
> orientations to the world, rather than simply commanding a
> body of knowledge. These persons will be able to navigate change
> and diversity, learn-as-they-go, solve problems, collaborate, and
> be flexible and creative. Finally, new learning will be increasingly
> *interdisciplinary*, requiring deeper engagement with knowledge
> in all its complexity and ambiguity. The new basics are about
> promoting capability sets, reflexive and autonomous learning,
> collaboration, communication, and broadly knowledgeable
> persons (Kalantzis & Cope 2001).

The Middle Years are fertile ground for curriculum innovation, negotiation and integration for a number of key reasons. The content-laden curriculum that characterises the later years of schooling that are driven by high-stakes assessment (usually in the form of tertiary entrance assessment and examinations) is largely absent from the Middle Years. In addition, the specific characteristics and learning needs of adolescents lend themselves particularly to a curriculum that takes account of the 'whole person' rather than just the academic sphere or domain. Finally, the independence that most adolescent learners are eager to experience and develop provides an ideal context in which to develop metacognitive and learning-to-learn skills.

APPROACHES TO THE MIDDLE YEARS

Middle Years reform in Australia has occurred on two fronts: at the grassroots level, whereby individual schools or segments of school systems have reformed their structures and processes, and at the level of state and national education authorities and organisations. On a national level, a growing awareness of disengagement in early adolescence has sparked a variety of reports and projects relating to schooling in the Middle Years, including in the mid 1990s the National Middle Schooling Project (Barratt 1998) and From Alienation to Engagement (Australian Curriculum Studies Association 1996), and in the late 1990s, the middle school stream of the Innovation and Best Practice Project (Cuttance et al. 2001). A number of key national reports on middle schooling and Middle Years learners have been commissioned over the past decade, including those by the Australian Education Union (Chadbourne 2001), the Commonwealth Department of Education, Science and Training (Luke et al. 2003) and the Ministerial Council on Education, Employment, Training and Youth Affairs (Pendergast et al. 2005). We are not here to investigate the processes and findings of these reports, but to point to their very existence as evidence of the recent focus on the Middle Years.

State and territory education departments, sectors and professional associations have also commissioned reports on Middle Years curriculum and education, and covered principles of middle schooling in curriculum documents and syllabuses. A brief survey of the landscape of Middle Years education in Australia at the time of writing follows, although it should be noted that this summary is not intended to be exhaustive. An excellent more-detailed summary can be found in *Teaching Middle Years: Rethinking Curriculum, Pedagogy and Assessment* (Pendergast & Bahr 2005).

Across the board, the advocated reforms generally focus on transition issues for students moving from primary to secondary school, curriculum innovation in the form of structures for learning that are less subject-focused and more flexible and integrated, and pedagogical innovation in the form of student-centred, negotiated, collaborative teaching and learning practices.

In general, states and territories have each followed one of two approaches to Middle Years reform, exemplified by those of Queensland and New South Wales. While states such as Queensland, Victoria and Western Australia have developed and implemented specific strategies in the form of Middle Years reforms, other states, such as New South Wales, Tasmania and South Australia, have implemented specific strategies for Middle Years learners as part of broader curriculum reform across primary and secondary schooling.

Two approaches to Middle Years reform

The case of Queensland

In Queensland, following the *Education and Training Reforms for the Future* White Paper, a ministerial advisory committee for educational renewal was established to provide advice to the education minister on the 'Middle Phase of Learning'. The principles identified by this committee and formulated to underpin Middle Years reform in Queensland are:

- Students in this phase have particular characteristics that warrant the recognition, maintenance and establishment of a distinctive phase of learning that meets the unique needs of this group of learners. The need to develop as autonomous learners and the physical, intellectual, social, cultural, economic, technological and educational factors that impact simultaneously on early adolescence require particular consideration by educators.
- A distinctive middle phase requires the reframing of curriculum, pedagogy, assessment, and school ethos, environment and organisation.
- Accordingly, an effective middle phase should focus on student engagement, learning and achievement, and can occur in the full range of school contexts including:
  - P–7 schools and 8–12 schools, working collaboratively
  - P–10 and P–12 schools
  - purpose-built facilities.

- Partnerships and effective communication between schools (including state, Catholic and independent), parents and local communities enable a shared responsibility for the learning of all students and are an essential component in supporting students in the middle phase.
- Effective pedagogy involves identifying students who require particular support to succeed or require additional challenges in their learning in this phase, followed by timely intervention strategies and ongoing monitoring of achievement related to explicit expectations.
- Effective practice in the Middle Years is contingent on a teaching workforce being able to respond to the distinctive and diverse needs of students and to changing economic, social and technological conditions, and who have a strong desire to work with students in this phase.

The four strategic directions identified in the report relate to meeting the distinctive and diverse needs of Middle Years students, creating partnerships between and within schools and systems, achieving student engagement and success in learning in the Middle Years and building workforce capability through sustained and effective professional development initiatives for teachers.

Subsequently, in 2003, a Middle Phase of Learning State School Action Plan was developed in which 13 actions for Queensland state schools were outlined. The actions, organised within five key areas – focus and accountability, curriculum, teaching and assessment, achievement, transition and teachers – are currently in the process of being implemented.

The case of New South Wales

In 2000, the New South Wales Board of Studies commissioned a literature review on middle schooling (Arnold 2000), around the time when the principles informing the K–10 curriculum framework were under preparation. While at the board level the conversation about middle schooling has been limited over the past five years, it is interesting to note how these principles connect and overlap with ideas of middle schooling:
- Learning occurs at different rates and in different ways.
- Learning and teaching should take place in a context of high expectations.
- Students use their current level of learning to discover, construct and incorporate new knowledge, skills and understanding.
- Teacher instruction and assessment together influence student learning.
- Students can develop and use a range of strategies to actively monitor and evaluate their learning and their learning strategies.
- Strategies for learning are taught, learned and refined in a range of contexts.
- Students need learning experiences with appropriate time to explore, experiment and engage with the concepts underpinning what they are learning.
- Frequent feedback from teachers is critical for learners to gain insight into their learning and understanding, and to enable them to map their progress in relation to defined standards.

In New South Wales state schools, a number of Middle Years initiatives have recently been implemented, largely growing out of the key findings of the 2004 Consultation on the Future of NSW Public Education and Training. The report, *Excellence and Innovation*, recommended that professional development initiatives for teachers focus more explicitly on the needs of Middle Years students, and that teachers and schools be encouraged to 'implement innovative Middle Years strategies' (NSW Department of Education and Training 2004) in various forms. Since the publication of the report, a variety of professional learning opportunities have been developed for teachers, including funding a number of schools to undertake action research projects focusing on student learning in the Middle Years.

Schools in the Catholic and independent sectors, which tend to be more autonomous than their state school counterparts, have also implemented reforms in the Middle Years to respond to current thinking around the specific needs of early adolescents.

The International Baccalaureate Organization (IBO) has developed a program for students in the Middle Years (defined by the IBO as ages 11 to 16). According to the IBO (2005), there are currently over 40 state, Catholic and independent schools across all states and territories in Australia utilising this program. The Middle Years Program (MYP) aims to enable students to:

- build upon their spirit of discovery to develop an understanding and enjoyment of the process of learning, independently and in cooperation with others
- acquire knowledge and understanding and prepare for further learning
- recognise the extent to which knowledge is interrelated
- learn to communicate effectively in a variety of ways
- develop a sense of personal and cultural identity and a respect for themselves and for others
- acquire insights into local and global concerns affecting health, the community and the environment
- develop a sense of individual and collective responsibility and citizenship, through a program of study based on the key concepts of holistic learning, intercultural awareness and communication.

Designing curriculum for the Middle Years

As for all school curricula in Australia, while the states provide the foundation for what is to be taught in the form of syllabus documents, the role of teachers and schools is to develop and implement a curriculum at school level that satisfies both the imperatives of the state and the needs of their students.

Robert Marzano (2003) writes of a 'guaranteed and viable curriculum', which he describes as the single most important school-level factor in the improvement of student learning outcomes. Marzano's argument is that, in the context of the overcrowded curriculum, it is essential for teachers at the school level to decide about those parts of the state-developed curriculum that are essential learning and construct learning experiences that enable students to effectively develop their understanding within the time available to them, utilising pedagogies that are student-centred and allow authentic and deep learning to take place.

This approach requires teachers to move away from a transmission model of teaching and learning, with teacher as 'bus driver' (Mockler 2004), responsible for all decisions about the content and form of the learning journey, and the stops to be made along the way. Instead it requires that we embrace conceptualisations of ourselves as 'designers' (Atkin 2001) or 'architects' (Little 2000) of the learning environments we oversee, engaging in the hard intellectual work of bridging the gap between the big picture of the curriculum dictated by the state and the immediate context of our own schools, classrooms and students. Such an approach integrates well with the approach to pedagogy that has both a critical and transformative intent, as discussed in Chapter 4.

APPROACHES TO CURRICULUM DESIGN

Many different varieties of models for designing and planning student work are available, ranging from those aligned with specific subjects and disciplines to those aligned with particular approaches such as multiple intelligences, webquests or the integral learning model based on Ned Herrmann's (1989) 'whole brain model', made popular in Australia by Julia Atkin (2001). While many models would serve the development of curriculum for Middle Years learners well, that developed by Grant Wiggins and Jay McTighe (1999) in the late 1990s, and refined over the past decade, is of particular appeal for a number of reasons. Implicit in the model is the notion that in designing curriculum, we should 'begin with the end in mind' (Wiggins & McTighe 1999: xx), a notion compatible with the outcomes-based curriculum being implemented across Australia at present. The model is not aligned with any particular subject or discipline area, and includes a variety of worked examples across all disciplines (McTighe & Wiggins 2004), and nor is it tailored to or representative of any particular approach or set of pedagogies, despite an obvious bias towards pedagogies that encourage student responsibility and agency in learning, and assessment practices that are embedded within such pedagogies.

In essence, the model requires teachers to move through three phases in their planning of student work: in the first identifying (using both the state-developed syllabus and their expertise in their subject) the desired results of the unit of work, in the second determining acceptable evidence of student learning in relation to the desired results, and in the third planning learning experiences and instruction. While the model appears simple, it is deceptively so, as so very often in planning we are drawn to think about tasks and activities that will engage students before we decide on the endpoint of the unit. The 'backward design' model asks teachers to consider a range of questions at each stage in order to create units of student work that are both effective and engaging, reaching towards the aims of Marzano's 'guaranteed and viable curriculum'.

Many worked examples of units of student work across the curriculum are found in *Understanding by Design* (Wiggins & McTighe 2004) and the *Professional Development Workbook* (McTighe & Wiggins 2004). In addition, there is an online community of educators using this method for curriculum design at the Understanding by Design Exchange (Association for Supervision and Curriculum Development 2006). A series of recent works has emerged considering the Understanding by Design model in light of, for example, ideas about the differentiation of the curriculum (Tomlinson & McTighe 2006).

NEGOTIATING THE CURRICULUM

The notion of a curriculum negotiated between teacher and student grows not only out of ideas about new pedagogy and learning but also from its roots in critical and democratic education (Boomer et al. 1992). Student agency and decision-making in learning, and partnership between students and teachers in the learning process, are important aspects of the negotiated curriculum, and thus it is in essence an enactment of transformative intent. The negotiated curriculum is in its approach to the design and processes of learning the antithesis of the 'one size fits all' curriculum.

June Maker's (1982) model of curriculum modifications is useful when starting to think about negotiating curriculum. Implicit in Maker's model is a conceptualisation of learning as comprised

Table 3.1   The 'backward design' model

Stage 1: Identify desired results from the unit of work

Student learning outcomes (from syllabus document):

Enduring understanding:	**Essential questions:**
Students will understand that …	Students will grapple with essential questions that …
Does this idea:	• have no one obvious right answer
• represent a big idea having enduring value beyond the classroom?	• raise other important questions, sometimes across discipline boundaries
• reside at the heart of our discipline?	• address or reflect the philosophical or conceptual foundations of a discipline
• involve actually *doing* the subject?	• recur naturally throughout a learner's life
• offer potential for engaging students?	• are framed to ignite and sustain learner interest

Knowledge (from syllabus document):	**Skills** (from syllabus document):
Students will know …	Students will be able to …

Stage 2: Determine acceptable evidence of learning

Performance tasks:	**Other evidence:**
• feature a setting that is real or simulated	'Academic prompts':
• require students to address an identified audience	• require constructed responses
• are based on a specific purpose that relates to an audience	• are open-ended – there is no one single answer
• allow students opportunities to personalise the task	• involve analysis, synthesis or evaluation
	Quizzes and tests:
	• assess for factual information, concepts and discrete skills
	• use selected-response or short-answer formats
	• typically have a single or best answer

Stage 3: Plan learning experiences and instruction

Learning activities and resources:
What learning experiences and instruction enable students to achieve the desired result? How will the design:
- help the students to know **w**here the unit is going and what is expected? Help the teacher to know where the students are coming from (prior knowledge, interests)?
- **h**ook the students and hold their interest?
- **e**quip students, help them experience the key ideas and explore the issues?
- provide opportunities for students to **r**ethink and revise their understandings and work?
- allow students to **e**valuate their work and its implications?
- be **t**ailored to the different needs, interests and abilities of learners?
- be **o**rganised to maximise initial and sustained engagement and effective learning?

(Adapted from McTighe & Wiggins 2004)

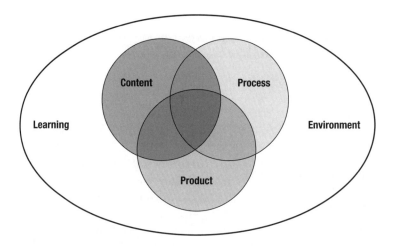

Figure 3.1 Maker's model of curriculum modifications

of content, processes and product, framed by the learning environment itself (see Figure 3.1). While Maker's central proposition is that a range of strategies can increase complexity for gifted and talented students across the content, process and product domains, for students of varying abilities, the model can be the basis of designing curriculum in which students are encouraged to make decisions about their learning in one of the three domains at a time, based on both their interests and abilities, while the remaining two domains are set by the teacher. Once students develop proficiency in making decisions, setting goals and meeting outcomes in each of the three domains, the capacity for student decision-making can be expanded to two of the three, and then eventually to all three. So students become highly proficient and skilled at navigating their own learning landscape.

PROVOCATION: NEGOTIATING THE CURRICULUM

Much in the way that education is structured in Australia at present might lead teachers to the conclusion that a 'one size fits all' approach is preferable to a negotiated curriculum. Who benefits, however, from a 'one size fits all' approach? Think about the positives and negatives of both approaches from the point of view of both the student and the teacher. Now think about it from the point of view of different kinds of students. Who are the 'winners' and the 'losers' from the 'one size fits all' approach?

MODELS OF INTEGRATION

Curriculum integration has long been seen as an apposite innovation for students in the Middle Years as it eases the transition between primary and secondary school (through slowing the move towards discipline-based study) and offers opportunities for the curriculum to connect to big issues and real-life questions. It also goes some way towards redressing the fragmentation of the curriculum, which is problematic in secondary schools, and encouraging students to link different pieces of knowledge and different ways of thinking.

A range of approaches to curriculum integration exists, from those that require little structural change in the school context to those that require radically different organisation of school structures. Generally speaking, these approaches are seen as multidisciplinary or interdisciplinary or transdisciplinary, each differing in their aims, methodology, required structure and outcome, as well as how they integrate the key learning areas (KLAs). While some advocates of middle schooling (Beane n.d.) argue for integrating all curriculum as the only way to adequately and authentically meet the needs of Middle Years learners, we believe, along with others (see, for example, Jackson & Davis 2000), that there are a variety of ways to structure curriculum in order to rise to this challenge. We provide here a broad overview of models of curriculum integration rather than a detailed analysis. For a more in-depth discussion see, for example, Beane (n.d.) or Wallace, Venville and Rennie (2006) for examples from the Australian context.

The multidisciplinary approach

In a multidisciplinary approach to curriculum integration, subject areas or disciplines act as 'mirrors' on a chosen theme or topic, each reflecting the aspect of the topic that relates most closely to the subject content as established in the syllabus. This approach requires each subject to draw relevant links to the chosen content area, as well as between the various mirrors. A multidisciplinary approach to an integrated curriculum generally requires only minimal structural changes to school organisation, as the integrated curriculum is taught in regular subject classes by subject specialists. The key structural changes required for this approach relate to the reorganisation of the subject curriculum so as to bring about alignment across subjects and a more collaborative approach to planning than that which traditionally takes place in secondary schools.

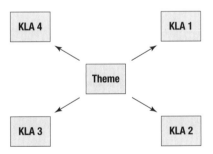

Figure 3.2 A multidisciplinary approach to an integrated curriculum

The interdisciplinary approach

An interdisciplinary approach to an integrated curriculum relies on subject areas or disciplines 'giving over' some of their designated content and skills outcomes to the integrated curriculum. In this approach, the disciplines become co-contributors to a joint enterprise, generally constructed and taught collaboratively by a team of teachers as an adjunct to the subject-based 'regular' curriculum. This approach relies upon establishing the integrated curriculum as a designated and separate part of the school repertoire, with the attendant structural changes that allow time and space for the innovation to occur, both in planning and implementation.

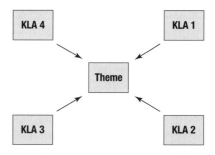

Figure 3.3 An interdisciplinary approach to an integrated curriculum

The transdisciplinary approach

A transdisciplinary approach to an integrated curriculum looks beyond the immediate curriculum established by the state to real-life issues and problems, beginning with a range of 'enduring understandings', common foundations or metacognitive skills and broad pathways. These are the basis of a curriculum that is built using the disciplines as 'lenses' through which students view the issue or topic under consideration. In structural terms, this approach to an integrated curriculum is the most demanding, requiring not only a larger commitment in terms of time and space than that required by an interdisciplinary approach, but also a commitment to the creation of new knowledge, ways of working and approaches to learning on the part of the teachers undertaking the design task.

The rich tasks developed in Queensland as part of the New Basics Project (Education Queensland 2001) are an excellent example of this approach. In the context of each of the rich tasks, students learn essential skills and gain essential knowledge while grappling with some of the big questions currently confronting Australian society and the global community. We return to further discussion of rich tasks in later chapters.

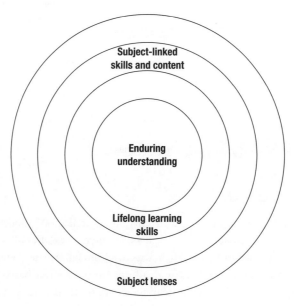

Figure 3.4 A transdisciplinary approach to an integrated curriculum

CASE STUDY
Three approaches to an integrated curriculum

This case study was developed for secondary school teachers at a school that was contemplating different approaches to integrating the curriculum in the Middle Years. The scenarios, each set in the fictitious Flobbertown, show how three schools have constructed an integrated curriculum for Middle Years students.

You may be familiar with the Dr Seuss book *Hooray for Diffendoofer Day*, where Miss Bonkers's class, having been the beneficiaries of a somewhat unusual approach to curriculum, are suddenly required to take a test:

'To see who's learning such-and-such –
To see which school's the best.
If our small school does not do well,
Then it will be torn down,
And you will have to go to school
In dreary Flobbertown'.
'Not Flobbertown!' we shouted,
And shuddered at the name,
For *everyone* in Flobbertown
Does *everything* the same.
Miss Bonkers rose. 'Don't fret!' she said.
'You've learned the things you need
To pass that test and many more –
I'm certain you'll succeed.
We've taught you that the earth is round,
That red and white make pink,
And something else that matters more –
We've taught you how to think'.

Of course, Miss Bonkers's class passes the test admirably and their school is able to stay open, but these three scenarios are set in a Flobbertown that is trying to cast off its reputation as a place of 'one size fits all' learning, and implement some changes in the Middle Years.

St Mary's College

Year 7 students at St Mary's have spent Term 1 contemplating the big question 'Who am I?'. Looking at the complex issue of identity from a range of perspectives, they have studied the influence of magazines and television shows on their perception of themselves, reflected on their spiritual development and identity, looked at the links between the environment and identity, and measured and checked their level of fitness against targets for teenagers. Rotating in groups between activities led by a cross-disciplinary group of Year 7 teachers, students have spent a week on work drawn from each of eight subject areas. Last week a Year 7 teacher was overheard having an 'animated discussion' with the Head of Human Society and its Environment (HSIE), Sheila Sherman, about how it had been difficult to fit a depth study of the bushrangers into a unit of work designed around 'Who am I?', despite the expectations of the HSIE department.

Flobbertown High School

Year 7 students at Flobbertown High are in the process of developing an understanding of the relationship between natural and built environments by designing a house for bushfire-prone areas. Having spent a number of weeks learning independent research skills and conducting group experiments on appropriate materials and designs, students are required to construct a scale drawing and model of their house, while at the same time work in pairs to keep a video-journal of their learning. While their learning has been guided by a small cross-disciplinary group of teachers, they also have had access to specialists across a range of areas. Despite some small setbacks, such as a student in Mavis Milton's group producing some asbestos out of his schoolbag to contribute to a group experiment, and a student in Geraldine Stout's group taking experimental learning a little too far by creating her own small bushfire at the back of the Science lab, the unit has run well.

Flobbertown Grammar School

Students in Year 7 at Flobbertown Grammar have been studying 'water' for five weeks. In Science they have boiled it, in PDHPE they have swum in it, in English they have written odes to it, in D & T they have made receptacles for holding it, in Geography they have looked at its existence in rivers, oceans and lakes, and in LOTE they have learned how to ask for a glass of it in four languages. And the list goes on. While some teachers feel that they may never bring themselves to drink water again, students have been assisted to make valuable connections across the curriculum. Herbert Hingledinger, for example, has noticed that students in his Year 7 English class are much more likely than those in years past to draw on their knowledge from Science or History in class discussions, and the TAS department has noted how useful students' newly acquired water-boiling skills from Science have been in their first practical lesson in the kitchen.

DISCUSSION STARTERS

1 For each scenario, consider:
   a Is it a multidisciplinary, interdisciplinary or transdisciplinary approach?
   b What are the strengths of the approach?
   c What might be the weaknesses of the approach?
   d What about the approach do you find interesting?
2 Overall, which approach do you think best responds to the challenges of 21st century learning and why?

CONCLUSION

This chapter has focused on the nature of curriculum reform in the Middle Years, and the context within which such reform occurs. While we acknowledge that there are many ways that curriculum can be adapted and changed to meet the needs of learners in the Middle Years, and that Middle Years curriculum reform should not itself be 'one size fits all', we do believe that a significantly different approach to curriculum in the Middle Years can meet the particular needs of this group. Transformative learning requires curriculum that is artfully constructed and provides opportunities for students to take many paths in their learning, to be key decision-makers in the learning process and to engage actively and rigorously with the curriculum. Pedagogy and assessment practices that are aligned with the intent of such a curriculum are, however, vital to the transformative intent, and it is to these elements that we now turn.

References

Apple, M.W. (2000) *Official Knowledge: Democratic Education in a Conservative Age.* New York, NY: Routledge.

Apple, M.W. (2001) *Educating the 'Right' Way: Markets, Standards, God and Inequality.* New York, NY: Routledge.

Apple, M.W. (2002) 'Pedagogy, patriotism and democracy: the educational meanings of 11 September 2001'. *Discourse: Studies in the Cultural Politics of Education,* 23(3), 299–308.

Arnold, R. (2000) *Middle Years Literature Review.* Sydney: New South Wales Board of Studies.

Association for Supervision and Curriculum Development (2006) Understanding by Design Exchange website. Accessed 5 February 2006 from www.ubdexchange. org.

Atkin, J. (2001) 'Learning by design'. Unpublished workshop materials. Harden, New South Wales.

Australian Curriculum Studies Association (1996) *From Alienation to Engagement: Opportunities for Reform in the Middle Years of Schooling.* Canberra: Australian Curriculum Studies Association.

Barratt, R. (1998) *Shaping Middle Schooling in Australia: A Report of the National Middle Schooling Project.* Canberra: Australian Curriculum Studies Association.

Beane, J.A. (n.d.) *Organizing the Middle School Curriculum.* Westerville, OH: National Middle School Association. Accessed 22 October 2006 from www.nmsa.org/ Publications/WebExclusive/Organizing/ tabid/651/Default.aspx.

Boomer, G. (1999) 'Curriculum and teaching in Australian schools, 1969–1990: A tale of two epistemologies'. *Designs on Learning: Essays on Curriculum and Teaching.* Canberra: Australian Curriculum Studies Association, 127–46.

Boomer, G., Lester, N., Onore, C. & Cook, J., (eds) (1992) *Negotiating the Curriculum: Educating for the 21st Century.* London, UK: Falmer Press.

Chadbourne, R. (2001) *Middle Schooling for the Middle Years: What Might the Jury be Considering?* Melbourne: Australian Education Union.

Cuttance, P., Angus, M., Chadbourne, R., Crowther, F., Hann, L., McMaster, J., Russell, J., Hill, P., Jones, G., Mackay, A., Stokes, S., Zbar, V., Olney, H. & Jane, G. (2001) *School Innovation: Pathway to the Knowledge Society.* Canberra: Department of Education, Science and Training.

Donnelly, K. (2004) *Why Our Schools are Failing: What Parents Need to Know About Australian Education.* Sydney: Duffy & Snellgrove.

Donnelly, K. (2006a). 'Let's go back to basics, beginning with the three R's'. *The Australian,* 31 January, 12.

Donnelly, K. (2006b) 'Why our greatest story is just not being told'. *The Australian,* 28 January, 24.

Education Queensland (2001) *The Why, What, How and When of Rich Tasks.* Brisbane: Education Queensland.

Herrmann, N. (1989) *The Creative Brain.* North Carolina: Ned Herrmann.

International Baccalaureate Organization (2005), IBO website. Accessed on 1 February 2006 from www.ibo.org.

Jackson, A.W. & Davis, G.A. (2000) *Turning Points 2000: Educating Adolescents in the 21st Century.* Westerville, OH: National Middle Schools Association.

Kalantzis, M. & Cope, B. (2001) *New Learning: A Charter for Australian Education.* Canberra: Australian Council of Deans of Education.

Little, J. (2000) 'Teacher as architect? How to describe what we do in technology-rich learning environments'. Accessed on 12 January 2006 from www.jennylittle.com/Issues/JL7_TEACHER_AS_ARCHITECT.HTML.

Luke, A., Elkins, J., Weir, K., Land, R., Carrington, V., Dole, S., Pendergast, D., Kapitzke, C., van Krayenoord, C., Moni, K., McIntosh, A., Mayer, D., Bahr, M., Hunter, L., Chadbourne, R., Bean, T., Alverman, D. & Stevens, L. (2003) *Beyond the Middle: A Report about Literacy and Numeracy Development of Target Group Students in the Middle Years of Schooling.* Canberra: Commonwealth Department of Education, Science and Training.

Maker, C.J. (1982) *Curriculum Development for the Gifted.* Austin, TX: Pro-Ed.

Marzano, R.J. (2003) *What Works in Schools: Translating Research into Action.* Alexandria, VA: Association for Supervision and Curriculum Development.

McTighe, J. & Wiggins, G. (2004) *Understanding by Design: Professional Development Workbook.* Alexandria, VA: Association for Supervision and Curriculum Development.

Mockler, N. (2004) Architects, travel agents and bus drivers: images of teacher professional identity. Paper presented to the Australian Association for Research in Education Annual Conference, University of Melbourne, December.

NSW Department of Education and Training (2004) *Excellence and Innovation.* Sydney: NSW Department of Education and Training.

Pendergast, D. & Bahr, N. (2005) *Teaching Middle Years: Rethinking Curriculum, Pedagogy and Assessment.* Sydney: Allen & Unwin.

Pendergast, D., Flanagan, R., Land, R., Bahr, M., Mitchell, J., Weir, K., Noblett, G., Cain, M., Misich, T., Carrington, V. & Smith, J. (2005) *Developing Lifelong Learners in the Middle Years of School.* Melbourne: Ministerial Council on Education, Employment, Training and Youth Affairs.

Tomlinson, C.A. & McTighe, J. (2006) *Integrating Differentiated Instruction and Understanding by Design.* Alexandria, VA: Association for Supervision and Curriculum Development.

Wallace, J., Venville, G. & Rennie, L. (2006) 'Integrating the curriculum', in D. Pendergast & N. Bahr, *Teaching Middle Years: Rethinking Curriculum, Pedagogy and Assessment.* Sydney: Allen & Unwin, 149–63.

Wiggins, G. & McTighe, J. (1999) *Understanding By Design.* Alexandria, VA: Association for Supervision and Curriculum Development.

Wiggins, G. & McTighe, J. (2004) *Understanding By Design*, 2nd edn. Alexandria, VA: Association for Supervision and Curriculum Development.

NEW PEDAGOGIES FOR THE MIDDLE YEARS

Usually on the first day of term people romp light-heartedly around the room and fights break out about who's sitting where and the teacher tears her hair and fusses about maths books and such. But Miss Belmont had all that organised before school even started, and you'd never believe the work we got through that first morning.

She seemed to have eyes like a fly, with multiple sections that could see sideways and backwards, and into things that hadn't happened yet. Such as into Barry Hollis's desk where he had a packet of cigarettes and a copy of *Playboy* (Klein 1998: 4–5).

INTRODUCTION

Miss Belmont is the Grade 6 teacher at Baringa East Primary in Robin Klein's novel *Hating Alison Ashley*, written in 1984. It has been a popular read for young adolescents over the last 20 years, with its amusing and touching insights into the characters in the class: Alison Ashley, the girl who can do no wrong; Erica 'Yuk' Yurken, who resents Alison's seeming perfection in everything; Barry Hollis, the inveterate troublemaker; and Miss Belmont, the only teacher in the school who can handle the 'ratty' Grade 6 class. Not only does Miss Belmont have eyes like a fly, but also she can freeze students into silence with her 'iceberg-that-sunk-the-*Titanic* look' (Klein 1984: 17). Our purpose here is not to hold up Miss Belmont as a guru of classroom management, rather to say that Klein does a brilliant job of presenting Miss Belmont with a challenge faced by all teachers – teaching groups of students with diverse backgrounds, abilities, interests, emotions, relationships, aspirations and responses to school.

This diversity of students, manifest in any class, requires complex pedagogical strategies for teaching practices that support, enable and extend students' learning. The need for such pedagogical strategies is keenly felt in the Middle Years in which there is considerable concern about student disengagement from schooling and there are numerous questions about the degree to which current approaches to teaching are meeting the needs of young adolescents. There is a demand for pedagogy that better prepares young people for the rapidly changing world outside school (Barratt 1998a; Carrington 2003; Pendergast 2005).

In the previous chapter we considered the 'what' of learning. In this chapter we extend this by thinking about the 'how' of learning.

The key question guiding this chapter is: If we want learning to engage students in the Middle Years – in other words, if we want learning to be meaningful and enjoyable – then what pedagogical practices can we employ?

To respond to this question, this chapter:

- develops a working understanding of pedagogy, teaching, learning, student engagement and disengagement
- examines research related to pedagogy and student engagement in the Middle Years
- discusses some pedagogical models and strategies relevant to the Middle Years.

We are not offering advice on how to develop an 'iceberg-that-sank-the-*Titanic*' look – read *Hating Alison Ashley* for the details of this classroom-management strategy!

WHAT IS PEDAGOGY?

Pedagogy is a term that is now commonly used in educational circles, but what does it mean? Is it just a fancy way of talking about teaching? The concept of pedagogy cannot be pinned down to one simple definition and, indeed, the meanings attached to pedagogy in educational systems and practices vary between countries and across cultures (Alexander 2000). Deriving from ancient Greek, the term literally means 'to lead children'. Dictionaries often define it as the 'science of teaching' or the 'science and art of teaching'. Conceptualising teaching as a science and an art is useful because it presupposes knowledge about teaching and a set of skills necessary for the practical application of that knowledge. A working definition of pedagogy is that it is the interaction between teaching and learning and associated theories, beliefs and values.

Alexander (2000) argues in *Culture and Pedagogy* that pedagogy is an extremely useful concept because at its heart is the 'nitty gritty' of classroom practice: communication and relationships between teachers and students, and the dynamic between teaching and learning. He compares teaching practices across five countries (England, France, the United States of America, Russia and India), providing fascinating insights into the cultural values that underpin teaching in these countries. Alexander suggests that 'pedagogy encompasses both the performance of teaching together with the theories, beliefs, policies, and controversies that inform and shape it' (2000: 540). The act of teaching – the interactions, methods, tasks, activities and judgements teachers use to enable students to learn particular concepts and practices – does not exist in isolation from values, theories, beliefs and debates about education. Likewise, teaching methods are not separate from the people, relationships, structures, cultures and purposes that make up classrooms, schools and school systems. The nature and quality of teaching can only be understood in relation to the cultural values, beliefs, theories and purposes that underpin it.

Some examples illustrate this point. First, in the preface to this book, we expressed our values and theories about pedagogy, calling for an approach to teaching that is concerned with the quality of education for *all* students, that is underpinned by an ethical stance and that is transformative in its potential. It is impossible for us to write about teaching in a value-free way, but by putting our values on the table, we invite you to discuss and debate them. Second, if you ask any teacher, pre-service teacher, student, parent, teacher educator or indeed person on the street to outline their beliefs about good teaching, you will no doubt hear a variety of points of view. There are many views on what makes for good teaching. Put this question to a number of people and their beliefs expressed will always provide food for thought, particularly when you compare them to your own beliefs about good teaching.

We provide some ideas, illustrations, problems and possibilities that we hope are useful for building teaching and learning practices relevant to the Middle Years contexts in which you work, and in ways that help you articulate the beliefs that underpin your own teaching practice.

PEDAGOGICAL REFORM IN THE MIDDLE YEARS

There have been strong calls to reform teaching and learning practices in the Middle Years. The reasons for reform centre on the following issues.

Student disengagement from learning

As indicated earlier, local and international studies have noted the ways in which young people in the Middle Years are disengaged from learning and from school (Australian Curriculum Studies Association 1996; Jackson & Davis 2000). It has been suggested that the social, emotional and physical changes that are part of adolescence increase the risk of disengagement. Others argue that the changes and transitions from primary school to secondary school increase the potential for disengagement. The structures and practices in some secondary schools mean that students do not have a close relationship with one teacher, any problems may go unnoticed, there is a greater focus on performance at a time when students are very self-conscious and the teaching approaches used discourage student autonomy (Eccles & Roeser 2003). Another perspective is that the modes of teaching and the nature of the curriculum in the Middle Years disengage students. While there are no doubt many reasons for disengagement, systemic changes to teaching and learning practices, rather than strategies that try to 'fix' individual disengaged students (Batten & Russell 1995; Newmann 1996), are now seen as important.

Achievement slump

In Victoria a large-scale longitudinal study mapping student learning documented the following results about the early years of secondary school:
- there was overall no improvement in literacy skills
- reading skills plateaued for most students and in some cases declined
- underachievement was greater and persisted for longer among boys
- students' attitudes towards school were more negative than in other years and this rating was higher for boys than girls
- there was a decline in overall enjoyment of school (Hill & Russell 1999).

The quality of pedagogy

A large-scale study of teaching and learning practices in Queensland classrooms found that there was a drop in the quality of pedagogy from Year 6 to Year 8, particularly in schools in lower socioeconomic areas. The quality picked up again in the senior years. The study analysed pedagogy in relation to both academic and social learning (Lingard et al. 2001).

Technology, popular culture and 'new times'

Young people engage with new technologies, mass media, popular culture and consumer culture in new and often sophisticated ways (Kenway & Bullen 2001). This has clear implications for young people's sense of self and identity, patterns of communication and friendship, and learning inside and outside the classroom. It is perhaps not surprising that school learning is often seen to be 'boring' in comparison to popular forms of entertainment for young people. Moreover, in contrast to even 20 years ago, there is an increasing sense of unpredictability associated with the current social and economic milieux in which young people live and their post-school pathways (Carrington 2003). The changing world outside of school raises questions about the relevance and value of current pedagogies.

These issues create a set of imperatives for the design of pedagogical models and practices relevant to the Middle Years.

PEDAGOGICAL MODELS AND PRACTICES

The previous chapter examined 'backward design' as a planning and organising principle. We apply this principle here to an assessment task for students in the Middle Years and then work backwards to think about the task in relation to different facets of student learning, and how teaching practices can support and extend that learning.

TEACHING AND LEARNING — A RICH TASK

As you read the example below, test the ideas by thinking about their relevance to the teaching and learning contexts you are familiar with, as well as to your own beliefs about teaching. The example is a rich task or cross-disciplinary assessment task designed as part of the New Basics curriculum in Queensland. The task is for students in Years 7 to 9. The content for the task is Australian national identity. Students are expected to work in groups of three to five. Large-scale project work, rich tasks and integrated assessment tasks are employed in many Middle Years contexts; this is just one example. We hope that you can connect this example to your own specific teaching areas and to any assessment tasks that you plan. The task is:

> Through the creation, production and presentation of a powerful, filmed documentary that incorporates information gleaned from research and interviews with people from different cultural backgrounds, students will demonstrate knowledge and understanding of the different influences and perspectives on 'Australian national identity' (Department of Education 2004).

The learning goals in this task are complex; students are expected to demonstrate that they *know* and *understand* issues related to national identity and the people, events and practices that have combined to build a sense of what it means to be Australian. The question for a teacher then is what sort of teaching and learning activities will assist students to build the knowledge and understanding necessary to complete the task. The task offers some clues about how students can learn about the content and communicate their understanding: conducting interviews and research, and filming a documentary. But this is still fairly broad. How do students learn to conduct research and interviews? How do they learn to interpret data and present their ideas in a filmed documentary? How do they learn to work in groups? How do they build the conceptual tools to enable them to understand the historical, geographical, political and cultural factors associated with national identity? Careful planning is required to provide an environment in which students can build the *skills* and *knowledge* required to complete this task and extend their knowledge about the concept of identity.

Components of this task can be linked to large-scale assessment tasks in other disciplinary or cross-disciplinary fields. These components are a focus on student research, challenging content, the integration of technology and the need for strong literacy and communication skills. Thus, these components of an assessment task can be used as a starting point for thinking about the design of pedagogical activities across curricula.

To develop the backward mapping process, we now consider how the task can be linked to some key theories about teaching and learning, and inform teaching and learning activities.

Assumptions about learning

Active participation in the learning process

The task is designed to actively involve students in building knowledge about national identity. To complete the task students, at the very least, need to conduct interviews, interpret data, link data to concepts, talk to peers about their ideas and prepare a documentary. Students are not passively receiving and remembering knowledge passed on by a teacher, rather they are required to take responsibility for interpreting data and constructing a perspective. Learning through experience is a concept that was advocated by the American educational philosopher John Dewey (1916, 1938) early last century.

Knowledge building through inquiry and research

Activities such as rich tasks require students to engage in research processes that are central to building knowledge. Involving students in a research process is a means by which they can actively construct knowledge (Wells 1999). Disciplined inquiry involves analysis of data, presentation of ideas, critical review of those ideas by others, and using and building on ideas in other contexts (Wells 1999). In the given example, the goal is to encourage students to build knowledge about national identity through primary research.

Learning, individual cognition and social process

In education, there has been a shift away from the notion of learning as an individual act of cognition taking place in isolation from a social or cultural context (Bruner 1996). The design of the rich task certainly opens up the potential for learning to be mediated through interactions between students and students, teachers and students, and students and members of the community. The work of the Russian psychologist Lev Vygotsky (1978, 1997) has been influential in thinking about the social and cultural dimensions of learning. Vygotsky argues that learning takes place through the interaction between a 'psychological plane' (thinking and individual cognition) and a 'social plane' (exchange with others within a cultural context).

Challenging and connected work

Some recent models of pedagogy argue that both the quality and meaningfulness of learning can be extended when the content is both challenging and connected to students' lives outside school and/or future actions they may take (Newmann 1996; Lingard et al. 2001). Given that many young adolescents say that they are bored in classrooms, developing tasks that offer such challenge and connection is critical. A key goal for teachers is to consider how rich tasks can be adapted and refined to suit students' interests and local contexts.

Technological tools for learning

There is an increasing expectation for teachers to integrate the use of new technologies into their teaching practice. It is clear that communications technologies have changed how people access knowledge, interpret information and communicate understandings. Many students have technological knowledge far superior to their teachers, which has implications for traditional patterns of student–teacher relationships. In the example, teachers need to plan for using at least three types of technology: (1) a video or digital camera, (2) the internet as a research tool and (3) video-editing software.

Structuring teaching and learning activities

Given the complexity of the rich task, careful thought is required to structure class activities to enable students to develop the necessary skills and knowledge. Central to the initial design of the rich tasks in Queensland was the concern to align curriculum, pedagogy and assessment. By using the rich task as a starting point for planning a unit of work, the assessment becomes a vehicle for giving meaning to the knowledge and skills represented in the curriculum. The assessment task also is a starting point for thinking about pedagogy. Pedagogy related to an assessment task should take account of both the overall structure of a unit of work and the day-to-day lessons and activities. Pedagogical design, be it for a unit of work or a lesson, is in many ways a creative process – it requires thinking about how ideas can be represented and activities structured so that students learn something of worth. Some questions relevant to the design process are:

1 How would you introduce the topic? What could you do to build student interest in the idea of national identity?

2 How would you introduce the task? How could you provide both a sense of the goals towards which learning is directed and some expectations for the final product?

3 What specific knowledge, skills and practices do students have to learn to complete the task? How can activities be structured to support learning of specific knowledge, skills and practices? What knowledge, skills and practices require explicit teaching? What require self-directed learning on the part of the students?

4 How can activities be structured to enable students to connect the knowledge, skills and practices of the task's components with the big picture of the task?

Designing a unit of work associated with a large-scale assessment task requires teachers to identify the components of the task, provide opportunities for these components to be understood and be connected. The example has various components related to the topic of national identity, as well as to the skills, knowledge and practices required to both extend understanding of the topic and complete the task.

'Research' is one component of the rich task. How will students be taught and learn the necessary skills, knowledge and practices? In this case, the task may involve library research, internet research and field research, and the analysis and presentation of data. Think about how you learnt to do research. In part you probably learnt through practice, through actually doing research. Your knowledge and skills are then developed and refined over time. How can teachers support students to learn by doing? Some options are the teacher modelling, demonstrating and explaining; students starting with a small research task and then building up to a larger task; giving students opportunities to check interpretations with others; giving feedback on students' practice; and students applying skills in new or different contexts or with different sets of data. Within the context of a rich task, such support may be required before, during and after work on the task.

The approach to teaching and learning may vary with the skills and knowledge necessary for different practices. For example, a teacher may offer different supports and structures to assist students to learn a set of technological skills to those required for students to learn communication or research skills.

Opportunities to practice

Learning a complex practice does not happen overnight. With respect to the sorts of practices associated with the rich task, students would need multiple opportunities to actually 'practise' the practice; that is, to build skills and knowledge and to get feedback before presenting a final product. Practice in this respect does not mean mindless repetition, rather offering a range of opportunities to build skills and knowledge. An activity such as learning to drive a car is a useful illustration here. Many people start learning to drive on backstreets where there are few cars, traffic lights, people and other distractions. As their skills and knowledge build, learner drivers move from minor to major streets and then to busy three-lane highways. Learning to drive can mean moving from what Lave and Wenger (1991) describe as 'peripheral' to more 'legitimate' forms of participation in the practices required to drive a car. Full 'legitimacy' may come with passing a driving test. In a classroom context, legitimate participation may come with the successful completion of a rich task. The key for a teacher is to structure activities that support moving from peripheral to legitimate participation and that build and extend knowledge of the topic and engagement in the practices associated with the topic.

Opportunities to practise in a lesson or unit of work will vary depending upon the time, subject matter, teaching and learning strategies and students. Key elements of structuring lessons or units of work include:

- explicating learning goals and connecting parts of learning
- giving necessary explanations, demonstrations and instructions
- providing opportunities for practice in ways related to the overall task
- offering guidance and feedback throughout.

The role of teachers in the learning process

Vygotsky (1978) asserted that the potential for development is greater when there is guidance or 'scaffolding' provided by those with expertise. This has done much to highlight the importance of teachers' expertise in the learning process. In the example, there are many occasions in which teachers could take an active role in assisting students to build the knowledge and skills required to complete the rich task. This might involve working with the whole class, small groups or individuals. It might involve explanations and demonstrations. It might involve giving ongoing feedback. Teachers typically have to judge how they balance explicit teaching with opportunities for students to learn through their own inquiry. For example, the concept of national identity is complex and some explicit teaching may be required to assist students to understand this concept over time.

One way that teachers can guide learning is by making clear learning expectations and recognising achievement. Knowing what is expected in relation to the activities associated with a rich task, and defining standards of good practice, can be important in focusing student learning. Clearly defined assessment criteria can give students a sense of what they should be aiming for, as well as what constitutes good practice. The feedback and recognition associated with completion of tasks is also an essential part of the learning process (see Chapter 5). Without acknowledgement of achievement and effort, the worth of the project can be devalued.

Teachers' expectations of students are also a critical influence on classroom learning (Eccles & Roeser 2003). Building an expectation for success is an important motivator for student learning.

The role of student interaction in the learning process

We mentioned above the ways that learning can take place through social interaction. Key resources for learning in classrooms are the students themselves (Ainscow 1999). Teachers can draw on this resource in many ways. One common way is through groupwork. Clearly there are benefits from working together: resources can be pooled, tasks shared, ideas tested with peers, and knowledge generated through exchange. Yet, as you probably know from experience, not all groupwork is successful. Given that the rich task requires students to work in groups, it is worth thinking about how groupwork skills can be developed. Ainscow offers some useful strategies to enable students to work effectively in groups:

- begin by working in pairs on straightforward tasks
- pool work completed independently into a group task
- assign roles to group members
- assess collaborative and individual effort (1999: 66).

DIFFERENCES BETWEEN STUDENTS AND HOW THEY LEARN

At the start of the chapter we noted one of the central concerns faced by all teachers – teaching a whole class and, at the same time, catering for the range of abilities, aspirations and backgrounds of students in the class. Some students have specific learning difficulties; some may complete work more quickly than others; some are gifted in their academic capabilities; some struggle with a task because they do not have the necessary literacy skills; some may find a topic boring, others may be highly motivated to learn about the topic. Likewise, returning to the ideas raised in Chapters 1 and 2, we can think about student difference and learning in terms of social factors: for example, gender, social class, ethnicity and language background. It is an incredibly complex component of teaching. Considerable planning is required to design activities for the whole class and at the same time personalise the learning (Ainscow 1999). We consider below three ways that individual differences in relation to learning are often characterised and understood in schools.

EXISTING KNOWLEDGE AND SKILLS

Ainscow (1999) argues that one of the most fundamental starting points for learning is the knowledge and understanding that students already have. For teachers this means finding out and tapping into what students already know and then building on this. This can be as straightforward as beginning a lesson with an introduction to ascertain students' existing knowledge or it might involve a more formal written survey of students' knowledge as a precursor to designing a unit of work. Teachers build their knowledge of students' understandings and abilities over time through both formal and informal means of assessing and evaluating student work (see Chapter 5). In the previous example of a rich task, a teacher may need to ascertain students' skill and knowledge in relation to not only the content (Australian identity) but also skills related to, for example, using a video camera, interviewing people and creating a documentary. Students come to class with a surprising amount of knowledge and skills – this is a critical starting point for unit and lesson design.

LEARNING STYLES

Students' learning styles or preferences is a concept commonly talked about in schools. Learning styles are typically categorised in three ways: students as visual learners (learn by looking, reading and writing), auditory learners (learn by talking and listening) or kinesthetic learners (learn by doing). While these styles oversimplify the complex ways that students learn, they are an initial way of thinking about how learning activities can be structured not only to cater for such differences but also to build students' capacities across the styles. The activities associated with completing the example of a rich task accommodate different styles and enable students to build capacities across the styles. Consider how students could bring their learning preference to the tasks of conducting interviews, working in groups, preparing a script for a documentary, conducting web-based research, filming and editing a documentary, taking on a reporting role and being filmed for the documentary.

MULTIPLE INTELLIGENCES

The notion of multiple intelligences (MI), developed by Howard Gardner in the 1980s, is likewise widely discussed in schools as a way of understanding individual differences in relation to learning. Gardner's (1983, 2006) theory of multiple intelligences is based on the premise that each person has a unique range of intelligences and talents that are linked to different parts of their brain. These intelligences are concerned with linguistic, logical–mathematical, musical, spatial, bodily–kinesthetic, and interpersonal abilities.[1] MI is a useful framework for thinking about students' talents and abilities in broad and varied ways. The rich task example offers multiple ways for students both to build on their talents and to extend their abilities. Think about making a documentary film – the sound, script development, communication between all involved, the shooting of the video. Think about the range of intelligences that students would draw on to complete the documentary and how students with different talents could contribute to the production, as well as the ways that the range of individual talents and intelligences could be developed through making a documentary.

CLASSROOM STRATEGIES TO RESPOND TO DIFFERENCE

Offering choice and options

Choice of topics can be a useful way of acknowledging student difference. The example of the rich task is open-ended, so there are various ways that topics and modes of learning could be developed. This opens up the potential for student choice in ways that link to their abilities, interests and backgrounds. For example, some students may be interested in sport and so could discuss how sport is linked to Australian identity. Some students may be interested in their family background and could connect to local and national aspects of Australia's multicultural population as a way of understanding aspects of identity.

Varying strategies

Variation in the use of teaching strategies is another means of catering for the differing abilities, backgrounds and interests of students. For example, a teacher may employ whole-class, small-group and individual activities to assist students to build conceptual knowledge about national identity. The range of strategies that teachers can draw on is enormous and allows for considerable creativity. Some examples of strategies and tasks are:

- *Broad or named strategies*: problem-solving; inquiry approach; thinking tools: for example, six hats; webquests; simulations; rich tasks.
- *Common school tasks*: discuss, explain, debate, describe, argue, demonstrate, present, practise, design, create, report.
- *Specific activities*: reading and writing; speaking and listening; collaborating; groupwork or individual work; experimenting; constructing models; searching the internet; watching a video; completing worksheets, questions and answers; discussing as a class, playing a game, building skills, doing textbook exercises.

---

1. We strongly urge you to read Gardner's original work, as well as that of other key educational theorists, to fully understanding their ideas. Gardner is only one of many psychologists who have developed theories of learning. We chose his work because the concept of multiple intelligences is now widely used in many Middle Years settings and often informs the design of lessons and units of work. MI has also provided the groundwork for numerous developments that seek to understand how young people learn. Every so often, some educational ideas gain currency in school systems across a number of countries. 'Habits of Mind' by Costa and Kallick (2000) is an example that has recently taken hold in Australia as a way of supporting student cognition and thinking.

Personalising learning

There are a number of ways that teachers can build their knowledge of the learning needs and capabilities of individuals, as well as respond to those needs during the course of a day or lesson. Creating opportunities to talk to individuals can enable teachers to make connections between class activities and learning needs. Having a range of materials and resources also is a means of connecting and adapting to individual needs. Keeping both formal and informal records enables teachers to build sets of clues about students' capabilities.

Valuing difference

Hayes et al. (2006) develop the idea of recognising and valuing difference by suggesting that quality teaching that improves educational outcomes for all students acknowledges different forms of cultural knowledge, deliberately creates opportunities for all students to participate and fosters classroom cultures that value and legitimate social difference and diversity.

Using specialised knowledge

Many specialised educational fields are concerned with the learning needs of particular groups, such as gifted and talented students, students with special needs, students with learning difficulties or disabilities. Each field has developed theories and practices responsive to the needs of these groups. We do not go into the detail of these fields here; however, you may wish to extend your reading based on your interests and the particular needs of the students with whom you are working.

PROVOCATION: WORKING WITH RICH TASKS

In the previous section we have touched on ideas to help you to think about teaching and learning practices in a Middle Years classroom. Working backwards from an assessment task is a useful way of understanding how the pedagogical activities associated with a task can be developed. We briefly consider how some of these ideas might be built into lessons and a unit of work later in the chapter. At this stage, consider the following provocation about the given example of a rich task:

- Scenario 1 – introducing the rich task to students: the rich task is substantial and will require ongoing work by the students over a series of weeks. What could be done to build challenge and connections in the topic and the task?

- Scenario 2 – completing the task in groups: one group is having trouble working as a team. How can you help this group to work more effectively as a team? How would you implement the following options: agreeing on rules for communication, following models for negotiation and task-sharing, practising and giving feedback, setting consequences for not completing the task or not working effectively as a team?

- Scenario 3 – developing technology skills: a number of students in the class do not know how to use a video camera. How can students learn to use it? Consider the pros and cons of these options: reading and following the instructions, following a demonstration, trial and error, practise and giving feedback, peer coaching.

- Scenario 4 –using interpretation skills: one group shows you their initial interpretation of the interview data. It reflects that the students have only thought about the data in a fairly superficial way and you know that they are capable of much more. What could you do to extend learning in this case?

STUDENT ENGAGEMENT

We turn now to the concept of student engagement, which is useful because its breadth of meaning can encompass the academic, social and emotional dimensions of classrooms. As noted in Chapter 1, the concept of engagement encapsulates not just participation in and completion of tasks (behavioural engagement), but also reactions and feelings towards school, teachers and peers (emotional engagement) and the degree of commitment and sense of purpose related to schooling and education (cognitive engagement).

There are a number of reasons why students might be engaged or disengaged from school learning. Some may be related to schooling writ large, some to classrooms and some to factors outside school. Here we focus in particular on those factors within schools. Factors outside school are discussed in more detail in Chapters 1 and 2.

The research converges about the school and classroom factors that enhance student engagement or that disengage students from learning (for a detailed summary see Murray et al. 2004). These factors tie to the social and emotional dimensions of classroom life, the meaningfulness of work and learning, and the school climate. Table 4.1 reflects these dimensions.

Table 4.1   School factors affecting student engagement

CLASSROOM LIFE

- caring, fun and fair
- respectful relationships between teachers and students
- sense of belonging and membership
- varied types of interaction
- support of diversity and varied perspectives
- success for all students
- student voice heard and respected
- clear and agreed-on rules

WORK AND LEARNING

- purposeful and connected to other subjects and life outside school
- intellectually challenging; rewarding, interesting and fun
- intrinsic and extrinsic rewards
- high expectations of students; explicit expectations in learning tasks
- teachers have strong knowledge of subjects
- students involved in creating learning goals and assessment

SCHOOL CLIMATE

- transition from primary to secondary school well managed
- positive representation of students
- student participation and leadership
- community links
- fair disciplinary climate

(Newmann 1992; Murray et al. 2004; Hayes et al. 2006)

The literature on engagement is important because it attends to the social as well as academic conditions that support learning. The question of classroom life is often missing from discussions about student learning. While it can be a fairly nebulous concept, and while there are many different types of classroom climates and various ways that a positive climate is created, it is worth thinking about, particularly in the context of adolescent development and the transition to secondary school. Communication and relationships are key here: how can positive student–teacher relationships be created to both enable young people to make decisions, take responsibility and be autonomous and, at the same time, provide support and stability for that autonomy? We elaborate on this issue in the case study later in the chapter.

It is important to note that engagement and disengagement are not neat and discrete categories. There is no on/off button – engaged or disengaged. Rather, there are varied forms of engagement and levels of engagement. For example, a student might participate actively in an English class, but withdraw from activities in a PE class. Or a student might be engaged in class work by completing set tasks and achieving good grades, but they might be really unhappy at school.

Vibert and Shields (2003) make the case that it is problematic to view engagement or disengagement as a quality located within individual students. Rather, they argue, students (and teachers) are engaged in learning when schools and classrooms are engaging places to be. They further argue that there is no one program or package that can engage students, rather pedagogies that make classrooms engaging places should be developed to suit schools, their purposes and the people in them. Clearly, building the practices that make schools and classrooms engaging places does not happen overnight, but it is worth thinking about how some of these practices could be created during a fieldwork placement and developed more substantively when working with a class over longer periods of time.

TEACHING TO EXTEND STUDENT LEARNING AND ENGAGEMENT

Here we detail some specific teaching models and practices that support learning and engagement in the Middle Years. There are two important provisos. First, we emphasise that there are no sure-fire prescriptions for teaching that will definitely work in all classrooms. While there is a wide body of literature that details the knowledge and skills constitutive of good pedagogy in the Middle Years (and across all school sectors), adaptation, adjustment and development based on context and circumstances is always necessary.

Second, a number of pedagogical principles and practices have been developed to engage students in the Middle Years and attend to their learning needs and interests. Here we outline *some*. It is impossible in the scope of this book to detail a wide range of pedagogical strategies and approaches. Rather our intent is to give you some examples of principles and practices and then develop a framework that you can use to build your ideas about good teaching and learning in the Middle Years.

The examples below encompass both large-scale frameworks that guide the long-term goals and development of the classroom learning environment, as well as more immediate day-to-day strategies and practices.

Example 1: Middle schooling signature practices

During the 1990s the National Middle Schooling Project (see Barratt 1998a, 1998b) in Australia provided significant direction for current practice for the Middle Years. The project grew out of growing concerns about student disengagement, and research and innovation conducted in South Australia. The project identified key needs of young adolescents and developed a set of organisational, curriculum and pedagogical principles and practices relevant to those needs. These are documented in Table 4.2. (We ask that you keep in mind that these principles and practices are strongly connected to other parts of school organisation and curriculum development.) The ideas developed as part of this project have been influential in policy and practice related to Middle Years across all states and territories in Australia. Many schools – primary or secondary, central schools, clusters of schools or purpose-built middle schools – have drawn on ideas from this project to develop programs and strategies.

Example 2: Productive pedagogies

'Productive pedagogies' is a term now widely used in Australian schools. Developed in Queensland as part of the Queensland School Reform Longitudinal Study (QSRLS) (Lingard et al. 2001), the productive pedagogies framework has been used as a tool to analyse and inform teaching and learning practices in a number of schools. Extending the research conducted by Newmann (1996) in America on authentic pedagogy, the QSRLS research sought to develop a pedagogical framework that would capture not only the academic dimensions of pedagogy, but also its social justice and equity dimensions. The study identified a number of elements of pedagogy related to the social and intellectual purposes of schooling and then used these elements to observe and rate the teaching and learning practices in over 1000 classrooms in Queensland. Based on the analysis of the observational data, the elements were grouped into four main dimensions of pedagogy: intellectual engagement, connectedness, supportive classroom environment and working with and valuing difference.[2] A key argument developed through the research was the importance of teaching practices that:

*   attend to academic rigour and enabled students to build a deep understanding of content
*   connect in-school learning to students' lives out of school and connected students' learning across subjects
*   connect with students' existing knowledge
*   create a classroom environment in which students had a clear sense of behavioural and academic expectations and in which they regulated their own actions
*   value difference by recognising the needs of individual students and built upon a strong understanding of the cultures, backgrounds and experiences of students.

Some of the key findings of the QSRLS and the productive pedagogies model that are pertinent to the discussion of teaching and learning in the Middle Years are:

*   While lessons observed tended to rate reasonably well in terms of the supportiveness of the classroom environment, there were generally much lower levels of intellectual engagement, connectedness and recognition and valuing of diversity. Ratings were lower across these four dimensions for Year 8 classes (the first year of secondary school in Queensland).
*   In those classes in which there were high ratings on all four dimensions of pedagogy, there was strong correlation with student achievement scores. These correlations were high across a range of schools in varied locations and with students from varied backgrounds. These findings demonstrated that the quality of pedagogy can make a difference to student learning outcomes.

Given these findings, a number of schools and systems have developed the means by which teachers can draw on the productive pedagogies framework to improve the quality of their teaching practice and student learning outcomes. Some of the ideas developed in Queensland have been adapted and modified in other Australian states. In New South Wales, the Quality Teaching framework trialled in schools has as its antecedent the productive pedagogies framework. Likewise, other systems have

---

2. For a more detailed description and explanation of productive pedagogies, see Hayes et al. (2006).

Table 4.2 Key components of middle schooling principles and practices

NEEDS OF ADOLESCENTS	PRINCIPLES	PEDAGOGICAL PRACTICES	EXAMPLES
identity (sense of self in relation to groups and cultures)	learner centred	positive teacher–student relationships and student–student relationships	extended contact with small number of teachers; teaching teams; home rooms and home groups
relationships (respectful relationships with peers and adults)	collaboratively organised	student participation and responsibility	class meetings; negotiating curriculum
purpose (learning linked to present and future)	outcome based	flexible use of time and space	alternatives to rigid timetabling structures
empowerment (being able to work independently and responsibly)	flexibly constructed	cooperative learning	collaboration and communication that enables knowledge-building
success (range of opportunities to learn and demonstrate skills, knowledge and talents)	ethically aware	practical, real-life, relevant activities	rich tasks
rigour (challenging work, high expectations, honest feedback)	community oriented	higher order and critical thinking	learning beyond recall and remembering; opportunities to construct, challenge, apply, revise and practise
safety (safe and caring environment that is supportive of all students)	adequately resourced	pastoral care as part of pedagogy	acknowledging social and emotional dimensions of learning; teaching students *and* subjects
	strategically linked		

(Australian Curriculum Studies Association 1996; Barratt 1998a, 1998b; Cumming 1998)

developed principles and standards for teaching that draw on ideas from productive pedagogies. The Principles of Learning and Teaching (POLTS) developed in Victoria is an example.

The productive pedagogies framework is useful for designing a unit of work. It provides a language and framework for both the *academic* and *social* dimensions of pedagogy; for thinking about how teaching practices can foster intellectual engagement and connection by recognising the diversity of students' backgrounds; and for creating a supportive classroom environment. Hayes et al. (2006) argue that employing productive pedagogies in classrooms can extend the learning outcomes for *all* students.

Example 3: What students say about good teaching and learning

As noted, giving students an opportunity to have a voice in the operation of classrooms is an important component of many initiatives in the Middle Years. We should ask then, what are students' views on good teaching and learning in the Middle Years? Susan Groundwater-Smith (2005) has been working on a research project in which she asks young people to talk about what they see as good teaching and learning. In one of her interviews with Year 9 students, she asked them about how they liked to learn in Maths and English. The responses provide interesting insights. It was important for students to like the teacher, they didn't like work that was boring, they liked the opportunity to participate and be active (involving practical hands-on work, less writing and more discussing, and not just bookwork). Students also liked the teacher to give good explanations. Finally, they liked learning when the teacher could keep difficult students 'under control'.

The emphasis placed by these students on work that is interesting, that can be done in a range of ways (other than 'bookwork'), that involves active participation and in which the teacher has the pedagogical and content knowledge to offer good explanations is a good starting point for designing a lesson or unit of work and setting some useful conditions for learning.

In a similar vein, a study conducted in the United Kingdom (Riley & Rustique-Forrester 2002) asked some teenagers who were disaffected from school to put forward their perceptions of 'good' and 'bad' teachers. Again, their comments are an important perspective on the actions that teachers can take to engage students:

> *Good teachers*: helpful and supportive, take time to explain things, friendly, understanding, know the subject well, use a variety of strategies, fair, recognise and reward good work.

> *Bad teachers*: mean and unfair, unwilling to help, judgemental of family, rigid routines, inflexible and disrespectful, unaware or not sympathetic re problems, intimidating (2002: 30).

As a means of getting to know students and how they learn, we suggest that it can be instructive to seek their views on what constitutes good teaching and learning and the conditions under which they learn best. It can also be instructive to ask students after a lesson the main (two or three) things that they learnt. This is a useful way of considering whether your teaching goals align with student learning.

Example 4: Dealing with disengagement

Student disengagement in classrooms manifests in many ways from rowdy behaviour to quiet lack of participation. The best way to deal with disengagement is by making classrooms engaging places for all students and by developing pedagogical practices that are interesting and worthwhile. Indeed, a recent evaluation of the Priority Schools Action Program in New South Wales noted that in the classrooms in which teachers used productive pedagogies there was improved behaviour: 'Consistently, teachers reported that behaviour problems decreased substantially and that "predictably difficult" students were on task, motivated and learning' (Groundwater-Smith & Kemmis 2004: 66). The evaluation went on to suggest that behaviour management plans in schools were effective when aligned with plans for engagement and pedagogy, and when based on positive feedback and 'reward' rather than punitive measures. Two points to think about here are: (1) the development of a classroom engagement plan that incorporates issues of classroom management by focusing on ways of building respectful relations and setting rules and routines that are clear, consistent and fair; and (2) as noted earlier, developing engaging classrooms and building the routines and structures to guide a class takes time, but having a plan in place is a critical and important starting point for dealing with a range of student behaviours and for extending the participation of all students.

CASE STUDY
Taking risks in teaching and learning

The case study illustrates the strategies developed in one school to build student engagement with learning. Valley Central is a K–12 school in a small rural town. Like a number of rural towns in Australia, the town has experienced considerable change over the last decade – people have been moving to larger towns or cities; there are fewer jobs in the town and rising levels of unemployment. For Valley Central this has meant declining enrolments and a growing proportion of students whose families are facing social and economic hardship. Staff at the school have implemented some initiatives to encourage students' participation in school and, in so doing, broaden their post-school pathways. One component of the reform has focused on vocational education in Year 9 and Year 10. The other component of reform has been the development of a middle school from Year 5 to Year 8. Four teachers work in the middle school. Some of the practices employed by these teachers to engage students and extend their learning are outlined below.

Three important aspects of the middle school at Valley Central are:

- First, one core component of the middle school curriculum is a set of integrated units in Science, Maths, English and Social Science. These units are innovative in their design and focus on capturing student interest and imagination.

- Second, the teachers work as a team. Regular meetings are held to design the program, implement it and to evaluate, refine and improve it over a long period. There is a real dynamic to the middle school program because of these regular team meetings – the teachers can respond to issues straight away and generate new ideas through their collective commitment to the program.

- Third, two 'home' classes have been created and students from Years 5 to 8 are in both. The teachers work in teams of two with each of the home classes. This team teaching also enables teachers to talk through issues, build their understanding of classroom dynamics and take more risks with their teaching.

Class environment and relationships

Using the term 'home' to describe a class is important and it underpins a central part of pedagogy in the middle school at Valley Central: that is, to build a classroom environment that encourages students to 'have a go' with their learning. Teachers want the students to feel confident about their learning abilities, to be interested in the work and to take a few risks in developing ideas. The teachers see the first couple of months of the school year as crucial to building such an environment. During this time they work on developing positive relationships (between students and teachers, and between students) and the social skills associated with good relationships. For the teachers this means getting to know the students in the class. They aim to 'touch base' with each student in the class twice a day. This isn't a deliberate 'tick the list' to make sure they have interacted with each student, rather, in the ebb and flow of the day to create the conversational space to better understand each student, their likes and dislikes, their hobbies and interests, their skills and knowledge, their sense of humour. The interaction might only be fleeting – sharing a joke, commenting on a sport result or a television show – or it might be a more sustained interaction related to a class task, but these small-scale and day-to-day interactions with the students are a crucial part of building a classroom community. Teachers get to know students in ways that enable them to help students make connections between inside and outside school, and to ascertain any problems that may emerge. Students have regular contact with two adults who they trust.

Participation

A second component of pedagogy employed by the teachers at Valley Central is to encourage participation in class activities. Many of the students don't want to make mistakes in front of their peers and some students don't have a lot of confidence in their academic abilities. To address this, the teachers have worked on building students' social skills and their teamwork. At the start of the year the teachers run outdoor activities and games specifically designed to build trust and confidence. This is a starting point for encouraging students to participate in the activities in the integrated units of work. Having built a level of trust and respect between the students, the teachers are then in a position to extend the ways that students work together and learn from each other. Thus, in the integrated units, a number of tasks require students to work as teams or to present ideas to the whole class. They are able to do this because of the deliberate efforts to build student confidence. Students are willing to have a go, to learn through participation without feeling self-conscious or open to ridicule.

Sense of self as learner

During their time in middle school, students are given opportunities to develop their understanding of how they learn and build on their learning strengths. This sense of themselves as learners becomes increasingly complex. At the start of middle school students take time to think about their own learning styles – are they visual learners, auditory learners or kinesthetic learners? In the second and third year of the program the students identify the social and physical environments in which they best learn. In the fourth year students use the language of multiple intelligences to talk about their talents and how they draw on these talents to undertake tasks.

Student voice

The teaching team regularly get feedback from students about how the middle school is working. At the end of each unit of work the teachers conduct a more formal evaluation that provides feedback on teaching, as well as the ways that the curriculum is targeting student needs and interests. What is important is that students are able to see how teachers respond to the feedback. For example, students have made a lot of suggestions about the physical environment in the classrooms and, because of the home-room set–up, the teachers have designed the classroom so that there are different learning areas that students can use. One area has beanbags, another area has large boards for students to work on; there is a computer area, as well as an area with desks and chairs.

Differentiating teaching and learning strategies

A key goal for the teaching teams is to develop strategies that cater for student difference and, in particular, to work with the different abilities of students as well as their different approaches to learning. To do this, the teachers employ a planning pyramid so that they deliberately develop specific activities for students who need the most academic support, students who can work independently and students who will benefit from extension activities. Likewise, teachers plan their lessons and units of work so that there is variation in strategies, using some individual tasks, some group tasks and some whole-class tasks; tasks that enable students to draw on their learning strengths; and tasks that get progressively more complex or that require the sophisticated building of skills over time.

Teachers taking risks

What is important in the middle school is that the risk-taking occurs at two levels – both students and teachers take risks with their learning. Working in a team provides an environment in which the teachers are prepared to try new strategies and innovative approaches. The team meetings also offer teachers an opportunity to regularly evaluate and review their practice. The teachers have also had to build trust in each other. This willingness to develop ideas and learn from each other has been a cornerstone of the middle-school program.

DISCUSSION STARTERS

Given the dynamic nature of the middle-school program, the teachers are always facing new challenges. One challenge that they are currently working on concerns the transition from Year 8 to Year 9. Some of the Year 8 students do not want to be in the middle school. They would prefer to be in high school and show this by being disruptive in class. This raises questions about the management of transitions and about how to ensure that being in middle school doesn't feel like being held back from high school.

1   How the school can address these questions?

Sustaining pedagogical reform over time can be very difficult and it often depends on stability of staff. The team at Valley Central has changed over the six years and, each time there is a change, adjustments have to be made to both accommodate new members of the teaching team and to build levels of trust and commitment. This is easier said than done and the process associated with changing staff can take time.

2   If you were to join a team such as this, what sort of attributes do you think would be required to work in the middle school?

3   How could trust and respect be developed among team members?

CONCLUSION

This chapter has covered a lot of territory. Its main concern has been to explore conceptual and practical tools that are relevant to your teaching in the Middle Years. The term 'pedagogy' is important because it captures the dynamic interrelationship between teaching and learning. We encourage you to debate and discuss how the pedagogical practices that you employ can transform the learning of your students.

This chapter has focused on pedagogy in the Middle Years that attends to the *academic* and *social* dimensions of learning. More specifically, our analysis of the general research on teaching and learning, as well as the research specific to the Middle Years, emphasises these aspects as being critical to students' learning:

- learning tasks and practice are challenging, meaningful and connected
- whole-class and personalised activities and strategies are varied, with multiple opportunities to practise, and are structured to support learning
- classrooms are engaging and encourage participation, positive feelings and respectful relationships
- expectations are high, achievable and clear.

We do not suggest that this list is the final word on pedagogy. Other dimensions of pedagogy are developed throughout the book. Likewise, strategies, practices and expectations need to be explicated in light of the needs of particular groups of students, the subject matter and the school context.

Underpinning teaching and learning practices are sets of beliefs, values, theories and debates. In the middle of teaching a class, you might not be thinking 'what theory will I draw on to do this'; however, by making explicit the theories, values, beliefs and knowledge underpinning your pedagogical practices, you are in a good position to outline your perspective on pedagogy and explain and justify the teaching practices that you employ.

It can be much easier to talk about good teaching than to practise it. In this respect, our comments are framed by a strong respect for the demands and complexity of teachers' work, and for theories of pedagogy that are derived from practice.

And, finally, back to Miss Belmont and Grade 6 at Baringa East Primary School. By morning recess on the first day of school the class had 'mental exhaustion'. Miss Belmont, on the other hand, was 'quite calm and relaxed as she sailed into the staff room for morning coffee' (Klein 1984: 5). Staying calm and relaxed is also a good teaching strategy!

References

Ainscow, M. (1999) *Understanding the Development of Inclusive Schools.* London, UK: Falmer Press.

Alexander, R. (2000) *Culture and Pedagogy: International Comparisons in Primary Education.* Oxford, UK: Blackwell.

Australian Curriculum Studies Association (1996) *From Alienation to Engagement: Opportunities for Reform in the Middle Years.* Canberra: Australian Curriculum Studies Association.

Barratt, R. (1998a) *Shaping middle schooling in Australia: A report of the National Middle*

Schooling Project. Canberra: Australian Curriculum Studies Association.

Barratt, R. (1998b) 'The future: The shape of middle schooling in Australia'. *Curriculum Perspectives*, 18(1), 53–6.

Batten, M. & Russell, J. (1995) Students at Risk: A Review of the Australian Literature 1980–1994. Melbourne: Australian Council for Educational Research.

Bruner, J. (1996) *The Culture of Education.* Cambridge, MA: Harvard University Press.

Carrington, V. (2003) 'Mid-term review: the middle years of schooling'. *Curriculum Perspectives*, 24, 30–41.

Costa, A. & Kallick, B. (2000) 'Habits of Mind'. Accessed on 15 September 2006 from www.habits-of-mind.net/.

Cumming, J. (1998) *Extending Reform in the Middle Years of Schooling: Challenges and Responses.* Canberra: Australian Curriculum Studies Association.

Department of Education, Queensland (2004) *Rich Task – Australian National Identity: Influences and Perspectives.* Accessed on 15 September 2006 from http://education. qld.gov.au/corporate/newbasics/pdfs/ yr9rt4.pdf.

Dewey, J. (1916) *Democracy and Education.* New York, NY: Macmillan.

Dewey, J. (1938) *Education and Experience.* New York, NY: Collier Macmillan.

Eccles, J. & Roeser, R. (2003) 'Schools as development contexts', in G. Adams & M. Berzonsky (eds), *Blackwell Handbook of Adolescence.* Malden, MA: Blackwell.

Gardner, H. (1983) *Frames of Mind: The Theory of Multiple Intelligences.* New York, NY: Basic Books.

Gardner, H. (2006) *The Development and Education of the Mind: The Selected Works of Howard Gardner.* London, UK: Routledge.

Groundwater-Smith, S. (2005) Giving students a voice – Learning to listen: listening to learn. Paper presented to Australian College of Education, Sydney, August.

Groundwater-Smith, S. & Kemmis, S. (2004) *Knowing Makes the Difference: Learnings from the NSW Priority Action Schools Program.* Sydney: New South Wales Department of Education and Training.

Hayes, D., Mills, M., Christie, P. & Lingard, B. (2006) *Teachers and Schooling: Making a Difference.* Sydney: Allen & Unwin.

Hill, P. & Russell, J. (1999) 'Systemic, whole-school reform of the middle years of schooling', in R. Bosker, B. Creemers & S. Stringfield (eds), *Enhancing Educational Excellence, Equity and Efficiency: Evidence from Evaluation Systems and Schools in Change.* Dortrecht, Netherlands: Kluwer Academic.

Jackson, A. & Davis, G. (2000) *Turning Points 2000: Educating Adolescents in the 21st Century.* New York, NY: Teachers College Press.

Kenway, J. & Bullen, E. (2001) *Consuming Children: Education—Entertainment— Advertising.* Buckingham, UK: Open University Press.

Klein, R. (1998) *Hating Alison Ashley.* Melbourne: Puffin.

Lave, J. & Wenger, E. (1991) *Situated Learning: Legitimate and Peripheral Participation.* Cambridge, MA: Cambridge University Press.

Lingard, B., Ladwig, J., Luke, A., Mills, M., Hayes, D. & Gore, J. (2001) *Queensland School Reform Longitudinal Study: Final Report.* Brisbane: Education Queensland.

Murray, S., Mitchell, J., Gale, T., Edwards, J. & Zyngier, D. (2004) *Student Disengagement from Primary School: A Review of Research and Practice.* Melbourne: CASS Foundation.

Newmann, F. (ed.) (1992) *Student Engagement and Achievement in American Secondary Schools.* New York, NY: Teachers College Press.

Newmann, F. (1996) *Authentic Achievement: Restructuring Schools for Intellectual Quality.* San Francisco, CA: Jossey-Bass.

Pendergast, D. (2005) 'The emergence of middle schooling', in D. Pendergast & N. Bahr (eds), *Teaching Middle Years.* Sydney: Allen & Unwin.

Riley, K. & Rustique-Forrester, E. (2002) *Working with Disaffected Students: Why Students Lose Interest in School and What We Can Do About It.* London, UK: Paul Chapman.

Vibert, A. & Shields, C. (2003) 'Approaches to student engagement: does ideology matter?'. *McGill Journal of Education*, 38, 221–40.

Vygotsky, L. (1978) *Mind in Society*, (ed. M. Cole). Cambridge, MA: Harvard University Press.

Vygotsky, L. (1997) *Thought and Language* (trans. A. Kozulin). Cambridge, MA: MIT Press.

Wells, G. (1999) *Dialogic Inquiry: Toward a Sociocultural Practice and Theory of Education.* New York, NY: Cambridge University Press.

ASSESSING LEARNING

Teachers must deal with two basic issues that are the source of many of the problems associated with changing to a system of formative assessment. The first is the nature of each teacher's beliefs about learning. If the teacher assumes that knowledge is to be transmitted and learned, that understanding will develop later, and that clarity of exposition accompanied by rewards for patient reception are the essentials of good teaching, then formative assessment is hardly necessary. However, most teachers accept the wealth of evidence that this transmission model does not work, even when judged by its own criteria, and so are willing to make a commitment to teaching through interaction. Formative assessment is an essential component of such instruction. We do not mean to imply that individualized, one-on-one teaching is the only solution; rather we mean that what is needed is a classroom culture of questioning and deep thinking, in which pupils learn from shared discussions with teachers and peers. What emerges very clearly here is the indivisibility of instruction and formative assessment practices (Black & Wiliam 1998: 144).

INTRODUCTION

The Middle Years of schooling are fertile ground for the development of assessment strategies and practices that focus on promoting learning and deep understanding. Safe from the high-stakes assessment to be found at the 'pointy end' of secondary school, assessment in the Middle Years is unencumbered by the relentless demands of measurement, percentages and rankings. We believe that this should foster assessment practices that are embedded in the learning process itself. This chapter explores notions of 'formative assessment', 'authentic assessment' (Torrance 1995), 'assessment for learning' and 'productive assessment' (Hayes et al. 2006) in terms of their frameworks, their approaches and their implications for classroom practice.

Key questions guiding this chapter are:

1 What is professional judgement?
2 What are the purposes of assessment in the Middle Years and who are the stakeholders in assessment?
3 What are some innovative models of assessment that support learning in the Middle Years?

PROFESSIONAL JUDGEMENT AND ASSESSMENT

The professional judgement of teachers is the lynchpin of effective assessment. Our capacity to judge the effect and extent of student learning, to be confident in our judgements and to collaboratively develop our skills impacts directly on our ability to be involved in the kinds of formative assessment discussed in this chapter. In relation to the importance of professional judgement in the development of teacher autonomy and emancipation, Stenhouse writes:

> The essence of emancipation, as I conceive it, is the intellectual, moral and spiritual autonomy which we recognise when we eschew paternalism and the rule of authority and hold ourselves obliged to appeal to judgement. Emancipation rests not merely on the right of a person to exercise intellectual, moral and spiritual judgement, but upon the passionate belief that the virtue of humanity is diminished in man when judgement is overruled by authority (1983: 163).

The implications of this in terms of evaluation and the collection of evidence for assessment of student and teacher learning is discussed in more detail in Chapter 9, but we stress here that effective assessment, to a great extent, relies upon teachers having confidence in and authentic opportunities to exercise their professional judgement. This in turn relies on our schools being places where high levels of trust are fostered, a responsibility that falls to all of us who work in them and one that is examined in greater depth in Chapter 8. As a profession, the more confident we are in this capacity, the less we feel the need to rely on less authentic assessment techniques. But professional judgement does not become finely honed without practice, and neither does it become finely honed in isolation. Developing well-polished professional judgement is very much a collaborative enterprise, and one that can lead not only to better assessment for students but also to enhanced collegiality and professional learning for the teachers involved.

Assessment of student learning

Assessment of student learning has many purposes, some of which can sometimes be conflicting or even diametrically opposed, and many stakeholders. Because this area is quite contested and complex, it is useful to take a moment to consider what these purposes and who the stakeholders are and whose interests really should be looked after in student assessment.

The stakeholders

Students

Students, we believe, are the most important stakeholders in the assessment process. Ideally, assessment should be used to give feedback to students on their progress, make the goals of learning and students' progress towards those goals transparent and understood, and support students at each stage in the learning process towards the attainment of learning outcomes. In order to achieve these goals, assessment should be entirely embedded in the learning process itself, explicit and varied in its nature. The capacity of assessment to support the learning process is discussed later in the chapter.

Parents and carers

Parents and carers have an understandable interest in assessment processes and outcomes, and the reporting of student achievement, and, as a profession, it is important that we are accountable to parents and carers in assessing student learning, giving them a realistic, accessible and defensible picture of student progress. For most parents and carers, however, their experience as students informs their understanding of effective and 'objective' assessment, and we can hardly expect them to trust a more innovative and less 'objective' approach without understanding it. For this reason, it is essential that we take every opportunity to draw parents and carers into the 'learning conversation', helping them also to understand assessment for learning and to trust our professional judgement. Providing a range of authentic and meaningful opportunities for parents to engage with the processes of schooling, particularly where assessment is concerned, is one of the most vital tasks for schools and teachers.

Approaches to assessment that focus on reporting percentages and rankings of students are often defended by schools who claim that 'parents want them'. We argue that what parents and carers *really* want, on the whole, is to understand their child's progress, and while basing their understanding on percentages and rankings may feel more familiar, it is possible to present parents and carers with a much richer picture of student performance using other methods. As teachers, we are responsible for encouraging parents to support assessment (and reporting) practices that are both generative and clear.

Schools

In the 'audit culture' in which we are currently working, we are seeing a growth in the number and scale of 'external' examinations, even in the Middle Years of schooling. Literacy and numeracy tests, standardised aptitude and general reasoning tests, for example, are being implemented at both state and federal levels, and it sometimes seems that, with each step, we come closer to a system such as that of the United Kingdom, where schools are sorted and ranked in terms of student performance and funding is increasingly tied to 'success'. Thus, the school itself increasingly is a stakeholder in the assessment of student learning, as are state and federal governments.

In our view, while this ongoing review of student performance gives feedback on often narrowly defined skills and knowledge, it falls into the category of 'measurement' rather than 'assessment'. This is not a semantic issue, but rather points to the richer nature of 'assessment' compared to 'measurement'. Indeed, we argue that for assessment to be genuine and accurate, not only does it need to be embedded, explicit and varied, but also that it should be based on authentic learning relationships and finely tuned professional judgement. In the current era, standardised tests may be perceived as a necessary evil, but as educators we should recognise them as a means to an end rather than an end in themselves, and never as the 'main game' of assessment. In a performance performed in schools in the 1990s, Australian educator Julia Atkin suggested to scores of teachers that 'nobody ever made a pig fatter by measuring it', and this is a salient message. Improving 'standards' or student learning outcomes comes from improved teaching and learning practices, and is reflected in evidence collected via assessment practices that focus on deep and enduring learning.

Society

Ultimately, as members of society, we are all stakeholders in the assessment of student learning and as such have an interest in assessment that encourages students to develop a deep and robust understanding of what they are learning, values creative and critical thinking and encourages the development and exercise of independent and collaborative work skills.

VARIETIES OF ASSESSMENT

Before we consider how assessment in the Middle Years can rise to the challenge set by Black and Wiliam (1998) at the beginning of this chapter, it is useful to consider some of the key and different ways that assessment is conceptualised. While these conceptualisations are often represented as dichotomies (for example, summative versus formative assessment), in our view it is more helpful to think of them as a continuum upon which different assessment processes and practices are placed in relation to each other.

Summative and formative assessment

In simple terms, summative assessment takes place at the end of a learning process and generally represents how successful students have been at meeting the learning outcomes. Formative assessment, on the other hand, takes place 'on the way through' and gives students feedback on their progress to assist them in their learning. Wiliam (2000) provides a useful insight into the differences between summative and formative assessment, construing summative assessment as that which is 'retrospective' (looking back over the learning process), while formative assessment is 'prospective' (looking forward to the learning that will happen in the future). This, for us, is the essence of the difference between the two. Regardless of where an assessment takes place in the learning process (at the beginning or middle or end), the test of whether it is more summative than formative or more formative than summative has to do with the intent, construction and process of the assessment task.

The characteristics of summative assessment tasks are that they are:
- situated at (or even some time after) the end of a unit of work
- designed to assign a mark, grade or rank to students in order to compare and draw conclusions about a class or cohort

- accompanied by feedback that is usually limited to advice on how students might have done better on a test or task.

By contrast, the characteristics of formative assessment tasks are that they are:

- situated during (or even throughout) a unit of work
- designed to provide opportunities for teachers and students to consider progress towards student learning outcomes
- accompanied by rich feedback that takes into account the context of the student's learning and suggests improvement and further progress.

Norm-referenced and criterion-referenced assessment

The distinction between norm- and criterion-referenced assessment lies not necessarily in the construction of the task – although how a task is constructed and presented to students is often a reflection of its orientation – but rather in the evaluation and 'marking' approach taken to the task.

Norm-referenced or normative approaches to assessment focus on comparing students and ranking them in relation to their performance on the task, and thus their learning. The most normative approaches use numerical marks whereby the teacher decides in advance what mark represents the acceptable or average level of performance and proceeds to assign marks to students based on the model of normal distribution, otherwise known as the 'bell curve'.

Conversely, criterion-referenced approaches to assessment focus upon the extent to which individual students have met the criteria established at the outset of the task. Criterion-referenced assessment tasks use a grade or descriptor to feed back to students the extent to which they have demonstrated their performance on each outcome and, at the outset, provide a performance rubric that outlines to students the standard of performance required to gain each grade for the task. An example of such an assessment rubric is given in the case study later in this chapter.

It is worthwhile to consider here the links between types of assessment and methods of reporting student learning, for it is often the case that a particular approach to reporting drives a particular form of assessment. The 'plain English report card' (see Figure 5.1 on page 86) championed by the current federal government that is currently being implemented in schools around the country is an example of an approach to reporting that favours normative approaches over criterion-referenced approaches to assessment. While 'A to E' reporting in itself allows for criterion-referenced approaches to be used, including 'position in the year', data on the report card is congruent with forms of assessment that rank and sort students.

PROVOCATION: THE PLAIN ENGLISH REPORT CARD

Look at the plain English report card on page 86.

1 Josh's performance highlights that he has great strengths and also some weakness. Would this be the case for most students? What might be the impact on a student of consistently scoring Es?

2 Given that Josh is currently about 8 years old, what might be the pros and cons for him and his parents of being aware that he is in the bottom quartile in two KLAs?

3 What do you think this report card says about a vision for education in Australian society generally?

The Australian Primary School
PRINCIPAL: *John Smith*

STUDENT: *Josh Citizen - Class 3B*
TEACHER: *Emma Jones*

PLAIN ENGLISH REPORT CARD

Subject	Grade	Position in year				Teacher's Comment
		Top 25%	2ⁿᵈ 25%	3ʳᵈ 25%	Bottom 25%	
English	*B*	✓				*Josh is working well in English and I am pleased with his progress this term. He is a keen reader and is building a very good vocabulary.*
Maths	*D*				✓	*Josh is trying hard in maths and attempting his homework. However, he is not doing as well as last year and I would like to discuss further work he could do at home to improve. Please contact me.*
Science and Technology	*C*			✓		*Josh can do much better than this. Josh's progress in science is adequate, but he shows little interest in technology and is easily distracted when working on the computer. He is capable of more.*
Studies of Society and Environment	*A*	✓				*Josh is an excellent pupil with a particular interest in history. His project work across the board has been of a very good standard.*
Health and Physical Education	*E*				✓	*Josh is not interested in school sport or PE and has not enjoyed swimming this term.*
Creative and Practical Arts	*B*	✓				*Josh has participated well in our performance activities and his art work shows a good appreciation of colour and shape. Josh enjoys music although it is not one of his strengths.*

Explanatory Notes:
A = Excellent, considerably above the standard expected of the year
B = Good, above standard expected of the year
C = Satisfactory, standard expected of the year
D = Less than satisfactory, does not meet standard expected of the year
E = Poor, considerably below the standard expected of the year

Department of Education, Science and Training 2005

Figure 5.1 Sample report card

Divergent and convergent assessment

Created by Torrance (1995) and Pryor (Torrance & Pryor 1998) in their work on authentic assessment, the terms 'divergent assessment' and 'convergent assessment' are used to represent two conceptual models of student assessment upon which, according to their research, teachers generally draw.

Convergent assessment is seen as that which establishes *if* students have acquired predetermined knowledge and skills. The practical aspects of this approach, as defined by Torrance and Pryor (2001: 617), are:

- precise planning and an intention to stick to it
- tick lists and can-do statements
- analysis of the interaction of the learner and the curriculum from the point of view of the curriculum
- closed or pseudo-open questioning and tasks
- focus on contrasting errors with correct responses
- judgemental or quantitative evaluation
- involvement of student as recipient of assessments.

They align this view of assessment with a behaviourist view of learning and suggest that the approach views assessment as something that is accomplished by the teacher and not the learner.

By contrast, divergent assessment is seen as that which establishes *what* the learner has learned and, as such, does not begin with a predetermined list against which student learning can be 'ticked off'. According to Torrance and Pryor (2001: 617), the practical aspects of divergent assessment are:

- flexible planning or complex planning that incorporates alternatives
- open forms of recording (narrative, quotations, and so on)
- analysis of the interaction of the learner and the curriculum from the point of view of both the learner and the curriculum
- open questioning and tasks
- focus on miscues (aspects of a learner's work that yield insights into their current understanding and, on prompting, metacognition)
- descriptive rather than purely judgemental evaluation
- involvement of the students as initiator of assessment as well as recipient.

They see this approach to assessment as emerging from and aligning with social constructivist theories of learning, including Vygotsky's (1978, 1986) notion of the zone of proximal development, and a view of assessment as a task accomplished jointly by teacher and student. While Torrance and Pryor argue that convergent assessment practices are more clearly aligned with summative assessment than formative assessment, and that divergent practices align more with formative assessment than summative assessment, they also argue that both are valid approaches and tools. The task for the teacher is thus to understand the difference between the various practices and discern the most appropriate approach to utilise in each learning context.

We do not believe that all summative assessment is also norm-referenced and convergent, nor that all assessment that is convergent in style is also summative in process. Assessment is complex and nuanced, and while it is possible to somewhat classify practices, we argue that assessment is as much about approaches to learning as anything else. In the context of the Middle Years, a variety of

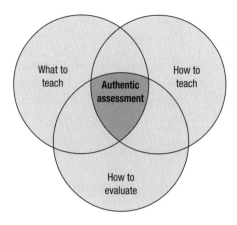

Figure 5.2 | Authentic assessment

(Kreisman, Knoll and Melchior 1995: 115)

formative assessment practices should be employed that take into account the understandings and principles discussed in previous chapters about learning in this stage of schooling.

INNOVATIVE ASSESSMENT

We note that all assessment practices that fall outside of the definition of authentic assessment should not be defined as 'inauthentic' or fraudulent in some way. Authentic assessment is authentic insofar as it focuses on the level of understanding a student has gained rather than the knowledge and skills they can remember. Figure 5.2 shows Kreisman, Knoll and Melchior's (1995) simple diagrammatic representation of authentic assessment. For them, authentic assessment is at the nexus of 'what to teach', 'how to teach' and 'how to evaluate' or, more simply put, at the crossroads of syllabus content, pedagogy and assessment (Kreisman, Knoll & Melchior 1995: 115).

This representation of authentic assessment contains two key assumptions and implications for teachers designing student assessment tasks and programs. The first is that, in any teaching and learning context, a range of options and choices exist for teachers in each of the three domains: what to teach, how to teach and how to evaluate. Earlier in this book, we have seen how these choices and options can be exercised in creative and innovative ways in the Middle Years. A similar range of options exists in the domain of assessment. The second is that for assessment to be truly authentic it must be seamlessly embedded in both the content of learning and in the learning process itself. In other words, to return to Black and Wiliam (1998), there should be 'indivisibility' between learning and assessment such that they occur concurrently and reflexively.

From their work on the Queensland Schools Reform Longitudinal Study, Hayes et al. (2006) have extended this notion of authentic assessment into 'productive assessment'. Productive assessment, they argue, connects productive pedagogies to productive student performance through the use of assessment tasks that are contextualised, demand high levels of student engagement and attend to issues of social justice through attentiveness to such questions as 'Whose knowledge is represented in this task and how?'

The productive assessment framework presented by Hayes et al. (2006) is a valuable insight into how productive pedagogies (outlined in Chapter 3) might be smoothly integrated into student assessment.

TASKS FOR ASSESSING LEARNING

As observed in Chapter 2, it is important that teachers conceptualise themselves as designers of the learning experience, doing the hard intellectual work of bridging the gap between the state-developed syllabus and local needs at the school and classroom level. This design work also extends into the realm of assessment. Tasks that offer scope for teachers to collect diverse and rich evidence of student learning are embedded in the learning process such that students see no difference between 'assessment' and 'business as usual' in the classroom. Black and Wiliam's study (1998) focused on formative assessment as a lever for 'raising the standard' of student learning, as an alternative to the ongoing and increasingly state-based 'measuring the pig', and suggests that if we are serious about raising standards of student learning, formative assessment, not external summative assessment, is crucial.

It is also salient to remember, drawing on the message of Torrance and Pryor (1998, 2001), that even when improving student learning on an individual level is seen as the most important purpose of assessment, that different types of assessment serve different purposes. We are not advocating that *only* assessment tasks of a particular nature and purpose should be used with students, rather that teachers should understand and recognise the different types and purposes, and choose their tools according to the needs of the students and the particular context.

Wiggins and McTighe (1998: 14) offer a 'continuum' of assessment methods that are construed in a hierarchy of increasing complexity, adapted in Table 5.1 on page 90.

The discussion of backward design in Chapters 2 and 3 highlighted the importance of assessment as a key consideration in the design and planning of the learning experience. Planning assessment up front as an integral part of the design of the curriculum raises the likelihood that assessment processes will be embedded in the pedagogy and learning processes of the unit of work, as well as ensuring that the mad rush to develop an acceptable means of assessment that sometimes occurs at the end of a unit is circumvented. Furthermore, planning assessment alongside and integrated with teaching and learning strategies means that assessment requirements are more likely to be explicit to students from the outset, a factor that research suggests is highly significant in improving student learning outcomes, particularly for students from less advantaged backgrounds (Hayes et al. 2006).

While including a range of assessment approaches into any unit of work is desirable, the use of tasks such as tests and quizzes, for example, need not be formal and summative. Particularly in classrooms where students have access to technology, doing short 'test your knowledge' quizzes, or puzzles and games that require students to have acquired a level of knowledge of a topic to complete, using programs such as Hot Potatoes[1] or the Microsoft® SharePoint™ or the Moodle software currently in use by many schools around Australia, is a valuable and fun way of providing feedback to both students and teachers on knowledge acquisition and 'gaps'. Furthermore, if such opportunities are built so that students can have more than one attempt to demonstrate that they have acquired the required knowledge (particularly if tasks are constructed and conceptualised in such a way that students do not feel that their level of attainment is 'carried with them'), then the assessment practices

---

1. Hot Potatoes is produced by Half-Baked Software and is available at www.halfbakedsoftware.com/.

Table 5.1 Hierarchy of assessment forms

QUIZ AND TEST ITEMS

Simple, content-focused questions that:
- assess for factual information, concepts and discrete skills
- use selected-response or short-answer formats
- are convergent (typically they have a single best answer)
- may be easily scored using an answer key (or machine scoring)
- are typically secure (not known in advance)

ACADEMIC PROMPTS

Open-ended questions or problems that:
- require a student to think critically, not just recall knowledge, and then prepare a response, product or performance
- require constructed responses under school or exam conditions
- are open (there is no single best answer or strategy for answering or solving them)
- often are ill-structured, requiring the development of a strategy
- involve analysis, synthesis or evaluation
- typically require an explanation or defence of the given answer or methods used
- require judgement-based scoring, based on criteria and performance standards
- may or may not be secure

PERFORMANCE TASKS AND PROJECTS

Short-term tasks to long-term tasks or multi-staged projects that:
- are authentic because they involve complex challenges that mirror the issues and problems faced by adults
- require the production of performance

They differ from prompts because they:
- feature a setting that is real or simulated (that involves the kinds of constraints, background noise, incentives and opportunities an adult would find in a similar situation)
- typically require a student to address an identified audience
- allow a student greater opportunity to personalise the task
- are not secure – task, criteria and standards are known in advance and guide students' work

are indeed truly formative, although they may fit more readily into what Torrance and Pryor (1998, 2001) consider 'convergent' assessment practices.

RICH TASKS

At the other end of Wiggins and McTighe's continuum of assessment strategies, we find performance or rich tasks. Rich tasks have been the subject of much discussion in education throughout Australia in recent times. They are one of the three key components of Education Queensland's New Basics Project, were embedded in the Middle Years Numeracy Research Project in Victoria, and have formed part of recent discussion about pedagogy and assessment in Western Australia, Tasmania, the ACT and New South Wales. It is in Queensland that this model is currently most embedded in the culture and practice of Middle Years education and thus in explaining and defining rich tasks, it is from here that we shall predominantly draw. An example of a 'home grown' rich task is given in the case study at the end of this chapter, while one of the tasks developed in Queensland is the starting point for the backward-mapping of pedagogy in Chapter 4.

According to Education Queensland (2001), the model of rich tasks integrates the principles from the work of educators such as John Dewey, Paolo Freire, Lev Vygotsky and Ted Sizer in that it is part of a conceptualisation of learning that assumes, for example, that:

- new knowledge is actively constructed by learners
- learner or student agency is paramount to the learning process
- deep learning occurs when the learner is substantively engaged with both content and the processes of learning
- learning occurs for different learners at different rates and different times (for each learner there exists at any time an optimal zone for learning and that, to be effective, learning should be appropriately set within this zone).

A generic and streamlined set of principles for the development of rich tasks in diverse contexts might look like this. Rich tasks:

- emphasise 'connectedness', presenting students with real-world problems
- position and engage students as creators, builders and evaluators of knowledge
- are trans-disciplinary, cross-disciplinary and inter-disciplinary, and exploit naturally occurring links between disciplines
- develop students' capacity to empathise with others and understand multiple perspectives
- utilise a range of strategies for assessment of student learning, both divergent and convergent, throughout and at the conclusion of the task
- focus partly upon the development of broad skills and key competencies that can be drawn on across the K–12 curriculum
- embed lifelong learning skills, which are explicitly taught and scaffolded in ways appropriate to the specific context of the task
- are structured so as to allow students to make key decisions about the content, process and products of their learning, and to be supported in those decisions
- provide opportunities for students to work independently and in groups of varying size and composition.

Rich tasks are *not* projects that have been rebadged for the 21st century context and run in parallel with class work; instead, they are complex and multidimensional units of work that require students to engage collaboratively and independently and take responsibility for their learning.

It is difficult to conceptualise how these principles would converge to form a task that provides the substantive material for a significant part of student learning time, for the intention with student learning and assessment tasks such as these is not that they are an add-on to the work undertaken in class, but rather that they form the bulk of the teaching and learning experience for students. In this way, to return Figure 5.2, they represent the seamless integration of what to teach, how to teach and how to assess. The case study below is an example of a rich task and assessment rubric, developed independently by a teacher working with students in the Middle Years in New South Wales.

CASE STUDY

Rich tasks for enhanced learning and assessment

This example of a student assessment task responds to the challenge of integrating pedagogy and assessment. It was developed using the principles and ideas discussed above as a starting point.

Climate change and us: creating sustainable community

Overview

> We have to act *together* to solve this global crisis.

Al Gore, on climate change

One of the most significant challenges facing humanity in our age is that of climate change. Our response to this challenge relies on our understanding of the ways that we impact upon our environment and our willingness, as local, national and global communities, to do something about the problem.

In this task, you will work individually to investigate the problem of climate change. Then, as part of an 'awareness-raising team', you will design a set of community guidelines based on your findings and a series of awareness-raising tools for use by different groups in the community. These tools could include a website, brochures, a short film, research papers, newspaper articles, podcasts or any other suitable tools.

Your guidelines and tools will be showcased at the Sustainable Community Expo to be held at the end of September. At this time, they will be judged by a panel of experts from the United Nations Framework Convention on Climate Change.

This unit of work is based upon the following NSW Board of Studies syllabus outcomes:	
English 1	responds to and composes texts for understanding, interpretation, critical analysis and pleasure
English 2	uses a range of processes for responding to and composing texts
English 3	responds to and composes texts in different technologies
Geography 4.7	identifies and discusses geographical issues from a range of perspectives
Geography 4.8	describes the interrelationships between people and environments
Science 4.3	identifies areas of everyday life that have been affected by scientific developments
Science 4.11	identifies where resources are found, and describes how they are used by humans
Science 4.20	uses an identified strategy to solve problems
Science 4.21	uses creativity and imagination to suggest plausible solutions to familiar problems

Student learning outcomes

These learning outcomes are the framework for this unit of work, as well as the basis of assessment for the unit. The assessment guidelines that follow link with these learning outcomes.

Students will:

- investigate and develop an understanding of the problem of climate change, using the guiding questions for this unit and the information literacy process as key organisers
- work collaboratively to develop a response to the challenge of climate change in the form of guidelines and awareness-raising tools
- employ a range of technologies and approaches in developing awareness-raising tools for diverse community members
- plan, structure and monitor the processes of their learning in consultation with the teacher.

Guiding questions

1 What is climate change and what impact has it had on the global community so far? What impact is it likely to have in the future?

2 What steps have been taken to counter climate change and how successful have they been?

3 What can and should be done at a local level to counter climate change?

4 What tools might be effective in raising awareness and provoking action among different groups in the community?

Assessment guidelines

	UNSATISFACTORY	SATISFACTORY	GOOD	EXCELLENT
Investigate and develop an understanding of the problem of climate change, using the guiding questions for this unit and the information literacy process as key organisers	Understanding of the key issues not adequately developed and/or demonstrated	Understanding of the key issues developed and/or demonstrated in an elementary or superficial way	Substantial understanding of the key issues is demonstrated	Sophisticated understanding of the key issues is demonstrated
	Little evidence that information literacy process has been followed	Information literacy process has been partially followed	Information literacy process has been followed	Information literacy process has been followed with emphasis on the final two steps
	No reference to guiding questions	Brief reference to guiding questions	Response is structured around the guiding questions and attempts to answer them	Response to guiding questions is creative and well informed

	UNSATISFACTORY	SATISFACTORY	GOOD	EXCELLENT
Work collaboratively to develop a response to the challenge of climate change, in the form of guidelines and awareness-raising tools	Little evidence of group collaboration	Some evidence of group collaboration	Work has been fairly allocated and completed; group members have collaborated well	Evidence of superior teamwork in the development of guidelines and tools
	Guidelines and tools are inadequate or poorly presented	Guidelines and tools show an elementary or superficial understanding of the topic	Guidelines and tools demonstrate a substantial understanding and are creatively presented	Guidelines and tools demonstrate a sophisticated understanding and are presented creatively, innovatively and systematically
Employ a range of technologies and approaches in developing awareness-raising tools for diverse community members	Tools all use a single or similar approach	Some variety in the approaches used	A diversity of approaches is evident in the tools	A broad range of approaches is evident and tools are integrated as a 'suite' of resources
	Little evidence of catering to the diverse interests and understandings of different members of the community	Some attempt to understand and cater to the diverse interests of different members of the community	Tools reflect an understanding of diverse interests of different members of the community	Tools reflect a sophisticated understanding of diverse interests of different members of the community
Plan, structure and monitor the processes of their learning in consultation with their teacher	Little evidence that learning processes have been planned	Some evidence that learning processes have been planned	Evidence is provided of planning, structuring and monitoring of learning processes at each step of the unit	Evidence of planning, structuring and monitoring of learning is embedded in the products submitted
	Lack of documentation of learning	Some documentation of learning		

DISCUSSION STARTERS

1 How does the rich task reflect each of the principles outlined on page 91?
2 How far and in what ways does this task integrate pedagogy and assessment?
3 How would the classroom run if your class was doing this rich task for a period of ten weeks? What would be the implications for you?
4 Where does this rich task stand on the divergent–convergent, norm-referenced– criterion-referenced and summative–formative continuums?

CONCLUSION

Assessment is a learning matter. This chapter has highlighted the connection between curriculum, pedagogy and assessment, suggesting that only when assessment is considered in conjunction with curriculum and pedagogy does it play a generative role in the teaching and learning process. Various forms of assessment and some terminology have been considered, and we have argued for the employment of assessment philosophies and practices in the Middle Years that are about supporting and fostering – and not just measuring – deep and enduring student learning. Constructing assessment tasks that prioritise learning over measurement and reflect the richness and complexity of 21st century learning is not for the fainthearted. We have given you a substantial challenge in this chapter and one that will bring significant benefits to you and the students in your care.

References

Black, P. & Wiliam, D. (1998) 'Inside the black box'. *Phi Delta Kappan*, 80(2), 139–48.

Education Queensland (2001) *The Why, What, How and When of Rich Tasks.* Brisbane: Education Queensland.

Hayes, D., Mills, M., Christie, P. & Lingard, B. (2006) *Teachers and Schooling: Making a Difference.* Sydney: Allen & Unwin.

Kreisman, S., Knoll, M. and Melchior, T. (1995) 'Toward more authentic assessment', in A. Costa & B. Kallick (eds), *Assessment in the Learning Organisation: Shifting the Paradigm.* Alexandria, VA, Association for Supervision and Curriculum Development.

Stenhouse, L. (1983) *Towards a Vernacular Humanism: Authority, Education and Emancipation.* London, UK: Heinemann.

Torrance, H. (1995) *Evaluating Authentic Assessment: Problems and Possibilities in New Approaches to Assessment.* Buckingham, UK: Open University Press.

Torrance, H. & Pryor, J. (1998) *Investigating Formative Assessment: Teaching, Learning and Assessment in the Classroom.* Buckingham, UK: Open University Press.

Torrance, H. & Pryor, J. (2001) 'Developing formative assessment in the classroom: using action research to explore and modify theory'. *British Educational Research Journal*, 27(5), 615–31.

Vygotsky, L. (1978) *Mind in Society.* Cambridge, MA: Harvard University Press.

Vygotsky, L. (1986) *Thought and Language.* Cambridge, MA: MIT Press.

Wiggins, G. & McTighe, J. (1998) *Understanding by Design.* Alexandria, VA: Association for Supervision and Curriculum Development.

Wiliam, D. (2000) 'An overview of the relationship between assessment and the curriculum', in D. Scott, *Assessment and the Curriculum.* Greenwich, CT, JAI Press.

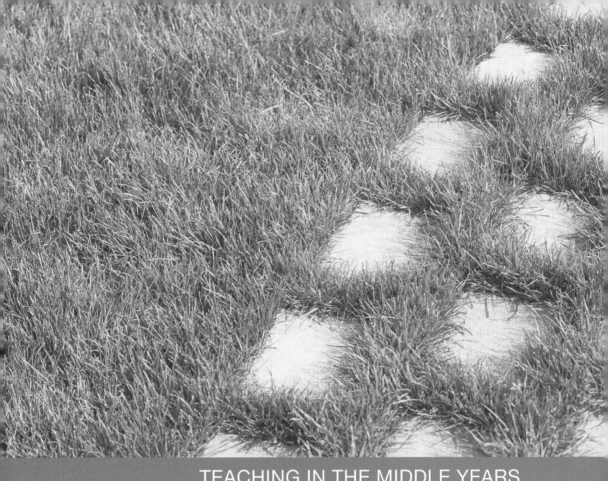

TEACHING IN THE MIDDLE YEARS

Pt 2

6

BEGINNING TO TEACH

Being a teacher is not just a matter of having a body of knowledge and a capacity to control a classroom. That could be done by a computer with a cattle-prod … Just as important, being a teacher means being able to establish human relations with people being taught (Connell 1993: 63).

INTRODUCTION

Connell's point is well taken – teaching cannot be done by a 'computer with a cattle-prod'. This chapter takes as its starting point the social and relational dimensions of teaching to explore why people choose to become teachers; the knowledge, skills and dispositions that underpin the relational processes of teaching; and the social processes associated with learning to teach.

For people beginning their work as teachers of the Middle Years there are a number of challenges – both exciting and daunting. The newness of the field means that there is much potential to be creative and innovative in the design of curriculum, pedagogy and assessment, and to be part of a new approach from the ground up. The newness of the field also means that a great deal of advocacy is needed to convince people of the merits of such things as integrated curriculum and rich tasks. Being a champion for new approaches in the Middle Years can be a hard call for beginning teachers, who are only just starting to find their way in schools and classrooms. The purpose of this chapter is to provide readers with frameworks by which to locate their teaching, their reasons for becoming a teacher and the process of learning to teach. These frameworks focus on some of the general aspects of teaching and learning to be a teacher, as well as some of the more specific aspects of being a teacher in the Middle Years.

Key questions guiding this chapter are:

1   Why do people choose teaching and why in the Middle Years?
2   What are some current trends in the supply and demand for teachers?
3   What are some of the social, ethical, emotional, intellectual and institutional frameworks that guide teachers' work?
4   What are key processes associated with learning to teach in the Middle Years?

THE TEACHING PROFESSION

WHY TEACHING?

Some of you are reading this book while undertaking teacher education. No doubt as part of your decision to enrol in a teacher-education program, as well in your discussions with peers, you have mulled over why you chose this career direction. Reasons that people consistently nominate for deciding to become a teacher include:

*   enjoy working with young people
*   enjoy teaching
*   to be a role model
*   to make a difference and contribute to social good
*   the employment conditions (Skilbeck & Connell 2003).

Are your reasons for becoming a teacher the same as any of these reasons? Clearly, many people choose teaching for a combination of reasons. Often teaching is something that people feel they are good at *and* something that is worthwhile. These broad reasons can also be complemented by more specific reasons pertaining to the conditions of work, such as job security, promotion potential, holidays, 'family friendly' conditions, and the potential to work in other countries. Unlike other careers, most people have a strong sense of what the job entails through their own experiences as a student. These experiences can play a big part in deciding to enter into teaching, as well as underpinning the sort of teacher that you want to be.

Why the Middle Years?

Entering into a teacher-education program or employment in teaching usually requires deciding about specialist options and pathways. Traditionally, the options have been primary or secondary teaching. However, reforms in Australian schools over the last decade, such as those listed below, have opened new employment and specialist options for those people who are particularly interested in working in the Middle Years:

- A growing number of new school campuses span all age groups (that is, K–10 or K–12) in Australia (Skilbeck & Connell 2003). Within these schools are options for programs and structures that break out of the primary and secondary division, and that include sub-schools for the Middle Years.
- School reforms in existing secondary schools, primary schools or K–12 schools are deliberately targeted towards students in the Middle Years. These include dedicated Middle Years programs with their own timetables, classrooms, curricula and teaching staff; transitions programs between primary and secondary schools; welfare programs that specifically target students in the latter years of primary school and/or the early years of secondary school; and interdisciplinary curriculum.

These reforms have led to a demand for teachers with specialist qualifications related to the Middle Years. Over the last five years, the number of programs of initial teacher education and ongoing professional learning that prepare teachers to work in the Middle Years has increased significantly. Thus, through formal study and programs of professional learning, as well as through workplace experience, teachers are gaining qualifications and skills relevant to working in schools and programs that focus on education in the Middle Years. Given the newness of the field, there is tremendous potential for teachers to be creative and innovative, to show initiative and leadership and to engage more broadly with professional associations, policy makers and researchers working in this field.

THE PROFILE OF PEOPLE ENTERING TEACHING

As well as thinking about *why* people choose teaching as a career, it is worth thinking about *who* chooses to enter the teaching profession. Below we discuss two current trends in the profile of those entering teaching and the implications of these trends.

Current trends

Career mobility

Discussions about teaching are often predicated on the assumption that it is a lifelong career. Certainly, for some people it is. However, current employment practices indicate that people are changing careers with greater frequency (Mayer 2006). One consequence of this has been changes to the profile of those entering teacher-education programs and seeking employment in schools. While many people enter into teacher education straight from school, the number of people entering teacher education as 'career switchers' is growing. Recent analyses of the profiles of students in teacher-education programs in three Australian universities indicated that over a third of students enrolled in postgraduate programs were 'career switchers' (Richardson & Watt 2006).

The fact that people are entering into teaching with varied levels of work experience has implications for both for the design of teacher-education programs, as well as induction practices employed by schools. Teacher-education programs and employers are increasingly attending to how they can be responsive to the diverse experiences of beginning teachers. Flexible pathways and program-delivery options (for example, part-time or off-campus), recognition of prior learning and targeted mentoring programs are examples of practices that more adequately meet the diverse needs of pre-service teachers.

Greater career mobility means not only that 'career switchers' are coming into teaching, but also means that people are switching out of teaching in search of other careers. For schools seeking stability of staffing, this movement can pose problems. In response, many employing authorities are examining how they can retain teachers in the profession through, for example, improved conditions of work. At the same time, it can be argued that movement across careers is beneficial for school systems if people move into, out of and then back into teaching. This could, in fact, assist teachers to build their expertise and develop skills in other workplaces that inform their teaching (Mayer 2006). Such movement is also part of new workforce patterns more generally (Skilbeck & Connell 2004).

Gender profile

Over the last two decades there has been a clear pattern in the gender profile of the teaching profession in Australia and other countries. The proportion of male teachers is declining. This is most noticeable in primary education. Key reasons suggested for the decline in the number of males in teaching are that (1) teaching has a low salary and status compared to other professions; (2) teaching is often portrayed as 'women's work'; and (3) there are negative connotations associated with men working with young children (Smith 2004). In the sphere of public policy, this decline has been seen as a problem, particularly in the Middle Years of schooling. It is argued that boys in the Middle Years need male role models (House of Representatives Standing Committee on Education and Training 2002). As a consequence, considerable attention has been focused on ways of attracting more males into teaching. Many commentators argue, however, that the concern to get more males into teaching is based on the problematic assumption that boys' performance and engagement will improve simply by having a male teacher. They also argue that it can be unrealistic to expect male teachers to be role models for boys (Mills, Martino & Lingard 2004; Smith 2004).

SUPPLY OF AND DEMAND FOR TEACHERS

Building a picture of who is entering the teaching profession and why is critically important for school systems to ensure that there is an adequate supply of teachers to fill available positions. The demand for teachers is obviously linked to the number of children attending schools. Therefore, schools and school authorities are constantly working with predictions related to student numbers and enrolments, both short-term and long-term, to plan employment policies and practices. This planning is also considered in light of the number of teachers in the profession; the movement of teachers out of the profession through, for example, retirement and 'career switching'; and the availability of new teachers to take up positions. Discussion about the supply of and demand for teachers is complex because of changing demographic, economic and social variables. Moreover, issues related to supply of and demand for teachers can vary across state and territory boundaries, school systems and sectors, geographic locations and within specialist fields. At the moment it is predicted that the current age profile of the teaching workforce in Australia (large numbers of teachers in the 45–55 age bracket) will mean high rates of retirement and thus a shortage of teachers over the next decade. This shortage will cause an increase in the demand for new teachers. In some areas there are already shortages, particularly in rural and remote areas, and in subject areas such as Mathematics, Science and languages (Ministerial Council for Education, Employment and Youth Affairs 2004).

To ensure an adequate supply of teachers, employer authorities in Australia have begun to look closely at how they can attract people into the teaching profession and, more particularly, to those areas in which there are shortages. Issues related to the nature and status of teaching, teacher salaries, working conditions, job satisfaction, school type and location, and incentives to enter teaching, all have a bearing not just on the number but also the quality of applicants for teacher-education programs and teaching positions. A number of employing authorities have programs and incentives that encourage people to work in rural and remote areas or in other areas of teacher shortage. Likewise, some have developed strategies to enhance the status of the profession and attract well-qualified people into teaching. We consider some of these below.

Depending on how teacher-education programs are structured, teachers with Middle Years qualifications – be it a specialist qualification related to the Middle Years or a Middle Years unit as part of a primary and secondary qualification – have employment options in both the primary and secondary sectors, as well as K–10 or K–12 sites with a separate middle school. The curriculum developments taking place across Australia are emphasising not only broad interdisciplinary approaches to teaching, but also how key ideas and practices in areas such as technology, literacy, numeracy and thinking cross curriculum boundaries. The implementation of these curriculum initiatives opens employment opportunities for Middle Years teachers who are qualified to teach across traditional curriculum boundaries.

PROVOCATION: TEACHING IN THE MIDDLE YEARS

1   Why are you interested in working in Middle Years settings?

2   What sorts of skills, knowledge and abilities would you bring to a school that is just establishing a Middle Years program? How could you represent these in a professional portfolio?

UNDERSTANDING TEACHING AND TEACHERS' WORK

Your experiences as a student at school will have given you good insights into what teaching in a classroom involves. Lortie (1975) described it as an 'apprenticeship of observation'. It is a long apprenticeship, lasting a good 12 years for many people! Despite the length of the apprenticeship many pre-service teachers are surprised by all that the job entails both in and outside the classroom for a number of reasons:

- The task of teaching itself can be much more complex and intense than anticipated.
- The nature of teaching can vary enormously depending on the school, the classroom context, the curricula and the students.
- Working as a pre-service teacher in a school that is considerably different from the schools you experienced as a student can challenge and change your assumptions about teaching.

- There are 'hidden' components of teachers' work – the jobs that teachers do outside of classrooms. Planning lessons and units of work, assessing student work and participating in committees, professional activities and extracurricular activities constitute important yet sometimes unnoticed parts of the job.
- Patterns of rapid social and technological change, and intense reform, have created new dynamics in schools. There are shifting patterns of relationships between teachers and students, intensification of work and frequent calls to be responsive to new mandates.

To assist beginning teachers to build a conception not only of what teaching entails but also of some of the knowledge, skills and dispositions that underpin teaching, we present three different frameworks for understanding different facets of teachers' work. First is a descriptive framework, outlining the diverse and changing roles associated with teaching, particularly in the Middle Years. Second is a prescriptive framework, detailing some of the expectations held of teachers by institutions associated with teaching, teacher education and teacher registration. Third is a framework of qualities, characteristics and dispositions, based on perspectives held by students, former students and teachers.

FRAMEWORKS FOR UNDERSTANDING TEACHING

1   The multifaceted and changing nature of teachers' work

Teachers' work is complex and involves much more than standing at a whiteboard and issuing a few instructions. The complexity is in part related to rapid social, technological and economic changes that are placing new demands on teachers, on curriculum and pedagogical reform, and on school organisation. Some of the multiple roles that may be now part of teachers' work are:
- organiser and assessor of learning
- curriculum planner
- manager of behaviour
- role model
- values educator
- social worker and emotional support
- religious educator
- health educator
- home–school liaison
- risk manager
- administrator
- team worker
- community liaison, especially in rural and remote communities (Skilbeck & Connell 2004).

This list indicates the multiple roles that teachers may have, but is certainly not exhaustive and many more tasks and activities could be added. If you can imagine the specific day-to-day activities constitutive of these roles, you will begin to build a picture of the intellectual, emotional, relational, communicative and physical dimensions of teachers' work.

Given that many schools are in the process of designing and implementing reforms in the Middle Years, there may be additional dimensions to teachers' work. Reform can require teachers to conduct research into current programs; design new curricula, pedagogy and assessment; communicate reforms to parents, teachers and the community; and evaluate the effect of new programs.

One of the clear shifts associated with teachers' work over the last 25 years, and certainly in much of the Middle Years reform, has been an increased focus on student welfare alongside student learning. There is considerable debate about these dual roles. Some argue that the work of teachers should be focused primarily on student learning and not on welfare issues, as teachers' expertise is in the domain of teaching and learning, not welfare and social work. Others argue that to create the conditions for learning, teachers should be responsive to a range of contextual factors, including the social, emotional, health and welfare needs of students. How schools and teachers develop practices that are responsive to the social and academic needs of young adolescents is clearly emphasised in the literature on the Middle Years and student engagement. Moreover, a number of Middle Years teacher-education programs offer pre-service teachers opportunities to study not just teaching and learning practices relevant to young adolescents, but also broad issues related to the psychology and sociology of adolescence.

The range of tasks associated with teachers' work is also constantly evolving and requires those entering the profession to be responsive to these changes. Some major recent changes to teachers' work include:

- increased expectations to integrate new communication technologies into teaching practice
- growing concern about student welfare, behaviour problems and learning difficulties
- increasing cultural and linguistic diversity among students in some areas and schools
- greater inclusion of students with disabilities
- new curriculum content that extends beyond traditional discipline boundaries to include values, thinking, communication, literacy and numeracy
- new forms of teacher and school accountability (Skilbeck & Connell 2004).

Many of the reforms associated with the Middle Years have been in response to these changes.

2   Institutional standards and guidelines for teachers

All institutions associated with teacher education and the employment and registration of teachers have guidelines and expectations related to teaching practice. Some examples are:

- practicum or fieldwork reports contain criteria that supervising or mentor teachers use to evaluate the work of pre-service teachers
- school employing authorities typically specify selection criteria essential for employment
- employing authorities have codes of conduct and/or codes of professional ethics that govern and guide teachers' work
- state and territory teacher registration bodies have standards for professional practice.

One critical change affecting most teachers and beginning teachers in Australia has been the widespread introduction of teacher registration, coupled with the development and use of professional standards for teachers. Some of the key components of the process of teacher registration and the use of standards follow.

Teacher registration

With the exception of the ACT, all Australian states and territories now have independent bodies responsible for the registration of teachers. Teacher registration authorities have existed for many years in Queensland (Queensland Board of Teacher Registration, now the Queensland College of Teachers) and South Australia (the Teacher Registration Board of South Australia). Over the last five years, other states have established such bodies: the Victorian Institute of Teaching, the New South

Wales Institute of Teachers, the Western Australian College of Educators, the Teachers Registration Board of Tasmania, the Teacher Registration Board of the Northern Territory. A central purpose of these authorities is to ensure and extend the quality of teachers and teaching across *all* school sectors. Registration is one means of doing so.

Registration ensures that teachers have met certain requirements before they take on a teaching appointment in any school. Teachers must have minimum qualifications, satisfy a police record check and/or 'working with children' check, and meet a set of professional standards. Many beginning teachers are required to undergo a period of provisional registration (typically one year) before applying for full registration as a teacher. To meet the requirements for full registration, beginning teachers may need to provide evidence of their teaching capabilities and demonstrate how they have met appropriate professional standards.

Professional standards

Over the last five years in Australia there have been a number of major initiatives to define and use professional standards for teachers. The standards define the practices, skills and knowledge that constitute good teaching. They are the means by which the nature and quality of teaching can be promoted, recognised and ensured. A number of organisations have been involved in the development of standards. Some professional associations have defined standards for good teaching within particular disciplinary or curriculum fields: for example, the Australian Association for the Teaching of English has produced the 'Standards for Teachers of English Language and Literacy in Australia' (STELLA). Some employing authorities have developed standards for all teachers working in an organisation: for example, Education Queensland has professional standards for all teachers in state schools in Queensland.

All registration bodies have developed standards as a part of efforts to ensure the quality of teaching. The Victorian Institute of Teaching (VIT), for example, has statutory responsibility for promoting and regulating the teaching profession in Victoria. The VIT has developed a set of professional standards that describe the professional knowledge, skills and practices that are constitutive of high-quality teaching, as outlined below.

KNOWLEDGE	PRACTICE	ENGAGEMENT
Teachers know how students learn and how to teach them effectively	Teachers plan and assess for effective learning	Teachers reflect on, improve and evaluate their professional knowledge and practice
Teachers know the content they teach	Teachers create and maintain safe and challenging learning environments	Teachers are active members of their profession
Teachers know their students	Teachers use a range of teaching strategies and resources to engage students in effective learning	

(Victorian Institute of Teaching 2006)

There is considerable similarity between the standards developed by the different registration bodies. The key issue related to the professional standards is not so much their content, rather how they are used. Standards can be used for a number of purposes: to guide professional learning, to inform the design of teacher-education programs, to promote teachers' work by acknowledging its complexity, and to underpin the evaluation of teaching practice and registration of teachers. In Victoria, as part of the process of moving from provisional to full registration, all beginning teachers work with a mentor to develop their teaching practice. As part of this process, beginning teachers prepare a portfolio that provides evidence of the ways that they have achieved the professional standards.

There is debate about the standards and how they are used:

- Should professional standards be generic or specific to specialist areas?
- Should there be different standards for beginning and experienced teachers?
- Should standards be used to guide professional learning, as well as the assessment and evaluation of teachers?

Codes of ethics and codes of conduct

Teachers' work in the Middle Years is located within legal and ethical frameworks. In Australia teacher-registration bodies are increasingly taking the lead in developing codes of ethics. Ethical codes usually outline a broad set of principles that guide teacher action, as shown in the example of principles set by the Teachers Registration Board Tasmania (2006):

- *dignity* – to recognise the intrinsic worth of all people
- *respect* – to show regard for people's feelings, rights and traditions
- *integrity* – to be honest, trustworthy and accountable in fulfilling work obligations
- *empathy* – to be open-minded and compassionate in responding to people
- *justice* – to be fair and committed to individuals, the community and the common good.

Teachers are also subject to more specific legal codes that are part of state and territory legislative frameworks. Two codes central to teachers' work are *duty of care* and *mandatory reporting*. Duty of care is the legal responsibility of all teachers to take precautions to ensure the safety and welfare of students. This responsibility exists in the contexts in which there is a student–teacher relationship. Duty of care thus applies both inside and outside the classroom and at school inside and outside school hours. For example, the playground is one area in which schools and teachers are obliged to ensure a duty of care through adequate supervision. Detailed legal description of teachers' duty of care is beyond the scope of this book; however, all schools and systems have policies that outline specific legal responsibilities.

Mandatory reporting is part of a duty of care and is the legal obligation to report suspected cases of child abuse and neglect. There is variation across state and territory jurisdictions about which people are subject to this legislation, so it is important to check the detail for your state or territory. However, at the time of writing, teachers in all jurisdictions, with the exception of Western Australia and Queensland, are obligated to report *all* suspected cases of child abuse and neglect.

Employer expectations

Individual schools and employing authorities also have expectations related to teachers' work. These expectations can be both formal and informal, and can help teachers understand their duties and also develop career plans.

For example, the Victorian Department of Education offers a career pathway for teachers that focuses on classroom practice and delineates responsibilities based on levels of experience and expertise. The classifications are 'graduate teacher', 'accomplished teacher' and 'expert teacher'. The central responsibilities of graduate teachers, or teachers new to the profession, are to:

- plan and implement a range of teaching programs or courses of study
- teach an area of the curriculum or a general curriculum to a year level
- monitor, evaluate and report student progress in key learning areas
- implement strategies to achieve targets related to student learning outcomes
- maintain records of class attendance and record student progress
- implement effective student management consistent with the school charter
- work with a mentor to participate in professional development, planning, implementation and reflection and develop a professional portfolio (Department of Education Victoria 2002).

There are four levels within the graduate teacher category and each is subject to annual review. The first review process incorporates the registration requirements established by the Victorian Institute of Teaching.

It is important to note that, in relation to the institutional detail, there is variation across state and territory jurisdictions as well as differences between individual schools and employing authorities. It is extremely important to check the specific detail relevant to your local context.

3 Teachers who make a difference

The final framework considers the perspectives of students past and present. As a student you have probably been taught by teachers with quite different styles, approaches and personalities. Through this experience you have probably developed strong ideas about the qualities of a good teacher and what you want to bring to your teaching. Sociologists Andrew Metcalfe and Ann Game (2006) asked well-known Australians to talk about a teacher who had changed their life. One of the interviewees, the broadcaster and comedian Julie McCrossin, noted the qualities one of her inspirational teachers had: 'passion, patience and a boundless personal relationship with each girl, they're the three qualities of a great teacher like Mrs Miller' (Metcalfe & Game 2006: 65).

The word 'passion' is not often used to describe good teaching, yet it is one that many of us relate to when we think of an inspirational teacher. Passion in this context presupposes a love of learning and a love of teaching (Day 2004). A good teacher has qualities such as passion, commitment, enthusiasm, care, sensitivity and humour, and these qualities are central to good relationships between teachers and learners, yet they are impossible to prescribe and measure in formal institutional ways.

A recent Australian study canvassed the views of young people about their perceptions of the ideal teacher, offering useful insights into the dispositions, qualities and characteristics that adolescents see as important. The ideal teacher:

- has a caring attitude
- is committed to the job
- has a sense of responsibility to students
- makes work interesting and relevant
- builds a relationship of mutual respect
- is interested in students' lives beyond class
- supports student diversity
- balances fairness and fun in the way that they control the class
- knows their subject matter (Lingard et al. 2002).

Obviously the qualities and dispositions that people bring to their teaching vary greatly from person to person. Likewise, the effect of particular qualities and dispositions depends, to a large degree, on the relationships that teachers have both individually and collectively with students. We encourage you to make explicit the qualities that you bring to teaching and how they can make a difference to student learning.

LEARNING TO TEACH

One of the great surprises in learning to teach is how deeply an emotional experience it is … How easily one can move from elation and hope to embarrassment and blame, from feeling all is in control to becoming undone, all within a moment's notice (Britzman 2003: 22).

At the start of the chapter we noted that learning to teach was a social process. Britzman (2003) also suggests that it is emotional. Here we provide a context for the social and emotional, as well as the intellectual and professional, dimensions of learning to teach by examining some of the typical structures and practices that are part of teacher-education programs.

TEACHER EDUCATION

The process of learning to teach does not typically begin and end with a teacher-education program. The development of a professional identity takes place over many years and may begin well before enrolling in teacher education. Many people bring to a program of initial teacher education considerable teaching experience through parenting, childcare, coaching, mentoring, peer tutoring, work experience, community service and other activities in which there is a teaching and learning relationship between people. As mentioned, most people also have a set of assumptions about teaching based on their own experiences as a student. These experiences and assumptions are an important touchstone for interpreting the formal experiences of learning to teach as part of initial teacher education and the first few years of work.

While learning to be a teacher does not necessarily begin with a formal program of teacher education, it certainly does not end there. Most teachers acknowledge that the first one or two years of teaching are crucial by way of gaining knowledge, skills and confidence in teaching. Many, in fact, note that the learning curve is particularly steep during the practicum and in the first year of teaching.

Initial teacher education – structures and practices

If you are reading this as you undertake a program of initial teacher education, or having recently completed a program of initial teacher education, you no doubt have developed views about the value of the different parts of the program to your academic and professional learning. Your experience is a starting point for entering what is often a complex discussion about policy and practice (the structure, design, content and location of programs) in initial teacher education. The debate takes place between and among pre-service teachers, teacher educators, teachers, school administrators and policy makers, revolving around these questions:

- Is learning to teach a matter of training or education?
- What are the most important things that beginning teachers need to know and how are these best taught?
- What are the connections between campus-based coursework and field experience, between educational theory and teaching practice and between components of teacher-education programs?
- How should the campus-based and school-based parts of a program be balanced? Should a greater component of teacher education be located in schools?
- What is the minimum length of time for a teacher-education program, and for days of practice teaching?

The different positions taken to these questions are usually underpinned by assumptions about the nature of teachers' work. There has been a clear trend in Australia over the last 25 years to strengthen the notion of teaching as a professional endeavour and to highlight the complex knowledge and skills that teachers are to have. In this respect, there has been a deliberate move away from conceiving teaching as a technical activity, and of learning to teach as a matter of 'training'. Rather, teaching has been seen as an intellectual endeavour and learning to teach as a matter of 'education'. Such conceptualisations have been important by way of granting teaching professional status and requiring university study as part of entry into the teaching profession.

A program of university study in teacher education usually encompasses the following:

- content or curriculum knowledge
- pedagogy and assessment relevant to curriculum knowledge
- an understanding of children or young people and their learning, development and diversity
- an understanding of the social, economic and cultural contexts of schooling and their implications for teaching practice
- professional skills, knowledge, ethics and dispositions relevant to teaching practice.

In a Middle Years specialisation there may be particular emphasis on curriculum and pedagogy that spans disciplinary frameworks, and a particular focus on professional knowledge related to working in teams (Beane & Brodhagen 2001).

Teacher-education programs typically include a campus-based and a school-based component. Each component serves various purposes in preparation for the immediacy of classroom teaching, as well being as a foundation for understanding educational practice over a longer period.

Teacher-education programs will have different emphases. One of the specific issues in the design of programs that prepare teachers to work in the Middle Years is the relationship between generalist and specialist curriculum knowledge. Consider current models of initial teacher education for primary and secondary schooling – primary teachers are required to develop general knowledge of a number of curriculum areas and secondary teachers are required to develop specialist knowledge of one or two curriculum areas. The question then arises, can teachers in the Middle Years be both specialists and generalists? Is it possible, for example, to have the specialist knowledge required to teach Year 9 Mathematics, as well as the generalist knowledge to teach across a number of areas of the curriculum in Year 6?

Teacher-education programs for the Middle Years are typically aiming to give pre-service teachers the opportunities to develop both specialist and generalist curriculum knowledge. In some programs, pre-service teachers can take university coursework that enables them to build specialist knowledge, for example, of Mathematics and Mathematics curriculum and pedagogy. Along with this knowledge, pre-service teachers can also take general curriculum units in Science, Studies of Society and the Environment and English, as well as broad cross-curricula units concerned with literacy, numeracy and communication technology.

It is also worth noting that the staffing practices in many schools with a Middle Years program enable teachers to work together in cross-curricula teams. In this way teachers with different areas of expertise can work together to teach units with an interdisciplinary focus. It is not surprising that many programs of initial teacher education focus on offering pre-service teachers opportunities to work collaboratively with peers to build the skills for the teamwork now common in Middle Years school settings.

Practices that support teacher learning

What are some teaching and learning practices that assist beginning teachers to develop the professional knowledge, skills and dispositions required to work in Middle Years settings? Considerable research and program development in Australia and internationally has focused on teaching and learning practices in all parts of initial teacher-education programs. Given the newness of Middle Years teacher education there is relatively little specific research about preparing teachers for this particular phase. Yet the concern to respond to and generate new ideas for the Middle Years has meant that teacher-education programs themselves have sought to be innovative in their design.

Below we detail some of the key pedagogical practices employed in teacher education across all school sectors. Central to these are models of professional learning that enable pre-service teachers to actively construct their own knowledge of teaching and teachers' work. It is worth noting that many of the initiatives described below address one of the major criticisms of teacher education – the lack of connection between theory and practice, and between campus-based coursework and the school-based practicum.

Reflecting on practice

Many assignments that are part of teacher education ask pre-service teachers to reflect on an aspect of their learning or their practice. While acknowledging that the process of reflection can be overused in teacher education, it is worth noting the history of the use of this concept in teacher education. Of all ideas related to learning to teach and pre-service teacher education over the last 25 years, reflection has been one of the most influential. Its use in teacher-education programs marked a radical change in understanding the processes of learning to teach. This change involved a move away from technical models of teacher training towards models that acknowledged the ways that beginning teachers developed their own theories and knowledge of teaching through engaging in, and critically thinking about, teaching practice. Schon (1987) coined the terms 'reflection *in* action' and 'reflection *on* action'. Reflection *in* action described how much professional knowledge develops while *in* the middle of action at work. For example, while running a class discussion, a teacher may also be assessing the quality of discussion, thinking about why some students are not participating and framing the next question in order to extend student thinking. Based on this reflection *in* action, the teacher may decide to halt the discussion and move onto another activity or reframe the discussion so that more students participate. Thinking about an action while doing it is a means of building professional knowledge.

Professional knowledge also develops through reflection *on* action: that is, by careful analysis after an event. In the class discussion example, a teacher may talk to another teacher about the discussion, mull over why some students did not participate and then draw up a plan for the next lesson to extend participation. While this sounds relatively simple, and you may be thinking that this is what teachers do anyway, Schon's point was that through the process of reflection and through deliberate analysis of action, teachers build and make explicit their professional knowledge in ways relevant to their context. Instead of applying knowledge developed in a decontextualised research setting, learnt in a theoretical course of study or used by a supervising teacher, pre-service teachers can take responsibility for building their professional knowledge in ways that are meaningful to the settings in which they work.

Action research, practitioner inquiry and communities of inquiry

Closely aligned with the process of reflection is the idea of building professional knowledge through research and inquiry. This has become a central feature of many initial teacher-education programs. While the philosophies and practices associated with action research, practitioner research and communities of inquiry can be very different, some common themes underlie their use in teacher education:

- Teachers are involved in the development of knowledge through systematic inquiry.
- Practice is used to drive research. Knowledge developed as part of research is linked to a context.
- Action and improvement are central to the research. Research is used to inform practice.
- Collaboration and testing ideas in wider forums are central to the process.

Integrated and authentic tasks

A common criticism directed at teacher-education programs is the lack of connection between program parts, and the lack of practical or professional meaning attached to campus-based learning. In some ways, such criticisms are not dissimilar to the criticism of the fragmented school curriculum that reforms in the Middle Years are seeking to address. To address these criticisms, many teacher-education programs use assessment tasks that link program parts and have a degree of authenticity. Portfolios and learning logs that require students to write their reflections and provide evidence of their learning are an example (Darling-Hammond & Snyder 2000).

Practicum pedagogy

The practicum or fieldwork component of programs is an area in initial teacher education about which there has been major discussion and development. In part this is because the practicum is recognised by pre-service teachers, teachers and teacher educators alike as one of the most important, and also one of the most problematic, components of teacher education. Underpinning many of the developments have been efforts to ensure that the practicum is a time when pre-service teachers can focus on learning about teaching, rather than being burdened by the weight of performance and evaluation of teaching practice. The major areas of reform have focused on pedagogy in the practicum:

- *reconceptualising the role of school-based teacher educators* – pre-service teachers are typically allocated to work with one or two teachers, who are responsible for supporting pre-service teachers and evaluating their practice. For many beginning teachers the quality of their relationship with these school-based teacher educators is crucial to the success of the practicum. Over the last few years, how the role of school-based teacher educators is conceived has changed, with a greater focus on how they can *mentor* rather than *supervise* beginning teachers. This subtle shift helps to focus practicum relationships on supporting learning instead of overseeing and directing practice.

- *placing pre-service teachers in peer-mentoring teams* – some teacher-education programs place students in pairs to team-teach. This is useful for building confidence, learning to work collaboratively with others and getting peer feedback on teaching (Ryan & Brandenburg 2002; Le Cornu 2005).
- *extending practicum in the final year* – in some teacher-education programs, pre-service teachers have the opportunity to work in a school for an extended period of time, usually a full school term. This enables pre-service teachers to get to know a school, the teachers and students; feel more like a 'real' teacher than a 'student' teacher; and make a smooth transition into a teaching position (Mitchell & Dobbins 1998).

New communication technologies

Over the last decade there have been major developments in the use of new learning technologies in both schools and universities. Many teacher-education programs have used email and web-based discussions as part of coursework, in particular to provide a bridge between people during the practicum. Students who are taking units either by distance learning or who are placed in a school with few peers often find electronic communication invaluable as a way of keeping in contact, exchanging ideas and debriefing experiences (Mayer 2002).

The experience of teacher education

We now consider how to understand and prepare for the experience of teacher education. Many pre-service teachers note that the experience in a teacher-education program, be it campus-based coursework or the practicum, can be intense and emotional in both positive and negative ways. Some common experiences in teacher education that can cause this intensity and emotion are:

- juggling study alongside other work and family commitments
- experiencing pressures of returning to study after time in other fields of employment
- getting a sense of real satisfaction and achievement about giving a good lesson or seeing students engaged in an activity
- feeling a sense of despair when a lesson does not go according to plan
- working in a school and with a mentor in ways that confirm the decision to be a teacher
- working in a school and with a mentor in ways that do not match the ideals of teaching
- feeling the pressure to perform and/or conform during the practicum
- developing strong collegial relationships with other pre-service teachers in the program
- feeling isolated if the only pre-service teacher in a school or if studying by distance
- being nervous about classroom management and subject knowledge (particularly if asked to do things during the practicum that are outside comfort zones)
- establishing good working relationships with mentors or supervising teachers in a short period of time and within the routines of typically busy schools
- experiencing the degrees of alignment, conflict and contradiction between the ideals and reality of teaching; between what you want to be like as a teacher and the actions actually taken in class
- negotiating the 'conflicting realities' of learning to teach (Britzman 2003).

Many pre-service teachers regard the practicum as the most critical part of a teacher-education program. This is not surprising – learning about teaching and teachers' work through actual experience is obviously going to be important. Canadian scholar Deborah Britzman wrote a groundbreaking book in 1991 called *Practice Makes Practice*, which contains a detailed analysis of the experiences of two student teachers during their school-based experience. The study charts the process of learning to teach as a complex interplay between student teachers' biographies, emotions and sense of self; between student teachers' relationships with school personnel; and student teachers' negotiation of institutional cultures and expectations about what it means to be a student teacher and what it means to be a teacher. The study criticises the approaches to learning to teach that are individualistic and competitive, and that expect learning to teach to be mistake-free. Britzman (1991) questions the value that is often, and simply, attached to school experience in programs of teacher education. She argues that instead more attention should be focused on the 'meaning making' that is part of the practicum and the ways that student teachers negotiate the conflict of being both student and teacher.

A number of studies describe the stages that pre-service teachers go through in learning to teach. Furlong (2000) notes the shift in focus from one's own teaching performance to the learning of students. In a study of a one-year teacher education program, Loughran (2006) showed how pre-service teachers' concerns with program structure, teaching, learning and self changed and fluctuated over the course of the year. Not surprisingly the context for learning and the level of experience underpinned these changes and fluctuations.

For pre-service teachers gaining specialist qualifications in the Middle Years, there are additional things to think about as part of teacher education pertaining to the new ways that middle schooling is being developed in Australia. When pre-service teachers are placed in schools that have strongly established Middle Years programs, campus- and school-based learning become strongly aligned. However, if pre-service teachers are placed in primary or secondary schools with fledgling middle school programs or no specific Middle Years initiatives, then it can be much harder to connect campus- and school-based learning. Likewise, it can be hard for pre-service teachers to be learning on the job as well as trying to develop and justify specific models and philosophies associated with middle schooling.

PROVOCATION: LEARNING ABOUT TEACHING

If you are currently in a teacher-education program, what have been some of the key dimensions, emotions and stages in your learning about teaching?

THE FIRST YEARS OF TEACHING

PROFESSIONAL IDENTITY AND INDUCTION

We have sketched some of the issues facing pre-service teachers. The first year of teaching can be equally, if not more, emotional and intense. There is a sense of being 'on your own' in terms of responsibility for planning work, teaching lessons, building classroom routines, establishing patterns of communication, dealing with inappropriate behaviour, assessing student work, doing playground duty and so on. Alongside the responsibility of teaching is the intensity of learning a new workplace culture: new people, buildings, structures, practices and communities. The nature of that learning can be particularly challenging for beginning teachers placed in severely disadvantaged or isolated schools and communities, or those in which a beginning teacher's background and culture is very different from the prevailing culture (McCormack, Gore & Thomas 2006).

Many school systems now recognise the intensity of the experience and the need for the first year to not just focus on survival, but also support the professional learning of beginning teachers in their first appointment. Feiman-Nemser (2001) argues that the central tasks of learning to teach in the induction phase are learning the context, designing teaching practices responsive to needs of students, building classroom communities, putting into practice a repertoire of teaching practices and developing a sense of self as a teacher. Her argument is that structures need to be put in place to support this learning.

LEARNING SUPPORTS FOR BEGINNING TEACHERS

In a recent study of beginning teachers in Australia, McCormack, Gore and Thomas (2006) note some of the key practices that assisted beginning teachers:

* *formal mentoring programs* – many schools have in place formal procedures for mentoring beginning teachers in which an experienced teacher is appointed to work with a beginning teacher and give feedback and support during the initial phase
* *informal mentoring* – colleagues and peers from initial teacher-education programs also are an invaluable source of support, advice and feedback
* *meetings, conferences and induction programs* – organised at a system level for beginning teachers.

We elaborate on the final point by briefly describing some outcomes from an annual conference held for beginning teachers by the Western Australian College of Teachers. The Beginning Teachers Seminar is for teachers in their first three years of teaching. Large numbers of beginning teachers from all sectors and locations in Western Australia attend the two-day seminar. Keynote speeches, plenary and workshop sessions and opportunities to network are part of the seminar.

The report of the 2003 seminar (Western Australian College of Teaching 2003) gives detailed descriptions of focus group discussions in which pre-service teachers identified key issues they faced and possible strategies for responding to the issues. These focus groups identified the following key issues:

* managing student behaviour
* teaching strategies
* assessment
* managing workload
* planning
* curriculum content
* working with parents.

How do the concerns of beginning teachers at this conference align with your own concerns as a pre-service teacher or beginning teacher? Knowing that you are not the only one experiencing such concerns is important.

At the seminar, the focus groups specified the nature of one of these issues and developed workable responses from a system, school and personal perspective. Group responses were then collated and key ideas written up for dissemination. An example of the ideas developed by beginning teachers relating to behaviour management included the following:

PERSPECTIVE	ACTION AND IDEAS
system	provide models for behaviour management and professional development to support implementation of models
school	provide clear whole-school policies and practices; provide professional development opportunities
self	ask for support from mentors, school administration, colleagues, school welfare team; work out reasons for student behaviour; develop sets of management strategies and have these in place as part of lesson planning

(**Western Australian College of Teaching 2003: 7**)

This example illustrates two critical ideas for beginning teachers:
* the value of working problems through with peers
* the responsibilities that teachers have for behaviour management in their classrooms are also part of the responsibilities of schools and systems.

CASE STUDY
Beginning teaching in the Middle Years

The cases below detail dilemmas faced by two pre-service teachers during their teacher-education program.

Can some contradictions be resolved?

Michelle's experience during the practicum really sealed her interest in being a teacher and also working in the Middle Years. One of her practicums was in a large outer-suburban secondary school. The school had recently introduced a Middle Years initiative in Years 7 and 8 in an effort to address high levels of student disengagement. One part of this initiative was an integrated studies program that linked the key learning areas of Maths, English, Studies of Society and Environment and Science. The teachers developed units of work that went across these four areas. The timetable was designed to enable blocks of time for specialist studies and integrated studies.

For Michelle one of the first big challenges of her practicum was to stand in front of a class and actually teach. However, once over the awkward self-consciousness associated with her initial experiences of teaching, Michelle was able to turn her attention to the things happening in the classroom that she did not anticipate: large numbers of students seemed to have little interest in school and many students had low levels of literacy. Disengagement had been talked about in her university classes, but seeing it in real life was an eye-opener. She had also assumed that by the time students reached Year 7 they would have reasonable skills in reading and writing. In trying to understand and respond to this, Michelle grappled with a number of factors. She wondered about the degree to which her assumptions about students, what they should know and how they should behave were created by her age and her middle-class upbringing. But, more than this, she wondered what action she could take as a teacher. To take action she had to negotiate a number of contradictions.

Many of the methods of teaching that were advocated in her university course stressed higher order thinking, student inquiry, collaboration and negotiation. Yet how these activities were talked about and the examples given assumed that students would have reasonable literacy skills. The students in Michelle's classes didn't have such skills.

When observing some lessons at the school, Michelle noticed that some teachers used fairly traditional methods for teaching: completing worksheets, taking notes and practising skills. This structured form of teaching enabled the teachers to better manage the classes and focus on basic skills, yet at the same time the potential for students becoming bored and disengaged seemed to grow.

While Michelle worked hard to connect her lessons with students' interests and build students' intrinsic motivation in relation to tasks, she noted that students were most attentive when she brought in chocolate frogs to give as rewards for completing work.

Working with a supervising teacher

Troy really enjoyed his first practical experience in a large K–12 school that had a separate middle school program with its own timetable and teaching staff.

Teachers worked in teams with classes of 60 students. Troy was immediately treated as a member of the team. He really enjoyed being part of this team-teaching – there was a lot of scope for improvisation, small groupwork, a strong focus on action and activity, integrated studies, different interactions between teachers and students, and teachers to support each other and complement their areas of expertise. Troy got on well with his supervising teachers – they were young, easygoing and encouraged his involvement in all aspects of the class. This was exactly the sort of teaching situation Troy wanted to work in.

For his next practicum, Troy was located in a completely different context in a Year 6 class in a primary school. His supervising teacher, the deputy principal, ran the class in a very structured and ordered way when compared to the classes that Troy experienced in his first practicum. Troy and his supervisor were like 'chalk and cheese', even in their clothes: Troy wore jeans and a T-shirt; his supervisor always wore a suit and tie.

Troy struggled because he felt he had to fit in. He had to teach structured and individual lessons across all parts of the curriculum. In contrast to his other practicum where he could bring his specialist knowledge in Science and sport to integrated studies, Troy didn't feel particularly confident teaching English lessons and knew that his lack of knowledge in this area showed. He also had to stay within the routines and rules that the teacher had established with the class. He felt he was expected to be old and mature, but knew that this just wasn't him – he couldn't run a class in which there was no noise! The contrast in styles made it difficult for Troy and his supervising teacher to develop common ground in their views about how the class should be run. While they didn't openly disagree, there was an underlying tension. This worried Troy given that his supervisor would be writing his practicum report.

DISCUSSION STARTERS

1   How would you resolve some of the contradictions faced by Michelle?
2   How would you work through Troy's dilemma?

CONCLUSION

This chapter has offered frameworks for understanding how to be a teacher and learn to teach. The task of learning to teach requires complex negotiation of institutional contexts, the expectations that others have of you as a beginning teacher and your expectations about teaching and what you will be like as a teacher. This is the intensely social process of learning to teach. This process can be rendered more meaningful when you have a clear understanding of the institutional and relational components of programs of teacher education and induction.

For teachers preparing to work in the Middle Years there are some specific challenges. The newness of the field opens tremendous potential for creativity, leadership, curriculum design and pedagogical reform. At the same time, it can be difficult to take on the role of innovator while in the initial phases of learning to teach.

References

Beane, J.A., & Brodhagen, B.L. (2001) 'Teaching in middle schools', in V. Richardson (ed.), *Handbook of Research on Teaching*. Washington DC: American Educational Research Association.

Britzman, D. (1991) *Practice Makes Practice: A Critical Study of Learning to Teach*. New York, NY: State University of New York Press.

Britzman, D. (2003) *Practice Makes Practice: A Critical Study of Learning to Teach*. Revised edn. New York, NY: State University of New York Press.

Connell, R.W. (1993) *Schools and Social Justice*. Philadelphia, PA: Temple University Press.

Darling-Hammond, L. & Snyder, J. (2000) 'Authentic assessment of teaching in context'. *Teaching and Teacher Education*, 16(5–6), 523–45.

Day, C. (2004) *A Passion for Teaching*. London, UK: Routledge Falmer.

Department of Education Victoria (2002) Graduate Teacher. Accessed on 29 October 2006 from www.eduweb.vic.gov.au/hrweb/careers/teach/gradteach.htm.

Feiman-Nemser, S. (2001) 'From preparation to practice: designing a continuum to strengthen and sustain teaching'. *Teachers College Record*, 103(6), 1013–55.

Furlong, J. (2000) 'School mentors and university tutors: lessons from the English experiment'. *Theory into Practice*, 39(1), 12–19.

House of Representatives Standing Committee on Education and Training (2002) *Boys: Getting it Right. Report on the Inquiry into the Education of Boys*. Canberra: Commonwealth of Australia.

Le Cornu, R. (2005) 'Peer mentoring: engaging pre-service teachers in mentoring one another'. *Mentoring and Tutoring*, 13(3), 355–66.

Lingard, B., Martino, W., Mills, M. & Bahr, M. (2002) *Addressing the Educational Needs of Boys*. Canberra: Department of Education, Science and Training.

Lortie, D. (1975) *School-teacher: A Sociological Study*. Chicago, IL: Chicago University Press.

Loughran, J. (2006) *Developing a Pedagogy of Teacher Education: Understanding Teaching and Learning About Teaching*. London, UK: Routledge.

Mayer, D. (2002) 'An electronic lifeline: information and communication technologies in a teacher education internship'. *Asia Pacific Journal of Teacher Education*, 30(2), 181–95.

Mayer, D. (2006) 'The changing face of the Australian teaching profession: New generation and new ways of working and learning'. *Asia Pacific Journal of Teacher Education*, 34(1), 57–71.

McCormack, A., Gore, J. & Thomas, K. (2006) 'Early career teacher professional learning'. *Asia Pacific Journal of Teacher Education*, 34(1), 95–113.

Metcalfe, A. & Game, A. (2006) *Teachers Who Change Lives*. Melbourne: Melbourne University Press.

Mills, M., Martino, W. & Lingard, B. (2004) 'Attracting, recruiting and retaining male teachers: policy issues in the male teacher debate'. *British Journal of Sociology of Education*, 25(3), 355–69.

Ministerial Council for Education, Employment and Youth Affairs (2004) *Demand and Supply of Primary and Secondary School Teachers in Australia*. Melbourne: MCEETYA.

Mitchell, J. & Dobbins, R. (1998) 'Charles Sturt University extended practicum program: Deliberate and serendipitous learning'. *Mentoring and Tutoring*, 4(2), 32–40.

Richardson, P. & Watt, H. (2006) 'Who chooses teaching and why? Profiling characteristics and motivations across three Australian universities'. *Asia Pacific Journal of Teacher Education*, 34(1), 25–56.

Ryan, J. & Brandenburg, R. (2002) Refuelling the practicum: From 'neophytes' and experts to collaborative, reflective relationships. Paper presented at the Australian Association for Research in Education Annual Conference, Brisbane.

Schon, D. (1987) *Educating the Reflective Practitioner: Toward a New Design for Teaching and Learning in the Professions*. San Francisco, CA: Jossey-Bass.

Skilbeck, M. & Connell, H. (2003) *Attracting, Developing and Retaining Effective Teachers: Australian Country Background Report prepared for the OECD*. Canberra: Commonwealth Government of Australia.

Skilbeck, M. & Connell, H. (2004) *Teachers for the Future: The Changing Nature of Society and Related Issues for the Teaching Workforce*. Melbourne: Ministerial Council on Education, Employment, Training and Youth Affairs.

Smith, J. (2004) Male primary teachers: Disadvantaged or advantaged? Paper presented at the Australian Association for Research in Education Annual Conference, Melbourne.

Teachers Registration Board Tasmania (2006) *Code for Professional Ethics for the Teaching Profession in Tasmania*. Hobart: Teachers Registration Board.

Victorian Institute of Teaching (2006) *Standards of Professional Practice for Full Registrations*. Accessed on 26 August 2006 from www.vit.vic.edu.au/files/documents/787_standards.PDF.

Western Australian College of Teaching (2003) *Beginning Teachers 2003 Research Report*. Perth: Western Australian College of Teaching.

7

CONTINUING TO TEACH

Passion is not an add-on but is at the heart of teaching at its best. It must therefore be nurtured and sustained (Day 2004: 177).

INTRODUCTION

This chapter is designed to address the needs of both newly qualified teachers and teachers who have been working for some time but are meeting new and different challenges as Middle Years teachers. Some of you will come from the primary school sector and be reconsidering the demands of teaching early adolescents. It has been the policy of a number of schools introducing specific Middle Years programs to employ primary-trained teachers on the basis that they have the capacity to integrate learning across a number of disciplines. Probably the majority of you, however, will be secondary school teachers who have long been accustomed to teaching your subject in a given faculty or department. Your skills will have been developed in the method for teaching that subject, rather than for the broader needs of the adolescent learner. You may have found yourself in a Middle Years context in which you are working more closely with colleagues from a range of disciplines than was the case in the past. You may now be a member of a team of teachers, enjoying the collegiality but finding your allegiances somewhat split between your department and the sub-school of which you are now a member. You will be in the process of developing a new professional identity for yourself. This chapter, therefore, recognises that as teachers of students in the Middle Years you are experienced practitioners who are finding new ways to work effectively with young people.

Our focus is on professional learning *in situ*: that is, how more-experienced teachers develop their skills by enhancing well-established ones and discovering new ways of working. We look at formal courses and in-school arrangements, as well as professional learning that results from participating in national and state action learning programs. With the increased attention on teaching and learning in the Middle Years, some employing authorities, professional associations and universities have designed a range of strategies to support teacher learning in this area.

Key questions guiding this chapter are:

1   Why is professional learning so important in the context of teaching in the Middle Years?
2   How can professional learning for teachers be structured and supported in ways related to school and classroom reform in the Middle Years?

CONNECTING TEACHING AND PROFESSIONAL LEARNING

Teaching should never be boring. After all, if you, the teacher, are bored then probably so are your students, and boredom has never been a good condition for student engagement. However, teaching can be and often is tiring in both the short and the long term. It is important that teachers find ways of refreshing and reinvigorating their practice after some years in the profession.

LEARNING FROM THE START

International studies have indicated that the transition and adaptation of those beginning to teach can be a harrowing professional journey. Sabar (2004) likened it to the passage of immigrants to a new country. The metaphor is a powerful one in that normally a person does not choose to migrate alone – but in a new teaching appointment, you may find yourself in a strange place experiencing culture shock with little external support. Migration often involves desires and dreams; similarly, teaching carries the ideals and expectations of the newcomer to the profession. But, after some time, migrants adapt and become accustomed to what had appeared strange before. They find ways of fitting in. In effect they become socialised in their new land.

So, too, can be the case with teaching. What was questioned initially becomes taken for granted, even comfortable. An anecdote by Nicole Mockler describes the process of taking up a new appointment as an experienced teacher. She had asked why and how some of the prevailing rituals of her new school came to be so. A colleague remarked that she was noticing the metaphorical dead dog on the doorstep, but that after some time in the position she would cease to recognise its existence. Mockler promised herself that she would be alert to the hidden rituals, no matter how long she stayed at the school. We put to you the challenge of resisting stepping blindly over the dead dog on the threshold.

As Hebert & Worthy (2001) demonstrate, matching expectations with reality in terms of the culture of a workplace is not achieved by chance but requires great effort on the part of all involved. Much has been written about the need to support and mentor the beginning teacher; however, less has been documented about sustaining and renewing those who have been teaching for some time, particularly when the conditions for teaching and learning change as much as they have in developing Middle Years pedagogy and curriculum. Huberman (1989) has devised a typology for the progression of teachers through their careers, arguing that there are five phases: exploration and stabilisation, commitment, diversification and crisis, serenity and distancing, and, finally, conservatism or regret. While there is argument about whether these stages are as lockstep as Huberman suggests, there is no question that teacher professional learning should take account of the range of experience that a teacher has had. What may be appropriate for the early career teacher will not necessarily meet the needs of those who have been teaching for some time, many of whom may have a world-weary 'we've seen it all' attitude. It is clear from this book that while learning and teaching in the Middle Years has many features that are clearly recognisable, the overall approach is fresh and new.

A systematic approach to teacher professional learning is essential when it comes to significant change, particularly in the context of overall, ongoing, multilevel change such as is being experienced in Australian schools. Fullan warned that 'the greatest problem faced by school districts and schools is not resistance to innovation, but the fragmentation, overload and incoherence resulting from the uncritical acceptance of too many different innovations' (1991: 197). This view is strongly endorsed by Bredeson and Scribner in America and is amplified when they argue that 'research has clearly indicated that teachers-as-learners are critical to pedagogical, social, political and economic goals here in the US and other countries' (2000: 2).

A SYSTEMATIC APPROACH TO PROFESSIONAL LEARNING

Teachers' work changes in response to social, economic, technological and political developments and is influenced by changing understandings of the nature of learning itself. It is a profession that cannot stand still. The toolbag of knowledge and skills that teachers carry from their initial teacher education should be both well maintained and supplemented. It necessarily grows heavier as time goes by. Grundy and Robison, reporting upon recent trends in Australian teacher professional development, commented: 'Teaching is forever an unfinished profession . . . By its very nature, teaching is never complete, never conquered, always being developed, always changing. Far from signalling some flaw, the centrality of development to the profession of teaching should be viewed as a badge of honour' (2004: 146). Good teachers are ever alert to what it is that they need to know so that they may continually grow and develop.

Think about something you have learned recently that has made a difference to the learning of your students.

1   Where did you learn it? From whom or what?

2   What were the conditions under which you learned it?

3   Why did the learning take place at this time and place, and not in another?

4   How representative do you think this is of the way you learn?

5   Compare your example with that of your colleagues. Draw some conclusions about the way teacher learning impacts upon student learning.

Much of what teachers learn comes about through casual interactions, such as discussions around the photocopier, in the staffroom, even over a glass of beer at the local pub. Stories are told, events are relayed and strategies shared. However, not all learning is good learning – you may learn how to survive rather than how to professionally thrive. Duncombe and Armour (2003) distinguish between collaborative opportunities for professional learning and everyday discussions, a matter to which this chapter returns. Experience-swapping, sympathy and support may not, of themselves, be productive in enhancing teacher learning. The stories shared between teachers may 'need to be told and retold in different ways and with different emphases in order to meet teachers' different learning needs' (Duncombe & Armour 2003: 146). Experience-swapping may serve only to enhance prejudice and antagonism to certain students, groups of students and even colleagues, and may not have much basis. If you return to the second case study in Chapter 1 about the Inner West Girls' High School, when the evaluation of the innovation was proposed, it was argued by some members of staff that it was costly and unnecessary. It seemed that most people were unhappy with the Middle Years plan and wished it to be discontinued. However, once the evidence had been collected, analysed and interpreted, a very different story emerged. As one of the school leaders observed, 'I guess it was the squeaky wheels who were getting the attention'. It became clear as the study progressed that, while some improvements could and should be made, the innovation itself was worth continuing. Had the loudest voices around the photocopier or in the school carpark been the ones to prevail, the program could well have been terminated.

Clearly, professional learning for teachers should have at its heart the intention to improve the learning conditions for students. Sparks (2002) sees that keeping the vision of improved student learning at the centre of teacher development requires attention to be paid not only to the local conditions, including data about the students and their environment, but also to what research and literature has to say. As seen in the case study in this chapter, this is precisely what the school sought to do in its teams approach to middle schooling.

There are many ways that professional learning can be catered for, including:
* formal courses offered by accredited institutions
* conferences
* projects
* in-school support and assistance through such arrangements as reading groups
* networked communities of practice.

Each deserves attention in that they have attendant costs and benefits. We do not include here one-day discrete experiences that are sometimes characterised as 'spray-on' professional development, often offering recipes and so-called solutions to difficult and complex problems.

Formal courses

Teachers undertaking formal postgraduate studies may be seeking a number of outcomes, such as getting pedagogical content and knowledge, better meeting the needs of their students and understanding more deeply the beliefs and values behind significant developments in education (Harvey 2005). It is common, after a number of years of teaching, to have a more fully formed idea of what the profession is and what it entails. But care needs to be taken that this understanding does not harden into inflexibility. By engaging in formal studies it is possible to subject your beliefs and values about aspects of teaching, such as behaviour management, equity provisions, classroom organisation, literacy teaching, and so on, to scrutiny and review them alongside current research and practice.

While some states and territories allow salary sacrifice and give teachers opportunities to attend formal postgraduate courses full time, most do not and none at present reward teachers who have gained further qualifications by increasing their salary. The teacher who engages in a formal postgraduate course, usually in the evenings and over weekends, does so through a strong sense of professional commitment. Their drivers are intrinsic, rather than extrinsic. For those interested in middle schooling there are now specific courses: for example, Deakin University's Graduate Diploma in Education (Applied Learning) assists teachers who want to reorient themselves to teaching in middle schooling. The course is offered in a mixed and flexible mode, making it more accessible to teachers in remote areas. Monash University now offers a Graduate Certificate in Middle Years and has a school-based Master's program that involves 30 teachers in action research projects whose purpose is to develop and improve middle schooling in one site.

Formal courses require time and commitment. The former resource is finite and teachers' lives are already busy with their work becoming increasingly intense. As a colleague once remarked, 'you can take time, but you cannot make time'. In other words, if time is to be devoted to formal courses it is an 'opportunity cost'; the time is no longer available for some other activity that may be equally useful and worthwhile. Some teachers prefer the intensity of the conference, at which they meet their peers and get expert input that they can then build upon when they return to their workplaces.

Conferences

Enhancing understanding of learning and teaching in the Middle Years through conferences has attracted nationwide attention. The Middle Years of Schooling Association (MYSA), established in 1999, has been the hub of conference development for Australia. MYSA is dedicated exclusively to the education, development and growth of young adolescents. It offers an extensive professional development program, and produces the *Australian Journal of Middle Schooling* biannually. While MYSA was originally based in Queensland, over the past six years programs and activities have been expanded to take a national focus and a Victorian branch of the association began in 2005. It also maintains strong links with the US National Middle Schools Association. MYSA aims to:

- inform individuals, professional educators, parents and the wider community about the nature of response education in the Middle Years of schooling
- promote the achievements and efforts of individuals, professional educators, parents and the wider community in meeting the developmental needs and interests of young adolescents
- provide a voice for those interested in and committed to the education, development and growth of young adolescents
- identify and encourage relevant research in the areas of the Middle Years (Middle Years of Schooling Association 2006).

There is no question that conferences are an important medium for professional learning. As Bredeson and Scribner indicate, large-scale conferences serve an *establishment* function (2000: 8). They introduce to a wide range of participants the latest concepts and approaches to the matter in hand. Those attending have high expectations that they will be given basic information about the innovation or reform. They are looking for the concepts, theories and language; for models in practice; and for strategies for handling the associated challenges and difficulties. In the case of Middle Years conferences, MYSA offers regional conferences every second year. The alternate year is devoted to their international conference. The year 2006 was a regional conference year, with conferences held in Queensland and Victoria across the year.

There is clearly value in a group of people from one school attending such conferences as a collegial group. They can discuss the various inputs against the background of their school and its prevailing culture: what they would change, what they would maintain and what they would nurture. Such grassroots exchange is essential to the vitality of schools and ameliorates the isolation that can be experienced by those who are interested in innovation and development. Conferences also provide opportunities for schools to network with each other and arrange visits and exchanges. When federal government funding ceased for the early National Schools Network conferences, such as those conducted in the early 1990s, it was a great loss. These conferences were subsidised to the extent that teachers from every state and territory could attend, with their travel and accommodation expenses met. Teachers gave up a week of vacations to meet with colleagues from other areas, many of whom had very different policies about education. Many teachers today are trapped not only in the isolation of their own schools, but also in their states or territories; some of which are more conservative than others. However, it is true that some federally funded programs do have built-in opportunities for participants to meet, share and showcase their work, albeit normally within a given state or territory.

Projects within large-scale programs

A number of national and state programs have elements dedicated to middle schooling. The current rollout of the Australian Government Quality Teaching Program (AGQTP), 2006–2009, offers opportunities for ongoing and targeted professional development to meet individual and school needs. The aim of the program is to provide initiatives:

- to equip teachers with the skills and knowledge needed for teaching in the 21st century
- to provide national leadership in high-priority areas of professional learning
- to improve the professional standing of teachers and leaders[1].

Other programs are even more specific. Changing Places – Making Links (Callingham, Smith & Nicholson 2002) is a state-based program that focuses on improving outcomes for Indigenous students in the Middle Years in Tasmania. The associated professional learning themes are Indigenous cultural and community involvement and new approaches to assessment for Years 4 to 8. The specifications for the program are drawn from the Tasmanian Essential Learnings Framework (Department of Education Tasmania 2006), these being communicating, personal futures, social responsibility and world futures. The program proposes that these learnings are of particular relevance to Indigenous students in the Middle Years as they seek to establish their identity. Teachers undertake residential workshops with Aboriginal elders, which are designed to support the teachers undertaking projects in their schools.

---

1. The AGQTP gives the Northern Territory, for example, the opportunity to build learning communities that target the Middle Years. You can go to the AGQTP website for your state or territory to find out how the program addresses issues around middle schooling.

In reporting upon the AGQTP *Action Learning for School Teams*, Ewing et al. (2004) indicated that projects that successfully contributed to teachers' professional learning were ones in which:

- leadership was interactive (rather than line-managed and hierarchical)
- professional learning was a priority of the school
- communication was effective
- the community was collaborative
- enthusiasm, commitment and hard work were present
- curriculum initiatives were a feature of the school (2004: 34).

No matter who sponsors such initiatives, it is important that programs support teacher learning. It is difficult to engage in authentic innovation and change if sufficient time or resources are not devoted to the project. Furthermore, it is essential that schools are provided with appropriate systemic support. In their discussion of the NSW Priority Action Schools Program (PASP), Beveridge et al. (2005) indicated that not only were the conditions spelled out above necessary, but also that schools should be sustained and supported by committed and dedicated office management.

In-school professional learning

While the conditions for providing professional-learning funds vary from state to state, it is the case that schools budget in their annual plans for professional development. In the case of well-resourced schools enough may be set aside for teachers to participate in external training and/or engage in training that is exclusively for the school staff. Consider the following examples of schools that are members of the Coalition of Knowledge Building Schools[2]. In the case of the Independent Girls' School West, every second Wednesday the school day commenced half an hour earlier and finished earlier so that teachers could meet in what became known as commissions of inquiry. Each commission took an aspect of practice to investigate (K–12) with presentations of findings made at the close of the school year.

In the second case, Independent Girls' School North, a reading group of five teachers was given release time to consider readings on a given theme with a facilitator. The readers' circle, as it became known, was a voluntary group who met once a month to discuss such matters as assessment for learning, the changing nature of young people as learners and so on. Because time was given, there were high expectations that the time would be well spent and members would be well prepared. The readers' circle was one element of a complex professional-learning program designed to meet multiple needs in varying contexts across the school.

While it may not be possible for schools with limited resources to engage in such extended programs, there is evidence that teachers generally respect their colleagues as professional-development facilitators and find that they have a sound understanding of the school context. As Cripps-Clark and Walsh put it, 'Teachers' knowledge does not exist in isolation, they are part of a greater shared knowledge and practice and have a continuing dialogue with it' (2002: 5). It can be possible within the context of the school to tailor and differentiate professional learning in a manner that is difficult for external courses to accommodate. However, there are risks when schools become too inward-looking and are not open to ideas from outside. Ideally, schools would look for opportunities to bring in external people, from time to time, who will both affiliate with the school but maintain a more distanced stance.

---

2. For more information about the history and achievements of the Coalition of Knowledge Building Schools, refer to S. Groundwater-Smith & N. Mockler (2003) *Learning to Listen: Listening to Learn*. Sydney: University of Sydney and MLC School.

In-school professional learning has a great capacity to be collaborative. Teachers may visit each other's classrooms and engage in peer observation and feedback. They can plan together and clarify their understandings of practice through dialogue (MacGilchrist, Myers & Reed 2004). This is important in the context of such a great change as moving towards an authentic Middle Years program. For many, as we suggested, it means shedding years of particular practices such as teaching key learning areas in isolation, and taking on new approaches such as planning across the curriculum.

A perceived shortcoming of in-school professional learning is the concern that the prevailing culture of the school may not be challenged. While this is not necessarily the case, it is productive and worthwhile when schools form networks that enable them to share their experience and expertise and open themselves to outside scrutiny.

Networked learning communities

A complement to in-house professional learning is an increased trend to develop broader networked learning communities, such as those in England. The Networked Learning Communities (NLC) program brings together groups of schools, local authorities, higher education institutions and the wider community to work collaboratively to raise standards and improve opportunities for their students. Using information and communication technologies and other means, NLCs offer access to leadership learning, information and communication, and provide greater opportunities for school leaders to share good practice. There are currently 109 networks across the country, involving more than 1200 schools, 30 000 staff and 555 000 students.

The Australian National Schools Network (ANSN), established over a decade ago, is the only nationwide school-based professional development, research and curriculum support program, and since its inception it has successfully provided learning opportunities for some 5000 teachers across the country. It is a cooperative project represented by teachers' unions (satisfying a professional rather than industrial role), school authorities and academics working as 'critical friends'. Its espoused principles are to:

- adopt a sense of responsibility in and for the group
- attend to others and listen
- cooperate in good faith
- aim for consensus decision-making
- confront problems respectfully
- not allow and give no put downs
- accept where others are at
- share ethically
- suspend judgements.[3]

The network's focus on reform is conducted through examining school organisation – after all, the conditions under which teachers work are the conditions under which students learn. The organisational ramifications of establishing Middle Years schooling has fallen within its ambit. A major thrust for the ANSN was to support schools that were developing learning teams to restructure middle schooling (Currie & Groundwater-Smith 1998).

Networks can also be formed using electronic means. Education Queensland (2006) has introduced the Learning Place. Each course offered varies depending on its purpose. For example, the course 'Taking action in the middle phase of learning' takes 15 weeks of online and offline work. Online learning offers

---

3. The principles of the National Schools Network are published in postcard form.

the opportunity for participants to work at their own pace in their own space. Participants can form collegial groups with others who may be working in a different part of the state and under different conditions, ranging from metropolitan Brisbane to the most remote of outback schools.

This brings us to the matter of collegial professional learning: that is, learning as a member of a group. Well-articulated and coherently developed professional learning is not only a responsibility for each teacher, but also one for the school as a whole. Professional learning in a team composed of teachers from across faculties or from different KLAs can be a powerful catalyst for whole-school change. Moreover, when professional learning opportunities are created by focusing on an area such as pedagogy in the Middle Years, the benefits extend to the school community. Learning communities in the school context have a critical role to play in ongoing professional growth for teachers. Professional learning communities offer the teachers involved significant benefits and, consequently, impact upon student learning as a result of improved practices. A prerequisite for such teams to be successful is that they should be flexible to cater for issues that arise and centre on meeting the needs of the staff involved.

CASE STUDY
Learning is when …

… teachers help teachers, kids help kids, teachers help kids, kids help teachers

The title of this case study comes from a publication by Currie and Groundwater-Smith (1998). In it, they discuss five schools that had significantly restructured in the interests of better learning conditions for students and teachers. The study was commissioned by the National Schools Network. One of the schools has, over ten years, continued to consider its structures and provisions, in particular those that address the needs of Years 7 and 8. This case study outlines this school's earlier arrangements and the ones it is now addressing.

We have not nominated which of Australia's large cities the school is in on the grounds that, although we have strongly advocated recognising the influence of social geography, we believe that schools address common challenges. In this case, Madson High School for Boys (MHSB) is a single-sex, comprehensive inner-city school with a history spanning nearly 100 years.

At the time of the first restructure the school was facing falling enrolments and the sense that it was a place where boys 'tough it out'. The incoming principal was so concerned about the environment that she sought first to make the school a place students would want to come to. She said, 'I had this great urge to clean the place up. No school should look like a dump. I wanted it decently painted and carpeted. It was a matter of first things first. You learn better when your surroundings aren't run down and neglected. We had to have the courage to push forward and do things. It's important to see that these things can be quickly fixed so that we can move on to the real educational issues and not be distracted. First and foremost I wanted a "healthy school"' (Currie & Groundwater-Smith 1998: 78).

Having achieved this, the next step was to explore how learning in the Middle Years could be enhanced. Both Years 7 and 8 were divided into four groups with each group the responsibility of a team of four teachers, at least two of whom taught more than one key learning area. Teams met weekly for an equivalent of two periods to discuss student learning both in terms of achievement and need. The day was generally arranged with longer blocks of learning time, generally 80 minutes.

The teams were the central feature of the restructuring. Team meetings followed an agenda that was developed collaboratively and chaired on a rotational basis to reflect the different orientations of the team members. Action statements were recorded and ensured that decisions would be followed through. The process was not only one that ensured that all students were visible to their teachers, but also one that provided for teachers to learn from one another about how best to meet the needs of their students. Discussing strategies for teaching students with particular difficulties was regularly part of the agenda. Parents were kept abreast of the overall team's development through a regular bulletin.

Part of the work of the school was to regularly consult students; their voices were honoured and their ideas respected. Consider these insights from students about the characteristics of a helpful teacher (Currie & Groundwater-Smith 1998: 89–90):

They shouldn't <u>rush</u> us. They should give you a chance at trying and be positive.

Explain when I get something wrong, explain step by step – go slowly.

Cover fewer topics well.

Now, ten years on, the school is faced with very different circumstances. The school's demographics, its teaching staff and the structure of secondary schooling in the inner city have changed.

There are now more boys of South-East Asian origin, some of whom are in the school on a full fee-paying basis. The school is no longer a grantee in the Priority Schools Funding Program (a federally funded, broadly based equity program that provides supplementary resources for schools in need). Staff have moved on, with many not fully appreciating or realising the philosophy behind the team approach to assist students to make the transition from primary to secondary schooling. For some time, staff development was on an *ad hoc* basis, although it is now more structured.

The formation of a local collegiate with the senior high school and satellite junior secondary schools, as well as the dedicated streams for gifted and talented students and the selective high schools in the area, has meant that the school has to work hard to attract able students. (It is important to remember that all Australian states and territories have developed school-choice policies so that the notion of the neighbourhood school has all but disappeared.)

In response to the market-oriented environment of school choice, Madson High School for Boys has moved away from its former comprehensive policy. Using ACER tests to identify the abilities of Year 6 students, an extension class is offered, with remaining students placed in three parallel classes that are still taught by teams. The numbers of students that are eligible for the extension class appear to be dropping. However, the community expects that the streaming, such as it is, will be maintained. It would seem that there is a growing divide between the able Year 7 students and their peers.

Given the ever-changing environment and the ongoing discussion about the education of boys, it is timely that the policy of providing an extension class be reviewed. A first step for the school is to commission a discussion paper that focuses on boys' education and the conditions required for personalised learning, a phrase gaining currency in schooling. Currently, staff, students and parents are engaged in an evidence-based debate about what arrangements can best meet the needs of a comprehensive boys' high school, especially in the Middle Years.

DISCUSSION STARTERS

This case study is a complex one and its detail cannot be more than lightly touched on here. It is obvious that innovation and change must be ongoing. State and federal policies impact on what the school does and how it goes about its business. The burgeoning of the education marketplace is an issue for the school, as is the matter of boys' education. This school is in the grip of a genuine dilemma, both sides of which involve costs and benefits. If talented students are selected into an extension class for the critical Middle Years, what are the consequences for the remaining parallel classes? If the extension class is abandoned, what are the consequences for school enrolments? Debate these questions with other students or professional colleagues.

CONCLUSION

Our main focus in this chapter has been the ongoing professional learning of teachers. The case study highlights the fact that schooling does not stand still. Many teachers at Madson High School for Boys entered the profession when conditions were very different. Some can remember when recalcitrant boys were caned and boys' schools were a place where bullying was an accepted part of schooling. Others recall that many boys in such conditions left school at the earliest opportunity and that the preceding years merely kept them in a holding pattern.

We hope that this chapter is of value to beginning teachers, some of whom are mature-age students coming to teaching from different professions, as well as being a resource for teachers who have been teaching for some time and find themselves addressing new and exciting challenges.

References

Beveridge, S., Groundwater-Smith, S., Kemmis, S. & Wasson, D. (2005) 'Professional learning that makes a difference: successful strategies implemented by priority action schools in New South Wales'. *Journal of In-Service Education*, 31(4), 697–710.

Bredeson, P. & Scribner, J. (2000) A statewide professional development conference: useful strategy for learning or inefficient use of resources. *Education Policy Analysis Archives*, 8(13). Accessed 24 February 2006 from http://epaa.asu.edu/epaa/v8n13.html.

Callingham, R., Smith, P. & Nicholson, V. (2002) Changing places – making links: a framework for professional development for the middle years of schooling. Paper presented at the Australian Association for Research in Education Annual Conference, University of Queensland, 28 November – 2 December.

Cripps-Clark, J. & Walsh, J. (2002) Elements of a model of effective teachers. Paper presented at the Australian Association for Research in Education Annual Conference, University of Queensland, 28 November – 2 December.

Currie, J. & Groundwater-Smith, S. (1998) *Learning is When . . .* Milperra, NSW: National Schools Network, University of Western Sydney.

Day, C. (2004) *A Passion for Teaching*. London, UK: Routledge Falmer.

Department of Education Tasmania (2006) *Essential Learnings Framework 1*. Accessed 26 October 2006 from www.ltag.education. tas.gov.au/references.htm.

Duncombe R. & Armour, K. (2003) 'Collaborative professional learning: from theory to practice'. *Journal of Inservice Education*, 30(1), 141–66.

Education Queensland (2006) Learning Place. Accessed 3 May 2006 from http://education.qld.gov.au/learningplace/.

Ewing, R., Smith, D., Anderson, M., Gibson, R. & Manuel, J. (2004) *Teachers as Learners*. Australian Government Quality Teaching

Program Action Learning for School Teams Project Evaluation Report. Sydney: Faculty of Education, University of Sydney.

Fullan, M. (1991) *The New Meaning of Educational Change*. New York, NY: Teachers College Press.

Grundy, S. & Robison, J. (2004) 'Teacher professional development: themes and trends in the recent Australian experience', in C. Day and J. Sachs (eds), *International Handbook on the Continuing Professional Development of Teachers*. Maidenhead, UK: Open University Press.

Harvey, P. (2005) Motivating factors influencing teachers' engagement in postgraduate study. Paper presented to the Annual Conference of the Australian Association for Research in Education Conference. Parramatta, NSW, 29 November – 2 December.

Hebert, E. & Worthy, T. (2001) 'Does the first year of teaching have to be a bad one? A case study of success'. *Teaching and Teacher Education*, 17, 897–911.

Huberman, M. (1989) 'On teachers' careers: once over lightly with a broad brush'. *International Journal of Educational Research*, 13(4), 347–62.

MacGilchrist, B., Myers, K. & Reed, J. (2004) *The Intelligent School*. London, UK: Sage.

Middle Years of Schooling Association (2006) 'About MYSA'. Accessed 3 March 2006 from www.mysa.org.au.

Sabar, N. (2004) 'From heaven to reality through crisis: novice teachers as migrants'. *Teaching and Teacher Education*, 20(2), 145–61.

Sparks, D. (2002) *Designing Powerful Professional Development for Teachers and Principals*. Oxford, OH: National Staff Development Council.

8

BEYOND COMPLIANCE: LEADING TEACHING AND LEARNING

Studies of effective schools have consistently drawn attention to the importance of strong educational leadership. Good teaching may be possible in a school where there is weak and ineffective educational leadership, but it is harder to achieve. Change and sustained improvement are impossible without good educational leadership, particularly where whole-school change is sought (Fullan, Hill & Crevola 2006: 95).

The hardest part of sustainable leadership and improvement is the part that provokes us to think beyond our own schools and ourselves. We need to perform not merely as managers of organizations or as professionals who produce performance results, but also as community members, citizens, and human beings who lead to serve and promote the good of all (Hargreaves & Fink 2006: 16).

INTRODUCTION

In this chapter we focus on the leadership of teaching and learning in the Middle Years. While we direct our attention specifically to aspects of curriculum, pedagogical and assessment innovations we have discussed in earlier chapters, our comments about educational leadership relate just as readily to the leadership of primary, middle and secondary years. Messages about educational leadership, however, are particularly salient for those working in the Middle Years because of the particular challenges of grappling with new ideas and approaches, and implementing the educational change that is part of Middle Years reform.

We also mention at the outset that this chapter is not just for those who hold designated roles of responsibility in the school hierarchy, but rather for all who are involved in driving change within schools. Teaching well done, after all, involves the leadership of teaching and learning on a classroom basis, while some teachers additionally have responsibility for leading teaching and learning at faculty, policy and whole-school levels. Effective leadership must be enacted at all levels within our schools in order for generative teaching and learning environments to flourish.

Key questions guiding this chapter are:

1   What are the key dimensions of leadership in Middle Years settings?
2   What are some of the key leadership issues in Middle Years settings?
3   How can leaders in Middle Years contexts create cultures and communities that support learning for both students and staff?

'LEADERSHIP FOR THE SCHOOLHOUSE'

A wealth of literature about various models of school leadership exists, some of which has been 'borrowed' or adapted from business leadership models. Sergiovanni (1996), in *Leadership for the Schoolhouse*, argues that while, to some extent, models of leadership for the corporate world can be applied to the educational context, the challenges of leading schools in complex times demands something different of educational leaders.

Over the past 15 years, educational leadership literature has focused on the moral and ethical dimensions of school leadership, and the link between educational leadership and the fostering of particular approaches to teaching and learning in schools. In 1993, Fullan wrote that 'Teaching is at its core a moral profession. Scratch a good teacher and you will find a moral purpose' (1993b: 12), and a range of models of educational leadership have developed in the past decade that expand upon this idea and examine the role of the educational leader in fostering this moral purpose in the context of the school as learning community and more broadly within society. 'Moral leadership' (Sergiovanni 1992), 'ethical leadership' (Starratt 2004), 'distributed leadership' (Spillane 2005) and 'sustainable leadership' (Hargreaves & Fink 2005) are examples of this thinking in action. While we do not survey each of these in depth here, we consider some common themes and implications for us as leaders of teaching and learning in the Middle Years.

There are a number of key commonalities and overlapping components of these 'moral and ethical' approaches to leadership:

*   Leadership practices are framed by an awareness of the big picture: the social, political, economic and cultural context of schooling and education.
*   A developmental approach sees support and professional learning (for all) as vital to the leadership enterprise.

- A focus is on the 'common good', in action as well as in words, including authenticity and ethicality in relationships at all levels within the community.
- A commitment to cultivating a school learning community builds generative and critical cultures.

Leading teaching and learning in the Middle Years is largely about fostering the growth of a body of teachers who are willing to be innovative and embrace 'new learning' in their thinking, curriculum design, interactions with students and approaches to assessment. This, however, is much easier to name than it is to do, as there are many circumstances, government policies and cultural 'remnants' that can militate against teachers operating in such a way. The key task for the educational leader, then, is to be bold and courageous in creating conditions and opportunities in which teachers feel supported, encouraged and enabled to work critically and creatively. Such a task translates in practice into the kinds of 'transformative' (Sachs 2003) or, in the words of Hargreaves and Goodson (1996), postmodern professionalism. Abbreviated, the attributes of this kind of teacher professionalism are:

- increased opportunity and responsibility to exercise discretionary judgement
- opportunities and expectations to engage with the moral and social purposes and value of what teachers teach
- commitment to working with colleagues in collaborative cultures of help and support
- occupational heteronomy (accountability to each other and the profession) rather than self-protective autonomy
- a commitment to active care and not just anodyne service (that won't 'rock the boat') for students
- a self-directed search and struggle for continuous learning related to one's own expertise and standards of practice
- the creation and recognition of high task complexity (Hargreaves & Goodson 1996: 21).

To demonstrate how circumstances and politics might mitigate against the development of teachers who claim transformative professionalism, and how effective educational leaders may have to work counter-culturally, we look briefly at each of the attributes.

TRANSFORMATIVE TEACHER PROFESSIONALISM

Exercising discretionary judgement

The power given to teachers to exercise professional judgement has diminished over the past two decades, and along with it some of our capacity as a profession to build and develop our professional judgement. Attempts to reduce the teaching and learning process to a series of technical features or to replicate 'what works' (Hargreaves 1996) regardless of context and culture are representative of this diminution.

Engaging with the moral and social purposes of what teachers teach

Increasingly, curriculum content is being decontextualised from the broader moral and social purpose of education and wielded as a political weapon, as we have raised elsewhere in this book. Think about the 2006 'History Summit' held by the Commonwealth government, which focused on the importance of 'narrative' approaches to History in schools so as to provide students with an understanding of the 'true account' of Australian history. Given the current government's ongoing condemnation of what the prime minister terms 'black armband history', we can only but wonder whose version of the truth the adopted narrative might represent.

Working in collaborative cultures of help and support

Particularly in secondary schools, much works against collaboration cultures. Later we discuss the role of the leader in fostering school cultures that encourage such collaboration, but to cultivate true collegiality teachers need more than time together. They need a shared language with which to discuss their work and their own learning, time to work together on some of the hard problems and difficulties of their professional lives, and the confidence that comes from working in high-trust environments that enable them to take risks and innovate.

Having occupational heteronomy rather than self-protective autonomy

Linked to the attribute above, this attribute is about teachers having a sense of shared responsibility and accountability for the learning of their students. It relies also on teachers not being drawn into a sense of competition with each other but rather understanding their work as a joint enterprise. This is in some senses highly counter-cultural when you consider the individualistic, materialistic and competitive social and professional climate that characterises our time.

Committing to active care and not just anodyne service

The notion of 'active care' rather than an approach that does not 'rock the boat' is problematic in a litigious world in which risk is often frowned upon. Often the path of least resistance is mandated as the most 'sensible' course of action, even when, in our professional judgement, students may need something else.

Searching for continuous learning about expertise and standards of practice

As Fullan (1993a) has noted, generally speaking, teaching is not a learning profession, and this attribute represents an enormous cultural shift for most schools and teachers for whom, as we have previously noted, 'drive by' (Senge et al. 2000: 385) or 'spray on' (Mockler 2005: 738) professional development prevails. A significant portion of this chapter is devoted to discussing how educational leaders might make continuous learning a reality for teachers working in the Middle Years.

Creating and recognising high task complexity

Without suggesting that complexity should be created for complexity's sake, this attribute relates to the need for teachers to see their role in the teaching and learning process not merely as the 'bus driver' who sets the path and drives the 'learning bus' full of students, but rather as the 'architects' of the learning journey. The process of curriculum design, for example, is a complex one that teachers should engage in with alacrity and should be recognised both within and outside the profession as complex and multidimensional.

PROVOCATION: WHAT GETS IN THE WAY?

Think about the seven attributes of transformative professionalism, as previously listed.
1   What are the enabling factors and what factors 'get in the way' of teachers rising to this challenge?
2   What might teachers put into place to capitalise on the enabling factors and minimise the 'blocks'?
3   What might teachers in positions of designated responsibility do to 'open the doors' to this kind of professionalism?

THE CONTEXT OF EDUCATION REFORM

Much has been written about the broader social context of the 21st century. The move from industrial age to knowledge society (and knowledge economy); the fragmentation and isolation of modern life, particularly within urbanised areas; and the challenges of globalisation have all been considered in light of their implications for education, and we do not review this literature in any depth. As a prelude to discussing the work of those leading educational reform, however, it is important to look briefly at this broader social context as it has significant implications for the ways that educational leaders have to work in order to be wise and effective catalysts for change.

Manuel Castells (1997), in *The Power of Identity*, the second part of *The Information Age: Economy, Society and Culture*, makes an elegant analysis of the broad social impact of the move from the industrial age to the information age on group and individual identity. He argues that the growth of Western capitalism and globalisation over the last half of the 20th century produced a breakdown of civil society (due to the diminishing role of established social structures and norms), and a growth of uncertainty, leading to something of a crisis of identity. This, in turn, he argues, has produced a range of alternate and 'resistance' identities tied to such movements as Christian and Islamic extremism, market fundamentalism and right-wing nationalism. He suggests that these movements share a common thread in that they have eradicated the 'shades of grey' and provided simple, straightforward answers to the riddles and complexities of our time. As such, they appear as a safe foil to the need 'out there' to navigate uncertainty. Taking the feminist and environmentalist movements as key examples, Castells argues that the potential for social improvement lies in the development of generative and constructive identities that aim to reconstruct the social institutions of civil society in ways that represent and better serve the community – identities that grow out of shared enterprise rather than communal resistance.

In a similar vein, Michael Power (1997) argues that the rise of the audit society and audit cultures that seek to relentlessly measure and quantify human experience and endeavour are a response to 'manufactured uncertainty' – a term used by Anthony Giddens (1994) to describe the uncertainty that is not intrinsic to the human condition, but rather is a by-product of the organisation of human society. Central to Power's (1997) argument is the belief that this audit approach, particularly when undertaken in capricious or ill-considered ways (as he posits is often the case), has a detrimental impact upon risk-taking and thus innovation and creativity.

So, it is suggested that the enhanced uncertainty implicit in the postmodern world leads to increased fundamentalism of all varieties, while it is also suggested that the same uncertainty leads to an increased tendency to audit, count, measure and otherwise quantify. By no means, however, are these two outcomes mutually exclusive – quite the contrary in fact. After all, the narrower and more 'cut and dried' our approaches and understandings are, the more open we might be to the kinds of measurement and evaluation that fall into the category about which Power is writing.

Michael Apple (2006) is impassioned in his writing about the effect of these social patterns on schools and educators. In his recent analysis of the Bush administration's 'No Child Left Behind' policy in America, he traces the implications of audit cultures, market and religious fundamentalism, and the influence of neo-liberal and neo-conservative political agendas, on what he views as this most problematic of education policies. Apple writes:

Undoubtedly, within each and every institution of education at all levels, within the crevices and cracks so to speak, there are counterhegemonic practices being built and defended. But they are too often isolated from each other and never get organized into coherent movements and strategies. Part of the task is to make public the successes in contesting the control over curricula, pedagogy and evaluation and in reaching the children that our educational system has in fact 'left behind' – over all of our work. Although public 'storytelling' may not be sufficient, it performs an important function. It keeps alive and reminds ourselves of the very possibility of difference in an age of audits, commodification, and disrespect (2006: 121–2).

In very real, local ways, the prospect of good educational leadership promises to be a counterpoint to these social tides within our schools. For if we as a profession recognise that Dewey was right when in 1897 he wrote:

I believe that education is the fundamental method of social progress and reform.

I believe that all reforms which rest simply upon the enactment of law, or the threatening of certain penalties, or upon changes in mechanical or outward arrangements, are transitory and futile.

I believe that education is a regulation of the process of coming to share in the social consciousness; and that the adjustment of individual activity on the basis of this social consciousness is the only sure method of social reconstruction.

then the work of the educational leader is in fact to cultivate environments, communities and spaces wherein this kind of social reconstruction and transformation can occur. And the implications of this not only for our work as leaders, but also for our school cultures and how our profession constructs itself, are enormous.

Hargreaves (2003) considers the ways that the implications of the knowledge society or information age are being translated into educational practice in our schools. Hargreaves's argument is that the educational reality at present is such that teaching is becoming a 'casualty' of the knowledge society rather than a catalyst for it or a counterpoint to it (see Table 8.1 on page 137). This heuristic is a useful one for us as leaders, as it offers not only a sense of what the negative impact of the postmodern world could be for the education community, but also a sense of how we, as educational leaders, can resist it.

The challenge is for us to remember that the elements on the right side of the table represent not 'the way it needs to be' but rather more closely resemble the 'lowest common denominator'. In this age of compliance and institutional risk-aversion, it is essential for us as educators and for our students that we look beyond compliance to construct education as an enterprise far more rich and complex. A transformative teaching profession sees its primary responsibility as the development of critical, literate, socially aware citizens with a strong sense of civic responsibility, and through them the generation of social capital and the growth of civil society. The role of the educational leader

Table 8.1 Teaching in the knowledge society

	CATALYSTS (TEACHING FOR ...)	COUNTERPOINTS (TEACHING BEYOND ...)	CASUALTIES (TEACHING IN SPITE OF ...)
Learning as	deep cognitive	social and emotional	standardised performance
Professional	learning	development	training
Colleagues as	teams	groups	individuals
Parents as	learners	partners	consumers and complainers
Emotional	intelligence	understanding	labour
Tone of	change and risk	continuity and security	fear and insecurity
Trust in	processes	people	no one

(Hargreaves 2003: 81)

is to open doors to the development of such a profession. The key to doing so in the context of leading learning in the Middle Years relies upon developing school-based communities of practice and fostering professional learning for teachers in forms that are relevant and engaging. We now consider these two elements more deeply.

PROVOCATION: CATALYSTS, COUNTERPOINTS AND CASUALTIES

Think for a moment about your experience in teaching.
1   Where are we (as a profession) succeeding in responding to the challenge of the catalysts, pushing past the 'casualties' and moving beyond the counterpoints?

2   Where do you see the tensions or difficulties?

3   What is driving the casualties?

4   What further strategies can we put in place to push through them?

THE LEARNING COMMUNITY: FROM RHETORIC TO REALITY

Talk about the importance of schools becoming learning communities has been going on for at least the past decade. Sometimes connected to the problem of the professionalisation of the teaching profession (see, for example, Sergiovanni 1994: 139), and at other times seen as the panacea for an ailing occupation (see, for example, Fullan, Hill & Crevola 2006: 21, 85), at its heart, the concept of the learning community is neither. It is another of those concepts that is easy to name but more difficult to enact. We spend more time here thinking about the necessary conditions that leaders can work to create than describing the learning community, but a brief definition at the outset is necessary.

Drawing together a wealth of writing on school as learning organisation (see, for example, Fullan 1993a; Leithwood & Louis 1998; Mitchell & Sackney 2000), Giles and Hargreaves suggest that the school as learning community consists of three key tenets (represented in Figure 8.1): 'collaborative work and discussion among the school's professionals, a strong and consistent focus on teaching and learning within that collaborative work, and the collection and use of assessment and other data to inquire into and evaluate progress over time' (2006: 126).

Drawing on the work of Senge and colleagues (2000) on 'the fifth discipline' in schools, Giles and Hargreaves continue to extrapolate from these key tenets that there exists in such schools a capacity to adapt flexibly to change and develop sustainable innovation because 'through teamwork and dispersed leadership, they build the professional capacity to solve problems and make decisions expeditiously' (2006: 126).

COLLABORATIVE WORK AND DISCUSSION

Pushing way beyond the boundaries of 'contrived collegiality' (Hargreaves 1994), this kind of collaborative work and discussion engages teachers in the truly collegial endeavour that Wenger calls 'joint enterprise' (1998). It is about teachers working in collaborative ways to create and use professional knowledge, with all of the negotiation and hard critical thinking that it entails. It is also about a sense of mutual accountability (particularly for student learning) to each other, to students and to parents, and essential to its development is a shared language with which to discuss, critique and celebrate work and a commitment to do so as part of (not as an add-on) daily and weekly routines. We focus more on these conditions in subsequent sections of this chapter.

FOCUS ON TEACHING AND LEARNING

Much in the modern school detracts from teachers developing a consistent focus on teaching and learning in their collaborative work and discussion. Increasing administrative demands and the increase also in state-driven standardised testing, which can lead to more automated or instrumentalist approaches to teaching and learning, as well as the relentless pace of change and 'constant improvement' that

Figure 8.1 Professional learning community (Stage 1)

takes place in some schools can all contribute to diluting this learning focus. We should also recognise that such a focus is a demanding and difficult one for most teachers. To achieve such a focus, after all, teachers need to not only have a good knowledge of teaching and learning as it relates to the context of their teaching but also have the confidence to put their understandings and opinions 'out there'.

USE OF DATA TO INFORM PRACTICE

As we discuss at length in the next chapter, using assessment and other data as a 'springboard' from which to make judgements and decisions about teaching and learning is an important part of teachers' work. Such an approach not only increases the likelihood that decisions taken about the teaching and learning process will be wise, but also provides important opportunities for teachers to hone their professional judgement in collaborative and supportive environments.

These three elements, however, do not come to exist in isolation, and neither do they come into being via happenstance. Their effective formation and operation at a deep rather than superficial level relies upon the existence of a generative professional learning culture within the school, and it is here that educational leaders can play a major part, both as orchestrators and participants.

THE GENERATIVE PROFESSIONAL LEARNING CULTURE

As Hargreaves (2003) suggests, as represented in Table 8.1, the dominant tendency in our time in teacher education is the 'training' model. Despite all we know about engagement, points of readiness, constructivist learning, 'just-in-time learning', differentiation of the curriculum and active learning, most teacher professional learning takes place in an environment in which the learners are seen as passive participants; in which they make few decisions about the nature, duration and focus of

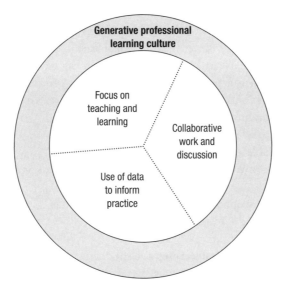

Figure 8.2 Professional learning community (Stage 2)

their learning; and in which there is little (if any) attempt to differentiate learning according to past knowledge and experience, career stage, learning style or the particular interests of the participants. Until teachers are able to become active agents of their own professional learning, it is unlikely that schools will become learning organisations or learning communities or, in fact, anything other than places where adult learning is stultified.

What might such a culture look like and how can we as leaders assist our school communities to develop one?

Cochran-Smith and Lytle (1999) argue that the development of teacher learning communities wherein the type of generative professional learning culture we are referring to is evident depends largely on the conception of teacher learning and teacher knowledge at its heart. They posit that there are three quite distinct conceptions within schools:

- *Knowledge-for-practice*: teacher knowledge is largely generated external to the profession (that is, as 'formal knowledge', predominantly created at university); the professional learning task for teachers is therefore to learn and integrate this knowledge into their professional repertoires to improve practice.
- *Knowledge-in-practice*: teacher knowledge is seen as 'practical', residing largely within the practical experience and capacities of teachers; the professional learning task for teachers is therefore to work with and learn from each other through action and reflection to improve practice.
- *Knowledge-of-practice*: teacher knowledge is not subject to the traditional formal versus practical divide, but is seen to be created through the process of ongoing critical inquiry whereby teachers use both systematic inquiry in their own classrooms and contexts, and interrogation of the knowledge created by others. 'In this sense, teachers learn when they generate local knowledge of practice by working within the contexts of inquiry communities to theorize and construct their work and to connect it to the larger social, cultural and political issues' (Cochran-Smith & Lytle 1999: 250).

Cochran-Smith and Lytle (1998) advocate adopting what they have termed 'inquiry as stance' as a framework for enacting this third conceptualisation of teachers' knowledge on a career-long basis, and as a methodology for integrating professional practice and professional learning within the generative professional learning community.

Approaching 'inquiry as stance' as a framework for professional learning, however, requires that we look closely at the nature of teacher professional learning and consider how much of what currently passes for 'professional learning' may or may not in fact be helpful. Susan Loucks-Horsley and colleagues posited a series of principles of effective teacher professional learning in 1987 that, almost 20 years later, we are (on a macro level at least) still to realise:

- collegiality and collaboration
- experimentation and risk-taking
- incorporation of available knowledge bases
- appropriate participant involvement in goal-setting, implementation, evaluation and decision-making
- time to work on staff development and assimilate new learnings
- leadership and sustained administrative support
- appropriate incentives and rewards
- designs built on principles of adult learning and the change process
- integration of individual goals with school goals
- formal placement of the program within the philosophy and organisational structure of the school (Loucks-Horsley et al. 1987: 8).

Writing in another context, Mockler has suggested the addition of another two principles:

- opportunities to (in the secondary school in particular) build both discipline knowledge and pedagogical expertise
- opportunities to develop an understanding of the broader social context of teachers' work and the implications of this context for pedagogy and practice (2005: 739).

The principles offered here offer some insights into the way that professional learning constructed with 'inquiry as stance' in mind might look, and equally have strong implications for those of us responsible for leading professional learning communities. Professional learning that is negotiated – offered as a 'smorgasbord' rather than a 'must do' – is constructed on the notion of teachers engaging with their practice via a broad range of naturally occurring critical questions, involves the creation of knowledge within the community while drawing on that created outside the community, and is taken seriously by those in key leadership administration roles in the school (it could be suggested that funding such professional development plays a crucial role in demonstrating this seriousness) and is an essential part of the development of a generative professional learning community.

TRUST – THE INCUBATOR OF THE LEARNING COMMUNITY

Cultivating a generative professional learning community, however, can never be merely a matter of constructing an effective professional learning program that responds to the challenges thrown out to us by the principles referred to above and the notion of 'inquiry as stance'. The very nature of this approach to professional learning requires that the participants have confidence in their capacities to learn, are able to be open and honest with each other, are unafraid to innovate and adopt new approaches and try new strategies, and feel supported to take risks generally. In short, the generative

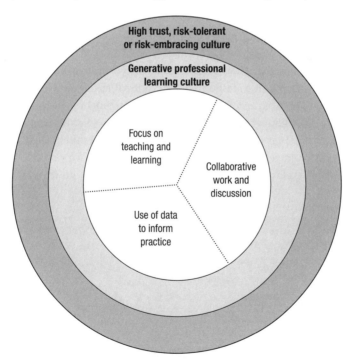

professional learning community relies on a culture comprising high levels of trust and a tolerance of or embracing of risk in order to work effectively.

The erosion of social trust within the broader social context has been the subject of much research and writing over the past decade (see, for example, Misztal 1996; Cvetkovich & Lofstedt 1999; Fukuyama 1999). A range of contributing factors are said to be responsible for this erosion of trust, including those referred to earlier in this chapter, such as the rise of the 'network society' (Castells 1997), the development of 'manufactured uncertainty' (Giddens 1994), the growth in global terrorism (Combs 2003) and the associated rise in fundamentalisms of all kinds.

Within education, this erosion of trust is reflected in worldwide moves towards 'standards', measurement and accountability to a set of rigid guidelines and 'norms', the current culture of compliance within which we see ourselves working. Giddens (1994) points to the need for the development of what he terms 'active trust' in response to the 'detraditionalising' of social institutions (such as education) whereby the expectation that practice will unfold in age-old and predictable ways can no longer be met. Construed by Giddens (1994: 14) as trust in people or in social institutions that has to be actively produced, active trust involves a deliberate leap of faith. This is a particularly salient message for us working in the context of educational institutions and Middle Years reform, in which the 'apprenticeship of observation'[1] (Lortie 1975: 61) experience prevails for many members of our school communities in the face of new and emerging pedagogies and approaches.

Directly linked to the development of active trust is an openness to risk-taking. Risk and trust go hand in hand in our social institutions, and the link between risk aversion and low trust cultures is quite well established (Misztal 1996). Furthermore, the minimisation or eradication of risk is one of the central aims of the audit society that we discussed previously. The overly managerial discourses that prevail in society generally, and are on the increase within the educational sphere, draw upon and build for the dogma of the audit society, and any of the increasing 'accountabilities' in our schools of recent years can be linked to this minimisation of risk.

One of the key challenges (possibly the ultimate one, in fact) for the educational leader at this time is this reinstatement of trust at a local level. In order for generative professional learning cultures that foster *real* learning communities to flourish, educational leaders working at classroom, school and system levels need to act courageously to create environments in which teachers, students and parents exercise trust and willingly take risks in innovating. No Middle Years reform, or any other educational reform, for that matter, will work without this cultural shift. Such a shift requires on the part of leaders not only courage but also creativity, commitment and a vision for education and for our society generally that pushes the boundaries and is not content with regimes of compliance.

PROVOCATION: BUILDING TRUST — EASY TO SAY, HARD TO DO!

Reina and Reina (1999) suggest that there are three kinds of trust in operation at the workplace:
- *contractual trust*, related to what we say we will do and undertake to do, both formally and informally

- *competence trust*, related to the trust we have that others and ourselves will be *able* and competent in carrying out that which we need to do

- *communication trust*, related to our interactions and communications with each other within our communities.

---

1. This term was used by Dan Lortie (1975) to describe the phenomena whereby prospective teachers undergo an 'apprenticeship' for an extended period as school students themselves.

Think about your own school community.

1   In which of these three domains do you see high levels of trust?

2   In which do you see room for improvement?

3   What do you think currently fosters trust and what erodes it in each of these domains?

4   What strategies could you and your colleagues put into place to build and expand contractual, competence and communication trust?

CASE STUDY
A tale of two schools

Both Bartlett School and Burton School embarked 18 months ago on a similar approach to a new way of constructing school for Years 6 to 8. Across the three years, students study an integrated curriculum for approximately 50 per cent of their learning time, and this curriculum is supplemented by specialist classes in each of the 'traditional' secondary-school subject areas for the other 50 per cent of learning time. The integrated curriculum is designed for each year group using the transdisciplinary approach to integrating curriculum, discussed earlier in this book, by a team of six teachers, who are also responsible for implementing the curriculum. Students are organised into a 'learning ring' of approximately 16 members, including 15 students and one teacher for the duration of each year. The 'learning rings' function in both the academic and pastoral domains of school life, with the 'learning ring leader' teacher integrating these two aspects of school life in their interactions with students.

Teaching team members meet daily for about 30 minutes to informally discuss the teaching and learning of their students, and they have a designated two-hour block of time put aside after school each week for curriculum design, assessment moderation, peer-led professional learning and other such activities. In addition, each team meets for five days over the course of the year during the school holidays. For the loss of time and flexibility, team members are duly compensated and remunerated in both schools.

In both schools, there are designated open-plan learning spaces designed and purpose-built for the Middle Years, where students have high-level access to technology (in the form of computers, digital cameras, interactive whiteboards and the like) and where furniture is set up in a range of configurations for different styles and types of learning.

The Burton School experience

At Burton School the team (in consultation with the school's Director of Teaching and Learning, to whom the team is ultimately responsible) choose the leader of each of the Middle Years teams (MYT). The MYT leaders then work within the structure of the school as the equivalent of KLA coordinators: they attend KLA coordinators' meetings and are responsible for 'keeping the team on track' when it comes to timelines and other requirements that impact upon the broader school operations.

MYT meetings are chaired by team members on a rotating basis and, while the director of teaching and learning sometimes attends some or all of a meeting on invitation from the team, each of the MYTs are autonomous when it comes to setting agendas and allocating time for tasks. Team members, however, feel well supported by the director, and know that they can count on his expertise and support. Although one of the requirements of team membership is that they meet for 30 minutes each day, they often meet for longer, beginning with breakfast at 7.30am and working through until school begins at 8.45am. At other times, when there is a 'lull', they might not meet at all for a few days. The director understands that this is their pattern and is happy for them to take a 'swings-and-roundabout' approach.

The five additional days over the holidays are usually conducted at a team member's house, unless the team needs access to technology or resources that require them to be at school. While the teams develop their own agendas and focus areas, the director is also drawn into the planning process, and is often invited to come along as a 'resource person' or to assist in leading or being involved in a session.

At the beginning of the second term in the year the new scheme was introduced, a group of Year 7 parents began to get nervous because they didn't really understand what an integrated curriculum is in the context of secondary school and are worried because their children seem to be spending a lot less time doing subjects such as English, Mathematics and Science than the children of friends at other secondary schools. The principal is confronted by parents wanting an assurance that things will change when their children get into Year 8. The principal asks the director to work with the Year 7 MYT to diffuse the tension and the team, along with their Year 6 and Year 8 colleagues, devise parent forums, school visits and other pathways for concerned parents to learn about the system in action and develop a language for discussing learning with their children. By the end of Term 3, while there are still a small number of unhappy parents, most parents are well informed and comfortable, and there is even a group of Year 7 parents developing and implementing a parent-led advocacy group in the school for parents of students in subsequent years.

The Bartlett School experience

At Bartlett School, each of the MYTs is led by the Curriculum Coordinator, who already had a more than full load before the new system came into being. For the coordinator to be available to chair all MYT meetings across each of the three year levels, the meetings are timetabled throughout the week and team members are unable to change them according to need. The agenda of each meeting is set by the coordinator, and while there is space under 'other business' for team members to raise issues or concerns, most of the agenda for the planning meetings is dedicated to responding to the administrative requirements and concerns raised at head teachers' meetings, which the coordinator both chairs and attends on behalf of the MYTs. Because it is necessary for teams to be accountable for what they do, and also because the coordinator needs to attend (and facilitate) all of the designated meetings during the school holidays, the dates for these meetings are plotted a year in advance and the meetings are held on campus.

Head teachers at Bartlett have been anxious about the new scheme since before its implementation, mostly because of the reduction of class time for their subjects, and this is often discussed at their meetings. The coordinator feels conflicted, for while she is the designated leader of the head teachers, she is also the designated leader of the MYTs and, as such, knows that she should be advocating for both groups. In addition, she is also slightly uneasy about the new scheme, having been the head teacher of Science when it was in the planning phase and only recently having taken on her current role.

When Bartlett is approached by a group of parents with similar concerns to those at Burton, the coordinator, who has been asked by the principal to prepare a response, convenes a team of head teachers who self-nominate to a committee to investigate a way forward. By the end of Term 3 of the same year, while the parents' concerns have largely dissipated – thanks largely to the Year 7 MYT who, sensing that there were issues, had worked hard to improve school–home communication and discuss with parents what was happening at school – the committee has developed a plan to change the structure for the following academic year so that students spend more time in specialist classes.

DISCUSSION STARTERS

For both Burton and Bartlett schools, consider:

1   Do the Middle Years reforms demonstrate the three key elements of learning communities in action? Where do the reforms 'fall down'?
2   What evidence is there of a generative professional learning community?
3   What evidence is there of a culture of high trust and risk-tolerance?
4   Where is the leadership courageous and where do you think it misses the mark? Why?
5   Return to Table 8.1 on page 137. What catalysts, counterpoints and casualties do you see in action here?

CONCLUSION

We began this chapter with a look at transformative teacher professionalism. Transformative teachers are creative designers of curriculum and are innovative in their pedagogy. Transformative teachers value 'risky thinking' and divergent approaches in themselves, their colleagues and their students, and in doing so they are powerful role models for students in developing their own capacity as critical thinkers and responsible citizens. Transformative teachers engage in critical thinking and collaborative inquiry into their practice not as a 'special project' but as routine, and necessary in adopting such an approach is a willingness to be open to change and transformation in themselves, a willingness that comes only with a readiness to take risks in opening up to others and in forging relationships that are open and authentic.

If as an educational community and a teaching profession we are to live up to all of the promise and possibilities inherent in Middle Years reform, we need to be boldly transformative in intent. Such bold transformation will not emerge without strong and daring leadership.

References

Apple, M. (2006) *Educating the 'Right' Way: Markets, Standards, God and Inequality.* 2nd edn. New York, NY: Routledge.

Castells, M. (1997) *The Power of Identity.* Oxford, UK: Blackwell.

Cochran-Smith, M. & Lytle, S. (1998) 'Teacher research: the question that persists'. *International Journal of Leadership in Education*, 1, 19–36.

Cochran-Smith, M. & Lytle, S. (1999) 'Relationships of knowledge and practice: teacher learning communities', *Review of Research in Education*, 24, 249–305.

Combs, C. (2003) *Terrorism in the 21st Century.* Upper Saddle River, NJ: Prentice Hall.

Cvetkovich, G. & Lofstedt, R. (1999) *Social Trust and the Management of Risk.* London, UK: Earthscan.

Dewey, J. (1897) 'My pedagogic creed.' Accessed 26 March 2006 from www.infed.org/archives/e-texts/e-dew-pc.htm.

Fukuyama, F. (1999) *The Great Disruption: Human Nature and the Reconstitution of Social Order.* New York, NY: Touchstone.

Fullan, M. (1993a) *Change Forces: Probing the Depths of Educational Reform.* Bristol, PL: Falmer.

Fullan, M. (1993b) 'Why teachers must become change agents'. *Educational Leadership*, 50(6), 12–17.

Fullan, M., Hill, P. & Crevola, C. (2006) *Breakthrough*. Thousand Oaks, CA: Corwin Press.

Giddens, A. (1994) *Beyond Left and Right: The Future of Radical Politics*. Cambridge, UK: Polity Press.

Giles, C. & Hargreaves, A. (2006) 'The sustainability of innovative schools as learning organizations and professional learning communities during standardized reform'. *Educational Administration Quarterly*, 42(1), 124–56.

Hargreaves, A. (1994) *Changing Teachers, Changing Times: Teachers' Work and Culture in the Postmodern Age*. New York, NY: Teachers' College Press.

Hargreaves, A. (2003) *Teaching in the Knowledge Society: Education in the Age of Insecurity*. New York, NY: Teachers' College Press.

Hargreaves, A. & Fink, D. (2005) *Sustainable Leadership*. San Francisco, CA: Jossey-Bass.

Hargreaves, A. & Fink, D. (2006) 'The ripple effect'. *Educational Leadership*, 63(8), 16–21.

Hargreaves, A. & Goodson, I. (1996) *Teachers' Professional Lives: Aspirations and Actualities*. London, UK: Falmer Press.

Hargreaves, D. (1996) *Teaching as a Research Based Profession*. London, UK: Teacher Training Agency.

Leithwood, K. & Louis, K. (eds) (1998) *Organizational Learning in Schools*. Downington, PA: Swets & Zeitlinger.

Lortie (1975) *Schoolteacher: A Sociological Study*. Chicago, IL: University of Chicago Press.

Loucks-Horsley, S., Harding, C., Arbuckle, M., Murray, L., Dubea, C. & Williams, M. (1987) *Continuing to Learn: A Guidebook for Teacher Development*. Andover, MA: Regional Laboratory for Educational Improvement of the Northeast and Islands and National Staff Development Council.

Misztal, B. (1996) *Trust in Modern Societies: The Search for the Basis of Social Order*. Cambridge, UK: Polity Press.

Mitchell, C. & Sackney, L. (2000) *Profound Improvement: Building Capacity for a Learning Community*. Downington, PA: Swets & Zeitlinger.

Mockler, N. (2005) 'Trans/forming teachers: new professional learning and transformative teacher professionalism'. *Journal of In-Service Education*, 31(4), 733–46.

Power, M. (1997) *The Audit Society: Rituals of Verification*. Oxford, UK: Oxford University Press.

Reina, D. & Reina, M. (1999) *Trust and Betrayal in the Workplace*. San Francisco, CA: Berett-Koehler.

Sachs, J. (2003) *The Activist Teaching Profession*. Buckingham, UK: Open University Press.

Senge, P., Cambron-McCabe, N., Lucas, T., Smith, B., Dutton, J. & Kleiner, A. (2000) *Schools That Learn*. London, UK: Nicholas Brealey.

Sergiovanni, T. (1992) *Moral Leadership: Getting to the Heart of School Improvement*. San Francisco, CA: Jossey-Bass.

Sergiovanni, T. (1994) *Building Community in Schools*. San Francisco, CA: Jossey-Bass.

Sergiovanni, T. (1996) *Leadership for the Schoolhouse: How is it Different? Why is it Important?* San Francisco, CA: Jossey-Bass.

Spillane, J. (2005) *Distributed Leadership*. San Francisco, CA: Jossey-Bass.

Starratt, R.J. (2004) Ethical Leadership. San Francisco, CA: Jossey-Bass.

Wenger, E. (1998) *Communities of Practice: Learning, Meaning and Identity*. Cambridge, UK: Cambridge University Press.

9

EVALUATING TEACHING AND LEARNING

We offer the term *inquiry as stance* to describe the positions teachers and others who work together in inquiry communities take toward knowledge and its relationships to practice . . . Taking an inquiry stance means teachers and student teachers working within inquiry communities to generate local knowledge, envision and theorize their practice, and interpret and interrogate the theory and research of others (Cochran-Smith 2003: 7–8).

INTRODUCTION

Teachers in the myriad of classrooms across Australia are daily engaged in practical problem-solving. Curriculum questions about what is to be taught and who decides, pedagogical questions related to how it is to be taught and assessment questions about what has been learnt – these are all matters that teachers address. Earlier chapters have considered these questions and looked at various strategies and methods to respond to them. In this chapter we argue for the approach to teaching and learning to be carefully considered, evidence-based and reflective.

We have encouraged you, as aspiring or practising teachers in the Middle Years, to act thoughtfully and responsively. In this chapter we concentrate upon encouraging you to act systematically when you ask yourself 'How effective am I as an individual teacher and as a member of the school community?' We challenge you to encounter teaching in new and sometimes quite disturbing ways. Decision-making in the classroom can be fast and furious; there is little time to stop and wonder if this is the best approach to take with Marina when she shouted above Josie, who hardly ever answers a question? Or, should I have stepped in with Mohammed's group and steered them in a different direction? We do what we think best at the time, because time is so short and precious. However, we also have to take the time to more systematically examine our decisions at both the macro and micro levels, and their consequences for ourselves, our colleagues and our students. This process can be disturbing, disruptive even, because when we take a step backwards we can see that our immediate solutions may not have been the best or most effective. Furthermore, we make the case for consulting students and engaging them as active agents in school-based inquiry. This, too, is risky business. Schools often find themselves reluctant to ask those who are most affected by their decisions and practices, those identified earlier as the 'consequential stakeholders'.

Key questions guiding this chapter are:

1   What are some ways that teachers can investigate and evaluate aspects of their classroom practice?
2   How can teachers build models of evidence-based classroom practice?

THE CRITICAL INCIDENT

To build our case we turn to an example outside the classroom.

> One of us lives with a small brown dog, who some years ago had to have her two back knees operated on simultaneously. After a general anaesthetic and a three-day stay at the vet hospital, we went to collect her to find ourselves greeted by a vet nurse who could hardly contain her glee. As she returned from the 'ward' with the dog, she announced that Maddy had learned a new trick while she had been there. The vet nurse popped the dog onto the floor, whereupon she lifted her back legs high into the air and scurried swiftly across the room on her front ones. Unsure of whether to laugh or cry at what was something of a sorry sight, we took her home for recuperation, which, because of her new-found skill, took almost three times longer than expected. Maddy was indeed so good at running and walking on her front legs that she was reluctant to use the

sore back ones to get about and thus it took much longer for them to heal. She had a similar effect on people who saw her: a pint-sized dog with a bandaged back happily charging around at full speed, eliciting both mirth and pity from those across whose path she scampered!

While we are not suggesting that teaching is as extreme as having pins inserted into your knees, it is and should be an activity in which the new and sometimes unusual are faced every day and require our attention and analysis. In the 'critical incident' related above, we were forced to examine our expectations about what can and cannot be achieved in a particular situation and observe the principle of mind over matter!

This incident was not 'critical' in the sense that it required an emergency response – it was not the kind of critical incident such as invasions by rival schools or serious drug events for which schools develop plans and procedures. Here we use the term 'critical incident' in the sense developed by Tripp (1993, 1996), whereby any small, normal incident can be used to analyse and examine some of the wider implications of an aspect of professional practice. His approach involves three distinct phases: the *description* of an incident, the *explanation* of the incident and the *broadening* of the implications of the incident to draw a more general meaning and interpret the events in the light of the broader context. When applied to an example of professional practice, this approach requires us to focus on the learning that occurred for us both during and after the incident, and to link this isolated incident with the immediate and general context. The critical incident approach depends upon the quality of the data available to us and how it might be used. In evaluating teaching and learning in our classrooms and schools (remembering that learning at school also takes place outside the classroom), we advocate a form of action learning based upon action research.

PROVOCATION: USING THE CRITICAL INCIDENT

Think about a recent incident that, in some way, impacted upon your learning. Use this methodology to reflect upon it: (1) describe the incident, (2) explain it and (3) link it to the broader context within which it occurred. How was it significant?

ACTION LEARNING AND ACTION RESEARCH

A FRAMEWORK FOR EVALUATION

For many, there is little difference between action learning and action research. We argue that the former can be seen as a subset of the latter. Action learning occurs when participants reflect upon and learn from data collected in settings in which a real problem has been identified (McGill & Brockbank 2004). It has quite specific characteristics in that – as it was devised by Revans (1980), who first developed and applied it in the coalmines in the United Kingdom in the 1940s – it is an explicit process for bringing together a group of people with varying skills and expertise to analyse a problem in a way that would bring about change. In school settings this might mean that those holding positions of responsibility, such as heads of department, work alongside those who may be new to teaching and relatively inexperienced or even work collectively with students in the school.

Action learning aims to find solutions to problems for which there are no ready answers. Working in a health setting, Dewar and Sharp (2006: 220) describe it as:

> a structured process whereby participants work within a framework which includes agreement to work within certain principles, such as an expectation of being challenged; this allows the development of new understandings about the situation, which in turn allows participants to take new actions.

Importantly, there is an expectation that participants, who are gathered together in 'sets', will make transparent their personal values, feelings and attitudes.

These precepts in no way contradict those of action research, so what, then, is the difference? If we take the now classic definition by Carr and Kemmis that action research is a 'form of self-reflective inquiry undertaken by participants in social situations in order to improve the rationality and justice of their own practices, their understanding of these practices and the situations in which they are carried out' (1986: 162), the difference is not immediately evident. However, action research has an additional expectation that it will actually contribute to the formation of professional knowledge beyond the immediate setting (Groundwater-Smith & Mockler 2006). In the Coalition for Knowledge Building learning cooperative, to which we have referred, the participating schools see that they have a responsibility to publish their inquiries, making them available for scrutiny and critique.

For the purposes of this chapter we take the action learning orientation as the one that most applies to schools choosing to systematically evaluate teaching and learning. The evaluation framework can best be seen as one that follows a series of steps:

- defining the problem that is to be addressed (this step may be revisited from time to time as the problem is reframed)
- forming an appropriate group to consider the problem
- analysing the context
- determining the appropriate data sources
- collecting the data

- analysing and interpreting the data
- reflecting on the learning
- developing an appropriate policy and/or practice to address the problem.

Each of these steps is important and should be considered in the light of the problem or challenge that is being addressed. However, collecting data requires particular attention in that the range of processes is much greater than many practitioners know or appreciate. We emphasise that no problem is too small when adopting the process. It may be that a teacher within his or her class, in partnership with students, investigates what seating arrangements best suit good learning or that a whole department or school inquires into the impact of bullying upon learning in the Middle Years.

COLLECTING AND USING AUTHENTIC DATA

Much of the data that is used in analysing and evaluating teaching and learning belongs to the 'business as usual' category: that is, the kind of data that is collected from students and developed in the course of planning and implementing a unit of student work or teaching and assessing students. This is not to say, however, that evaluation necessarily happens automatically or is ordinarily embedded in the everyday classroom experience. While the line between assessment of student learning and evaluation of teaching and learning can sometimes be blurred, it is very much the case that the effective evaluation of teaching and learning requires teachers to pose a different set of questions to those posed in assessing student learning. Also, while professional judgement is an integral part of both, evaluation of teaching and learning requires a 'meta' or 'macro' application of such judgement, while assessment of student learning generally requires a more 'micro' approach. As indicated in the previous chapter, honing professional judgement is an important and complex process, and one that relies on the development of collegial and collaborative links. More shall be said about this later.

If it is the case that evaluation requires a different set of questions to assessment, what might these questions be? When we are assessing student learning, we might pose such questions as:
- How far has student X met this outcome?
- What about this outcome has student X already mastered?
- Where does student X have room for improvement?
- Considering all that I know about student X as a person and as a learner, what might he/she do to consolidate learning and further improve?

The questions we pose in evaluating teaching and learning might be different:
- How far have students mastered the knowledge, understanding and skills intended in this unit of work?
- What factors have aided student learning?
- What factors have hindered student learning?
- What might I do the same and differently next time?

While the questions are similar, how they are framed necessarily narrows the focus in the case of assessment and broadens the focus in the case of evaluation. In answering the first evaluation question, we might employ a range of different tactics, relying on samples of student work and aggregated achievement (for example, '19 out of my 25 students achieved an excellent descriptor on outcome X, which might indicate …'). An analysis of student learning logs or learning journals might give some insight into the second and third questions, and perhaps a brief evaluation survey or questionnaire might assist in responding to the final question. In this way, you are using data you have already collected from students (that is, the work upon which assessment has been based, as well as their learning journals) and collect additional data as required. It is always a good idea to base our judgement on a range of sources of data rather than on one type, and this process is important not only in terms of validity but also in terms of ethical practice. As practitioners, we have an ethical responsibility to ensure that our professional judgement is grounded in the best quality of evidence possible, and part of the quality control process in this case is ensuring that judgements are based not merely on one source of information or data.

In addition, involving students in retrospectively considering their role, the teacher's role and the role of other factors in their learning offers benefits for both student and teacher. For students, it can be a powerful modelling of authentic reflection and the importance of 'taking time out' to think about what has gone before, prior to dashing off on new ventures. Additionally, it signals to students that their insights are taken seriously and their perspectives are valued. Over time, this fosters trust and openness (provided that students see that teachers are prepared to act upon their insights) in the learning relationship. We are yet to hear of a teacher who asked their students for their perspective on a learning experience and was not surprised by the response in some way. Sometimes it is not until we ask openly and explicitly that students feel free to tell us what they feel is or is not working for them in their learning.

There are many different ways that teachers can pose questions about learning to their students. We suggest a few ways here but encourage you to think creatively about methods that will work well for you and your students. There are certainly no hard-and-fast rules when it comes to driving the learning conversation forward.

Surveys and questionnaires

Surveys and questionnaires come in all kinds of forms and guises from the very lengthy and complex, involving different types of questions and links between questions, to those that are shorter and more straightforward. We advocate simplicity as, while it is surely important that we gather data from students, we do not want to use enormous amounts of student time in completing questionnaires nor teacher time in analysing the data. We suggest guidelines for using surveys and questionnaires to evaluate teaching and learning, but more discussion and 'how to' information can be found in Schratz and Walker (1995), Tripp (1996) and Burton and Bartlett (2005), for example.

On page 153 is an example of a brief survey developed by a group of Middle Years SOSE teachers who were conducting an investigation on learning in their subject area.

As a general rule, we keep questionnaires to one or two pages at a maximum. It is a good idea to ask a few different types of questions, combining questions for which the answers can be indicated by quantitative means (for example, using a Likert scale[1]) with questions that ask students to give

---

1. A Likert scale is a continuum upon which respondents place their level of agreement. An example of a Likert scale is shown in the 'Student learning in SOSE' survey.

Learning in SOSE: Student survey

→ → →

Your SOSE teachers are investigating the factors that help you to learn in SOSE.
Below is a list of things students have said in focus groups about learning in SOSE.

Please indicate how strongly you agree with each statement by choosing:
Strongly agree (SA)   Agree (A)   Disagree (D)   Strongly disagree (SD)

All answers will be anonymous.

1	Class discussions help me to learn.	
2	SOSE teachers should provide more structure for class discussions.	
3	I like to know where lessons and units of work are heading.	
4	Generally SOSE teachers do give me this information (see Q3).	
5	Groupwork helps me to learn.	
6	I learn well in independent project work.	
7	There is a good balance of group and independent work.	
8	I like to have choice in what I do.	
9	I like to have choice in how I do things.	
10	There is a good variety of assessment tasks.	
11	My learning is increased by doing assessment tasks.	
12	The feedback I receive after assessment tasks helps my learning.	

Please look at diagrams A, B and C below and answer the following questions:

13	In most of my SOSE classes, the room is set up like:	
14	I learn best in a room that is set up like:	
15	I prefer to do SOSE in a room that is set up like:	

16 Please give an example of something that helped your learning in SOSE recently and tell us how.

_____

_____

_____

_____

17 Please give an example of something that hindered your learning in SOSE recently and tell us how.

_____

_____

_____

_____

Thank you for completing our survey.
Student survey on learning in Studies of Society and Environment

more open-ended and explanatory responses. In the survey above, teachers have used a four-point Likert scale for the first 15 questions and then asked for a more extended response for the final two questions. While there is a vast literature on the statistical pros and cons of using a four-point scale as opposed to a five-point scale in which there is a mid or neutral point, we generally prefer to 'force' a choice rather than allow respondents to 'sit on the fence'. While in statistical terms this may not produce data of the highest possible level of validity, our purpose here is to gain an insight into the learning of our students, not to provide the kind of scientifically valid, generalisable data that might form part of a different type of research enterprise.

The steps in analysing the data gained from a survey such as this usually involve counting the number of responses at each point along the scale for each question and representing them on a frequency chart for a visual representation. Figure 9.1 is an example of a frequency chart.

Once the data is displayed in an easily accessible way, you might sit with colleagues and make observations and ask questions about the ways that different responses relate to, verify or contradict each other to come to some conclusions about student perceptions and understandings.

In terms of the open-ended responses, a simple approach to content analysis requires you to read the responses to each question through a number of times to become familiar with them and then ask what themes or trends emerge. The next step is to return to the data and check, by making a list and checking it off as you go, how far each of those trends or themes appears in the data. It is up to you to decide about 'significance', but if, for example, 8 of the 23 students surveyed indicated in Question 16 that their learning was helped when the teacher modelled how to solve a problem and then gave them examples to do themselves, you would probably rate this as quite a significant learning support for this group of students at this time. Remember, however, that the inverse is not necessarily true. That is, because the remaining 15 students did not mention modelling does not mean that they do not find it helpful – to find this out you would need to ask that question explicitly – merely that they chose to reflect on something else that supported their learning. The aim here is not to draw responses into percentages or represent them quantitatively, rather to generally assess significance and importance.

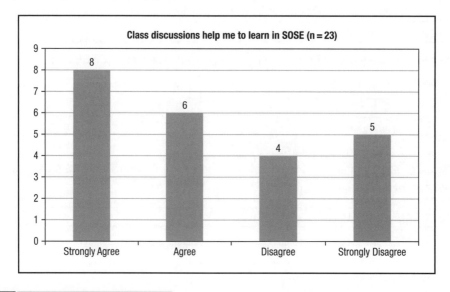

Figure 9.1 Example of a frequency chart

The 'minute paper'

A variation on the survey, the 'minute paper' poses a question to students at the end of a learning experience (perhaps a lesson or series of lessons) and asks them to comment briefly, in a paragraph or so, in only a minute or two. While a minute paper completed by a group of students gives an interesting insight into their perceptions on that occasion, a number of minute papers completed over a period of time can yield yet richer data and, depending on the focus, can perhaps function as a kind of learning log or journal. The type of simple content analysis used for open-ended survey responses can also be used to analyse minute papers.

Focus groups

First used by market researchers to elicit detailed data about consumers' attitudes towards different products, focus groups have, for some time, been adopted as a useful tool by educational and other social researchers. The focus group or focus group interview is an economical alternative to conducting individual interviews as more than one person at a time are interviewed and thus it uses much less of the researcher's time. Focus groups have an additional dimension to individual interviews that comes from the interactions of the participants, the 'bouncing around' of ideas and the general group dynamic. Focus groups are 'a way of listening to people and learning from them' (Morgan 1998: 9), while at the same time hearing the 'multivocality' (Madriz 2003: 364) or range of voices within any group of people.

Ideally, focus groups should have six to eight participants. Any less than six participants tends to make it difficult for a dynamic to emerge, while any more than eight can make it difficult for everybody to have their say. Questions for focus group discussions should be open-ended and the 'question route' should be loosely constructed so that the conversation can take natural twists and turns. Your role here is to facilitate discussion, not to lead it, and you should only really intervene when you feel that the discussion is heading off the track. It's also a good idea to think of a few 'prompting' questions (usually a slight rephrasing of the key question) for when the conversation gets stuck or you need to redirect it.

The question route chosen by the SOSE teachers conducting the investigation into learning in SOSE was:

---

1 When it works well, what does learning look like for you?
2 What needs to happen in order for learning to take place?
   a What should the teacher do?
   b What should you do?
   c What else needs to happen?
3 Is there anything else you would like to say about learning in SOSE that you haven't had the chance to say yet?

The focus group generally begins with the facilitator making a quick 'mudmap' of participants' first names when they enter the room, so if one participant has been quiet for a considerable time, or when another is dominating the conversation, being able to invite a person to speak by name can help break the pattern. There are two possibilities to record the conversation. Taking notes (albeit copious quantities of them) has the advantage of putting some participants at ease and allowing them to speak more freely than they might if the conversation was being taped. The disadvantage, of course, is that as the facilitator you only have your notes to rely on when writing up the discussion, so the writing up should take place promptly at the end of the focus group. While some participants can feel inhibited by the presence of an audio-recorder, the recording provides you a reference against which you can check your notes – a kind of 'safety net'. If you proceed this way, it is important that you make transparent the purpose of the recording and what method and timeline you will use to dispose of it when you are finished. Generally the recording should be kept until after the participants have had an opportunity to read and comment on your account of the discussion and then destroyed. What works well for one facilitator is not necessarily the preference of another. One of the authors, for example, prefers to facilitate focus groups without using a recorder because taking notes helps her to process what is being said, while another finds that having to take copious notes gets in the way of processing what is being said. You will develop your own style and preferences for doing this.

One of the important checks and balances in focus group research is the participant check. Once you have written an account of the discussion in which participants are anonymous, either in narrative form or in bullet points, it is important to return the account to participants for them to 'sign off' that it is a true and accurate account and to suggest any amendments that they would like you to make. The decision about whether to make the suggested amendments falls to the facilitator, but in our experience it is rare for a participant to suggest an amendment that does not enhance the account.

Once the participant check has been completed you are able to use the data, hopefully in concert with other data that you have collected and assembled, in order to make judgements and begin constructing a response to the questions you posed at the outset.

Later in this chapter we discuss how students might be involved not only as participants in this kind of evaluative research but also as active researchers themselves, and give some examples from schools in which this happens on a systematic basis.

Using photographs and drawings

Photography

Susan Sontag (2003) tells us that to collect photographs is to collect the world. Movies and television programs light up walls, flicker and go out, but with still photographs the image is also an object: lightweight, cheap to produce, easy to carry about, accumulate and store. If we look back, for a moment, to the photograph at the beginning of this chapter we can see how powerful a single image can be. As we see shortly, this is one of its great assets as an investigation tool in the hands of young people.

Photographs furnish evidence. Something we hear about we may doubt or question, but somehow it seems proven when we're shown a photograph of it. A photograph may be incontrovertible proof that a given thing happened; although, of course, with the technologies now available, it is possible to alter this evidence. What we examine here is how we might use photographs in what is normally seen as a discipline of words and how we can use photographs as a source of evidence when undertaking classroom inquiry.

These examples illustrate this exciting and challenging process. Walker and Wiedel's 1985 study of beginning secondary school drew on the multiple perspectives that different 'actors' bring to bear on an experience. They photographed young people beginning secondary school in various classroom and playground contexts. Six months later they conducted interviews with the participants, including the teachers, about the photographs and how they now felt about the experience of starting a new school. The process was a powerful means for understanding that events are not always 'read' in the same way. One particularly telling moment was when a young boy and his teacher are discussing his work. The teacher agonises over the fact that, at the beginning of the year, she had torn out a page of the boy's book so that he didn't have to carry such untidy work with him throughout the year. The boy draws attention to his arm in plaster and the excitement of meeting up with old friends and their signing and drawing on the plaster without a mention of the torn page – seemingly a trivial anecdote, but a telling one in terms of the range of responses that photographs evoke. You might consider using photographs in an inquiry that you are undertaking, asking questions such as who is in the photograph and what do they understand of the event? Too often photographs are used as celebratory tools, rather than as an opportunity to elicit multiple views.

The second example is that of a longitudinal study undertaken by Jon Prosser (1992) in which he documented the amalgamation of a grammar school and two secondary modern schools in the United Kingdom over a three-year period. The aim of the study was to understand how a new school defines itself. He nominated three phases that the study went through: *acceptance*, when his photographs were seen as 'safe'; *application*, when the photographs (current and historical) were used as an interview device stimulating recall; and *exploration*, when he used the photographs to engage in his own reflection of events. As he indicated, it is clear that the use of the photographs must be closely related to the particular needs of the inquiry and therefore closely aligned to the research process itself. While Prosser's study covered a significant period of time, it would be possible to adapt each of his phases when putting the camera into the hands of young people.

The final case that we draw on is a study undertaken by the SOS Children's Villages in various sites: Nicaragua, Colombia, Thailand and India (Schratz, Walker & Egg 2004). In this case, unlike the previous two studies, the researchers put the cameras in the hands of the young people. They gave digital cameras to young people who had been orphaned or abandoned (by reason of war, disaster or family violence) and were living in the care of the SOS villages to photograph the most positive aspects of their lives; the things, people and places that they liked and were important to them; places where they felt safe and protected; and where there were things that were fun. The purpose was to understand what was needed in care settings designed to provide security and comfort to young people who had experienced severe trauma. The researchers argued that the process enabled adults to see the world through children's eyes: 'it diminishes the power distribution between adult and child as it is not language, but image based' (Schratz, Walker & Egg 2004: 5). Using the photographs that the children took, they asked them to talk about the aspects of their lives that they most valued now. The insights were powerful and poignant.

Drawing

The classic study using drawing as an inquiry tool in education is Chamber's (1983) 'Draw a scientist test'. Students were asked to draw a scientist and explain what the scientist is doing in the drawing. A stereotypical view of scientists as male, bearded and most likely blowing things up emerged. When asked about their views of science in general, secondary-school students portrayed scientists as brilliant, dedicated and essential to the world. However, when asked about science as a career, they responded with a negative image of scientific work and scientists. They saw scientific work as dull and rarely rewarding, and scientists as bearded, balding, isolated and lonely. This image of scientists has also been documented among primary- and middle-school students.

Using drawings to provide contrasts can be a very powerful tool. Students have been asked to draw themselves reading at home and at school, and to produce drawings of teachers they liked and disliked (Groundwater-Smith, Ewing & Le Cornu 2007).

Most recently, working on a study of how young people see themselves as learners, one of the authors asked Year 9 students to draw themselves as they remember themselves in Year 6 and as they see themselves in Year 9. After discussing the drawings, students were asked to comment on the process. Most saw that there were fewer restrictions placed on them in the primary years and that they were required to join in a greater range of activities. Generally, secondary schooling was more academic and focused, and the peer pressures were greater. Independent rather than collaborative work was the norm. Several students observed that their teachers were more relaxed with them, but that primary school was more fun. Resources in secondary school were much better, especially in the area of ICT. Clearly, the curriculum and teaching were based on higher expectations and were, at times, more stressful. Teachers expected a better performance. There were divergent paths for students to take and greater choice. One student contrasted primary school as 'a small cup that is treasured but easily filled' with secondary schooling as 'a whirlwind moving at an ever-faster rate'.

When asked to reflect on the process of drawing, students thought the activity allowed them to think back: 'It came in flashbacks' and they could 'see ourselves as we were'. They thought the process was engaging and allowed for different ways to express themselves. While some were more amused about the request to draw, they indicated afterwards that 'it was ok', and that the process allowed them to look at things differently: 'it was more personal somehow'.

Student work as a basis for evaluation

One of the most effective ways to collect data for the evaluation of teaching and learning in the Middle Years is to closely consider student work. Sitting with a student, for example, and asking them to explain a piece of their work to you – their motivations for completing it in a certain way, the decisions they took in the course of completing the work and the reasons for these particular decisions, as well as how this piece of work links to their ongoing learning – can be truly illuminating. It is important, however, that such encounters are structured more as conversations than interrogations and that, while it is useful to prepare a series of open-ended questions to pose to students about their work, at the same time you should engage in a 'pedagogy of listening' (Rinaldi 2006: 65), perhaps writing up your observations and conclusions in the form of a reflection at the end of the conversation. Be guided by your own curiosity and interest in learning when constructing these experiences and your capacity to engage in authentic dialogue with students about learning will emerge and grow, enhancing not only your ability to use your professional judgement, but also students' capacity to describe and discuss their learning.

We believe strongly that wherever possible and feasible, students themselves should be seen as part of the process of action learning in relation to teaching and learning in the Middle Years.

Collecting data – the case for the student perspective

In Chapter 1 we discussed the concept of engagement in learning in the Middle Years, discussing how vital it is that young people are engaged behaviourally, emotionally and cognitively. Engaged students are fully participative in the life of the classroom, they interact with their teachers and peers with enthusiasm and optimism and they are persistent and willing to tackle complex learning processes. We drew attention to Munns (2004) concern for 'big E' engagement whereby it moves beyond the merely procedural 'doing as you are told' to the substantive 'doing what is worthwhile.' Perhaps one of the most difficult aspects of evaluating our effectiveness as teachers is to determine the extent of student engagement: how do students feel about what they are doing, why they are doing it and how they are going about it?

Here we look particularly at processes that allow us to examine student perspectives on their learning in general and their engagement in particular. We argue that when we consult young people and treat them seriously, it is possible to develop a learning process that has greater meaning for them and one they will find both relevant and enjoyable. The discussion that follows focuses upon ways in which you, as a Middle Years teacher or prospective teacher, can investigate *with* students, more deeply and profoundly, their learning. We advocate processes that are structured such that they are connected, dynamic, worthwhile and developed in a manner that recognises any ethical concerns. Contemporary understandings of pedagogy recognise that engagement is not merely a whim of the educational imagination but is critical to transforming learning in productive and positive ways. Students need to feel welcomed and supported and that:

* learning materials relate to students' lives and highlight how learning can apply in their own worlds
* they have some control over their learning and are involved in authentic problem-solving and inquiry tasks
* they are set challenging but achievable tasks
* they can question and reflect upon what they have learned
* their curiosity is encouraged
* they can share new knowledge with others in a multidirectional flow – student to student, student to teacher, teacher to student
* they can understand and employ the language of learning.

Here we argue for a form of student agency that not only feeds back into students' own learning but also into *your* professional learning. Mitra (2004) states that when students have agency and a sense of belonging, and are recognised as competent, they gain a stronger sense of their own abilities and build awareness that they can make changes in their schools, not only for themselves but also for others. Generally, however, students are not consulted about either their learning or the school or, at best, are treated only as a data source. Raymond (2001) notes that there are three possible steps for consulting students: *discussion* – students are active respondents; *dialogue* – students are co-researchers; and *significant voice* – students are researchers, initiating, inquiring, interpreting and developing actions. Groundwater-Smith & Mockler (2003) detail ways that schools can employ all of these practices, some of which we spell out shortly.

In his overview of school improvement based on student voice, Fielding asks important questions about how the relationship between school structures and culture can either facilitate or inhibit student voice:

> Where are the public spaces (physical and metaphorical) in
> which encounters might take place? Who controls them? What
> values shape their being and their use? (2001: 106)

In many cases, young people in our schools occupy a borderland where there exists an unnatural boundary between them and those who determine what their experiences will be. Others speak *on* their behalf, they speak *for* them, they speak *about* them, but they rarely speak *with* them. And yet, as Antoine de Saint-Exupéry wrote in *The Little Prince,* grown ups cannot on their own understand the world from the young person's point of view and therefore they need the young people to explain it to them.[2]

And yet there are those who advocate the right of students to be heard, for they are the witnesses to what takes place in schools, both within and outside classrooms.

> What pupils say about teaching, learning and schooling is not
> only worth listening to, but provides an important – perhaps
> the most important – foundation for thinking about ways of
> improving schools (Rudduck, Chaplain & Wallace 1996: 1).

Let us pause here to ask you when you were at school, how often were you consulted about the ways that teaching and learning were managed? How did you feel about how the day was organised? Did you have a say in how the curriculum was arrived at? Were you consulted about the criteria upon which your work was judged?

Of course, it should not be taken that, if and when they are consulted, young people will necessarily wish for more radical or innovative schooling. Howard and Johnson (2000) found, in the Australian context, that young people who were consulted about the possibility of changing middle schooling to assist them to make the transition from primary school more effectively generally opted for the status quo. It was argued that because the current conditions were the only ones that they knew and experienced, it was unreasonable to ask them to 'imagine how things might be managed differently, because it is asking them to put their present success at risk' (Howard & Johnson 2000: 8). The research results could partly be attributed to the researchers only seeking the views of 'resilient students'. However, the research raises an interesting ethical point: what are we to do if students themselves are the conservative forces?

While, in the main, it is true that schools rarely consult their students and take them seriously, there are schools in the United Kingdom, America and Australia where there have been systematic policies and practices to enable students' voices to be heard and the schools have even given students agency in designing, investigating, analysing and interpreting studies of learning (see, for example, Cook-Sather 2002; Needham & Groundwater-Smith 2003; Groundwater-Smith & Mockler 2003; Arnot et al. 2004; Danby & Farrell 2004; Johnson 2004; Rudduck & Flutter 2004; Flutter & Rudduck 2004). In Sydney, a network of schools, the Coalition of Knowledge Building Schools, has been developing authentic inquiry-based processes that involve students at every point in the research.

Michael Fielding (2004) has devoted much time to these concerns. His recent analysis of the very real difficulties in working in a consultative manner reminds us of the practical concerns that we must address if we are to move forward:

> [We need to] resist the constant pull for either 'fadism' or
> 'manipulative incorporation' . . . Fadism leads to unrealistic
> expectations, subsequent marginalisation and the unwitting
> corrosion of integrity; manipulative incorporation leads to
> betrayal of hope, resigned exhaustion and the bolstering of an
> increasingly powerful status quo (2004: 296).

He asks a series of penetrating questions, among them:

- How confident are we that our research does not redescribe and reconfigure students in ways that bind them more securely into the fabric of the status quo?

---

2. The full text of *The Little Prince* can be found at www.spiritual.com.au/articles/prince/prince_contents.htm#Top.

- How clear are we about the use to which the detail of data is likely to be put? Is our more detailed knowledge of what students think and feel largely used to control them more effectively?
- Are we sure that our positions of relative power and our personal and professional interests are not blurring our judgement or shaping our advocacy? (Fielding 2004: 302–4)

In effect, we might ask ourselves are we capturing students' voices in order to tame the unruly? As Cook-Sather asks, in the context of current American educational reform, are we 'authorising' student perspectives only to later ignore them: 'Most power relationships have no place for listening and actively do not tolerate it because it is very inconvenient: to really listen means to have to respond' (2002: 8).

PROVOCATION: PRACTICE UNDER THE MICROSCOPE

1   What might be positive and negative side effects of engaging students in research?

2   How might you put safeguards in place to minimise the negatives and maximise the positives?

3   How can you authentically understand and respond to students' feedback?

There are serious ethical questions to be asked about raising expectations that consultation with students will be ongoing and embedded in the culture of the school. If such consultation is to occur, schools must make ongoing plans about how they can nurture and sustain the student voice. Fielding & Bragg (2003) advocate developing students' roles and the identity of the work, and involving different staff and developing their roles. Similarly, continuity is dependent upon staff commitment. Nurturing an inquiring school culture and the capabilities of those within it to fully participate is clearly a significant but warranted challenge.

CONCLUSION

We are conscious that, in this chapter, we have made assumptions about how teachers, and teachers and their students, can work together. We have assumed that this will happen in a climate of trust and confidentiality. For instance, when we ask students in focus groups to discuss teaching and learning, we enjoin them to concentrate upon teacher behaviours and not on teachers. Asking teachers and students to work collaboratively to evaluate teaching and learning is to ask them to work ethically, according to the norms espoused by the Australian National Schools Network (see Chapter 7, page 126).

In addition we pose here a series of broad overriding ethical guidelines for action learning:

- *Inquiries should observe ethical protocols and processes*: school-based evaluation is subject to the same ethical protocols as other social research. Informed consent should be sought from participants, whether students, teachers, parents or others, and an earnest attempt should be made to 'do no harm'.

- *Inquiries should be transparent in their processes*: one of the broader aims of action learning lies in the building of community and the sharing of knowledge and ideas. To this end, action learning should be transparent in its enactment and action learners accountable to their community for the processes and products of their research.
- *Inquiries should be collaborative in nature*: action learning as a form of evaluation of teaching and learning in the school should aim to provide opportunities for colleagues to share, discuss and debate aspects of their practice in the name of improvement and development. Responsible 'making sense' of data collected relies heavily on these opportunities.
- *Inquiries should be transformative in their intent and action*: practitioner researchers engage in an enterprise that is, in essence, about contributing to both transformation of practice and of the lived social life of the school. Responsible action learning creates actionable and actioned outcomes.

References

Arnot, M., McIntyre, D., Pedder, D. & Reay, D. (2004) *Consultation in the Classroom: Developing Dialogue about Teaching and Learning.* Cambridge, UK: Pearson.

Burton, D. & Bartlett, S. (2005) *Practitioner Research for Teachers.* London, UK: Paul Chapman.

Carr, W. & Kemmis, S. (1986) *Becoming Critical: Education, Knowledge and Action Research.* London, UK: Falmer Press.

Chambers, D. (1983) 'Stereotypical images of the scientist'. *Science Education*, 67, 255–65.

Cochran-Smith, M. (2003) 'Learning and unlearning: the education of teacher educators'. *Teaching and Teacher Education*, 19, 5–28.

Cook-Sather, A. (2002) 'Authorizing students' perspectives: toward trust, dialogue and change in education'. *Educational Researcher*, 31(4), 3–14.

Danby, S. & Farrell, A. (2004) 'Accounting for young children's competence in educational research: new perspectives on research ethics'. *The Australian Educational Researcher*, 31(3), 35–48.

Dewar, B. & Sharp, C. (2006) 'Using evidence: how learning can support individual and organisational learning through action research'. *Educational Action Research*, 14(2), 219–38.

Fielding, M. (2001) 'Beyond the rhetoric of student voice: new departures or new constraints in the transformation of 21st century schooling?' *Forum*, 43(2), 100–9.

Fielding, M. (2004) 'Transformative approaches to student voice: theoretical underpinnings, recalcitrant realities'. *British Educational Research Journal*, 30(2), 295–311.

Fielding, M. & Bragg, S. (2003) *Students as Researchers: Making a Difference.* London, UK: Pearson.

Flutter, J. & Rudduck, J. (2004) *Consulting Pupils: What's in it for Schools?* London, UK: Routledge Falmer.

Groundwater-Smith, S., Ewing, R. & Le Cornu, R. (2007) *Teaching: Challenges and Dilemmas*, 3rd edn. Melbourne: Thomson.

Groundwater-Smith, S. & Mockler, N. (2003) *Learning to Listen: Listening to Learn.* Sydney: MLC School and Faculty of Education, University of Sydney.

Groundwater-Smith, S. & Mockler, N. (2006) 'Research that counts: practitioner research and the academy', in J. Blackmore, J. Wright & V. Harwood (eds) *Counterpoints on the Quality and Impact of Educational Research. Review of Australian Research in Education*, 6, 105–17.

Howard, S. & Johnson, B. (2000) Transitions from primary to secondary school:

possibilities and paradoxes. Paper presented to the Australian Association for Research in Education Annual Conference, Sydney, December.

Johnson, K. (2004) 'Children's voices: pupil leadership in primary schools'. *International Research Associate Perspectives.* National College of School Leadership, Summer.

Madriz, E. (2003) 'Focus groups in feminist research', in N. Denzin & Y. Lincoln (eds) *Collecting and Interpreting Qualitative Materials,* 2nd edn. Thousand Oaks, CA: Sage: 363–88.

McGill, I. & Brockbank, A. (2004) *The Action Learning Handbook.* London, UK: Routledge Falmer.

Mitra, D. (2004) 'The significance of students: can increasing 'student voice' in schools lead to gains in youth development?', in *Teachers College Record,* 106, 651–88.

Morgan, D. L. (1998) *The Focus Group Guidebook.* Thousand Oaks, CA: Sage.

Munns, G. (2004) A sense of wonder: student engagement in low SES school communities. Paper presented at the Australian Association for Research in Education Annual Conference, Melbourne, 28 November – 2 December.

Needham, K. & Groundwater-Smith, S. (2003) Using student voice to inform school improvement. Paper presented to the International Congress for School Effectiveness and Improvement, Sydney, January.

Prosser, J. (1992) 'Personal reflections on the use of photographs in an ethnographic case study'. *British Educational Research Journal,* 18(4), 397–411.

Raymond, L. (2001) 'Student involvement in school improvement: from data source to significant voice'. *Forum,* 43(2), 58–64.

Revans, R. (1980) *Action Learning: New Techniques for Management.* London, UK: Blond & Briggs.

Rinaldi, C. (2006) *In Dialogue with Reggio Emilia: Listening, Researching and Learning.* Oxford, UK: Routledge.

Rudduck, J., Chaplain, R. & Wallace, G. (eds) (1996) *School Improvement: What Can Pupils Tell Us?* London, UK: David Fulton.

Rudduck, J. & Flutter, J. (2004) *How to Improve your School: Giving Pupils a Voice.* London, UK: Continuum Press.

Schratz, B., Walker, R. & Egg, P. (2004) Photo evaluation: a participatory ethnographic and evaluative tool in child care and education. Paper presented to the Annual Conference of the Australian Association for Research in Education, Melbourne, 29 November – 2 December.

Schratz, M. & Walker, R. (1995) *Research as Social Change.* London, UK: Routledge.

Sontag, S. (2003) *Regarding the Pain of Others.* New York, NY: Farrar, Straus & Giroux.

Tripp, D. (1993) *Critical Incidents in Teaching: The Development of Professional Judgement.* London, UK: Routledge.

Tripp, D. (1996) *SCOPE: Self-Directed Collegial On-Going Personal Professional Effectiveness.* Perth: Education Department of Western Australia.

Walker, R. & Wiedel, J. (1985) 'Using photographs in a discipline of words', in R. Burgess (ed.) *Field Methods in the Study of Education.* London, UK: Falmer Press.

10

THE MIDDLE YEARS – MORE THAN A TRANSITION

Some believe that the notion of education for emancipation is utopian. I believe emphatically that it is not utopian to hope for education that emancipates students, teachers and societies from irrational forms of thinking, unproductive ways of working, unsatisfying forms of life ... or from unjust forms of social relations. (Kemmis, 2005: 12)

INTRODUCTION

Transition implies movement from one stage or state to another. Transformation implies an extensive change and growth. Our concern in this book has been to explain and analyse some of the practices that can transform students' learning in the Middle Years. This has required us to consider adolescents in transition: moving from childhood to adulthood, moving from one year level to another at school. Yet our goal has been to locate these transitions within a context of school and classroom practices that can transform learning, not only for students in the Middle Years but also for their teachers. In this chapter we summarise the main ideas developed in the book and point to new challenges and directions relevant to working in the Middle Years.

The book has two quite different yet related parts. The first focuses on aspects of student learning in the Middle Years: on young adolescents; on curriculum, pedagogy and assessment relevant to young adolescents; and on schools and the social contexts of which young people are a part. The second focuses on professional learning for teachers in the Middle Years: with content for beginning teachers, experienced teachers and school leaders. It is rare to bring together student learning and teacher professional learning in this way; however, it makes sense to do so because the design and development of transformative learning practices in schools depends on the professional knowledge and learning of teachers. Bringing these two areas together is also important because middle schooling is a new and growing field. Understanding the contexts and practices of student learning, and professional learning and leadership, is critical to the development of this field.

THE MIDDLE YEARS FOCUS

The focus on the Middle Years in Australia is fairly new. Interest in this phase of schooling really started to develop in the early to mid 1990s. The National Middle Schooling Project, funded by the Australian government and organised by the Australian Curriculum Studies Association, was a mechanism for drawing together key people, ideas and research related to the Middle Years and charting a direction for middle schooling. Key publications developed as part of this project include *From Alienation to Engagement* (Australian Curriculum Studies Association 1996) and *Shaping Middle Schooling in Australia: A Report of the National Middle Schooling Project* (Barratt 1998). Until this time, the Middle Years was almost a forgotten phase in terms of program development. Much attention had been paid to early childhood education and to curriculum in the senior years, but far less to the school practices and educational outcomes for those students in the middle. Given that the Middle Years field is relatively new, many are asking whether attention to this area is just a fad and whether reforms in the area can be sustained (Chadbourne 2001). Will it, like some other school reforms, last a few years and then be replaced by another wave of reform?

CONSOLIDATING THE FIELD

We suggest that the focus on the Middle Years has been sustained and it is more than a fad for the reasons outlined below.

Grassroots reform leading system-based policy

Reform in middle schooling in Australia has been primarily driven by grassroots development: teachers in schools working to develop specific practices to meet the needs of young adolescents. This has made the reform significantly different from many other types of school reform that involve implementing top-down policies and directives. It is of note that this grassroots reform is now being consolidated by system-based policy reform in many states and territories. Both top-down and bottom-up approaches strengthen the Middle Years as an important school focus and phase.

Middle Years as a stage of schooling

Focus has shifted to the Middle Years as a stage or phase of schooling rather than a special program. When conceptualised as a stage, students in Years 6 to 9 (with some variation either up or down a year) are considered to be in the Middle Years irrespective of whether they attend a primary school, a secondary school or a designated middle school. Likewise, teachers working in these year levels are considered Middle Years teachers. A variety of particular school and classroom practices are relevant to this stage of schooling.

Strong articulation of practices and philosophies

The notion of 'middle schooling' articulated as part of the National Middle Schooling Project has certainly been influential in defining many aspects of school and classroom practice in the Middle Years. Informed by ideas developed in North America, the middle schooling focus has as its core integrated curriculum, teaching teams and home groupings; a focus on social, pastoral and academic needs; collaborative learning; and smooth transitions across year levels. While noting the strength of this philosophical stance and the impact it has had on defining the Middle Years, there is a downside if it is taken as the only way through which to develop schooling practices in the Middle Years. There are many pedagogical, curricula and assessment practices that can be employed in worthwhile ways in the Middle Years that fall outside the scope of the specific practices of middle schooling.

Practices rather than structures

In Australia the focus of innovation in the Middle Years has been on school and classroom practices in existing school settings. This is quite different from the model of separate middle schools extensively used in North America. The focus on practices does mean that Middle Years innovations can be developed in primary schools, secondary schools and separate middle schools. That said, it is clear that in the schools that span K–10 or K–12 in which there are dedicated Middle Years timetables and staffing protocols, the Middle Years typically have a much higher profile. The fact that many new school developments span a wide range of age groups does open the door for specific middle-school options.

Students' lives outside of school

The circumstances in which young people are growing up are rapidly changing. Young people's take-up of new technologies, new forms of communication and popular culture, coupled with the fact that they are part of new patterns of social, cultural and family relations, creates an imperative for curricular response. Practices in the Middle Years have been seen as an important part of school responsiveness to the changing lives of adolescents.

Conferences, journals, professional associations and research reports

Over the last ten years there has been significant growth in the number of professional associations and conferences that focus specifically on the Middle Years. The national Middle Years of Schooling Association and state and local affiliations have promoted the exchange and building of ideas among teachers and have enhanced the profile of the field. Likewise, there has been growth in research about the Middle Years.

Specialist qualifications

A number of programs of teacher education prepare teachers to work in the Middle Years and teachers are now graduating as Middle Years teachers. Having such a professional identity is important in enhancing the status and position of the field.

KEY THEMES

This book has sought to both explicate and build on key reforms taking place in the Middle Years in Australia. Following are some key themes that have been developed in the book:

- *An exciting area of school reform* – the nature of reform taking place in the Middle Years does open wonderful opportunities for teachers. The work in the field encompasses understandings of adolescent psychology and sociology, innovation in school and classroom practice and commitments to teaching practices that transform learning for young adolescents. The nature of the reform presents an endless array of possibilities for teachers who want to develop school and classroom practices that are worthwhile and engaging.
- *Aligning curriculum, pedagogy and assessment* – British curriculum theorist Basil Bernstein (1990) talks about the 'message systems' of curriculum, pedagogy and assessment. These message systems carry the important matters of schooling: what is to be learned, how learning takes place and how learning will be evaluated. We have focused on aligning these messages systems by emphasising the *what* of learning in terms of knowledge that is worthwhile, relevant and engaging; the *how* of learning in terms of connections, variations and high expectations; and assessment as a process to not only measure but also support learning.
- *School and classrooms: academic and social* – engagement is a term commonly used in discussions of the Middle Years. Engagement means that students are doing more than just completing tasks, they find that being in class and at school is both worthwhile and enjoyable. Extending student engagement in the Middle Years requires a focus on both schools and classrooms, as well as on the academic and social components of classrooms that support learning. Good relationships between teachers and their students are a key here. Good relationships presuppose an understanding of context, sensitivity to student circumstance and recognition of differences between students.
- *Professional learning of teachers in the Middle Years* – central to the book has been the alignment between school reform in the Middle Years and reforms in the areas of teacher education and professional learning. Without this alignment, reforms will always be difficult to design and implement. Building and sustaining practices in the Middle Years can be strengthened through the establishment of strong professional learning communities and programs of initial teacher education.

NEW DIRECTIONS AND CHALLENGES

There are ongoing challenges in the Middle Years field as it attempts to establish itself. There are also exciting developments as the field branches in new directions. Below we outline some of these directions and challenges.

THE PROCESSES OF SCHOOL REFORM

School reform can be slow and faltering and developments in the Middle Years are no exception. It can take some years before practices become embedded in self-sustaining ways in the culture of a school. Many grassroots reforms in schools rely on the knowledge and enthusiasm of a small number of people. Changes to these teams can therefore have significant consequences for reform initiatives. Building practices that sustain reform over a long period is essential. In schools with entrenched secondary school or primary school cultures, developing programs with a Middle Years focus can be difficult, as can maintaining a strong identity as a Middle Years teacher.

ATTENTION TO THE TRANSITIONS

While much attention has focused on the transition from primary school to secondary school, little attention has been paid to new transitions created through practices in the Middle Years. Indeed, the transition from the Middle Years to the senior years of secondary school is rarely considered either in terms of academic learning or social learning. There is an urgent need for more research and practice about this transition.

There is a need also to examine transition from other angles and perspectives. For example, for a growing number of students and their parents, the transition from primary school to secondary school causes angst over choosing a secondary school (Tsolidis 2006). Likewise, for a growing number of students, the transition from primary school to secondary school involves moving from the government school sector to the non-government school sector. Into the mix of transitions come questions about an increasingly competitive school marketplace and shifting trends in school enrolments. How schools position their Middle Years programs in relation to such trends is an important issue to follow.

LITERACY AND TECHNOLOGY IN THE MIDDLE YEARS

We concur with Carrington (2003, 2006), who argues that literacy pedagogy needs to become a bigger part of the agenda for teachers in the Middle Years. Chapter 5 raised issues about literacy learning for boys and Indigenous students. Carrington talks about the 'techno-literacy' skills that many young people have acquired through gaming, texting, and chatting and blogging over the internet. Of critical importance for student engagement and learning are how teachers respond to the new forms of techno-literacy that students have, and how they respond to those students who are struggling with basic reading and writing.

LEARNING BEYOND THE CLASSROOM

Not surprisingly, most discussions about student learning in the Middle Years focus on the classroom context; however, one area of growing concern is the learning that takes place outside the classroom. Case studies in Chapter 1 illustrate whole-school learning programs. However, beyond this there are new developments for student learning in communities. In Victoria, the Department of Education runs the Alpine School, a residential school for students in Year 9, with a focus in curriculum and pedagogy on leadership, community building, peer-learning and self-understanding. The school is a unique opportunity for Year 9 students in government schools across Victoria to work together in an intense residential environment. Other smaller scale examples include after-school drop-in programs and homework help programs (Hayes & Chodkiewicz 2006). We suggest that learning outside the four walls of the classroom will be a fruitful area for new explorations for teachers in the Middle Years.

BUILDING THE EVIDENCE BASE

One problem with many educational reforms is that there are few studies that systematically evaluate their effect. Reforms in the Middle Years have been subject to this criticism – they have strong conceptual underpinnings but not necessarily a lot of evidence to show whether and how they extend student learning. There is a need for more practitioner research of the kind described in Chapter 9 as it will build the evidence base necessary to justify particular approaches. Likewise, there is a need for large-scale studies to analyse effects of programs on student learning across contexts and over time (Chadbourne 2001).

A FINAL FEW WORDS

Our aim in this book has been to open doors in your thinking and understanding of what it is to be a teacher of students in the Middle Years and how, in order to best meet the needs (however diverse) of adolescent learners, it is sometimes necessary to leave behind some of the old structures and processes that characterise industrial-age schooling and turn our faces bravely and courageously towards the new world of the 21st century – the century in which our students will live their lives and hopefully bring to fruition their own aspirations and dreams. Our hope is that we have sparked your interest and enthusiasm to find out more about the ways that we, as educators, can think outside the square in our ongoing quest to provide the best, the most relevant and the most engaging education possible for all of our students, whatever their circumstances.

Carlina Rinaldi, reflecting upon the educational philosophy of Loris Malaguzzi, the founder of Reggio Emilia Municipal Schools in Italy – a philosophy deeply transformative in its intent and vision – issues a challenge to us as educators thinking about the future and purpose of school, a challenge to which we hope we have gone some way to taking up. We invite you to continue constructing a response to this challenge throughout the days, weeks and years of your work as a teacher. Rinaldi writes:

> Pedagogy, like school, is not neutral. It takes sides, it participates in deep and vital ways in the definition of this project whose central theme is not [humankind], but [our] relations with the world, [our] being in the world, [our] feeling of interdependence with what is other than [ourselves] (2006: 170).

References

Australian Curriculum Studies Association (1996). *From Alienation to Engagement: Opportunities for Reform in the Middle Years.* Canberra: Australian Curriculum Studies Association.

Barratt, R. (1998) *Shaping Middle Schooling in Australia: A Report of the National Middle Schooling Project.* Canberra: Australian Curriculum Studies Association.

Bernstein, B. (1990) *The Structuring of Pedagogic Discourse.* London, UK: Routledge & Kegan Paul.

Carrington, V. (2003) 'Mid-term review: the middle years of schooling'. *Curriculum Perspectives*, 24, 30–41.

Carrington, V. (2006) *Rethinking Middle Years: Early Adolescents, Schooling and Digital Culture.* Sydney: Allen & Unwin.

Chadbourne, R. (2001) *Middle Schooling for the Middle Years.* Melbourne: Australian Education Union.

Hayes, D. & Chodkiewicz, A. (2006) 'School–community links: supporting learning in the middle years'. *Research Papers in Education*, 21(1), 3–18.

Kemmis, S. (2005) 'Participatory Action Research and the Public Sphere'. Keynote address to the Practitioner Research/Action Research (PRAR) 2005 Joint International Practitioner Research Conference and Collaborative Action Research Network (CARN) Conference, Utrecht, the Netherlands, 4–6 November 2005.

Rinaldi, C. (2006) *In Dialogue with Reggio Emilia: Listening, Researching and Learning.* New York, NY: Routledge.

Tsolidis, G. (2006) *Youthful Imagination: Schooling, Subcultures and Social Justice.* New York, NY: Peter Lang.

INDEX

and student disengagement 61
and supply of and demand for teachers 102
curriculum integration 52–6

D

data 139
collecting and using authentic 151–61
detainees 7
difference
ability differences 28
classroom strategies to respond to 68–9
the construction of 30–2
gender differences 11, 28, 32–5
individual differences and learning 67–9
politics and ethics of 30–2
race, culture and ethnicity differences 28
social difference 27–9, 30
teachers who make a 107–8
disengagement (from learning) 61, 71
dealing with 74–5
see also engagement (student)
divergent assessment 87–8
diversity 5, 18
and social justice 31–2
Donelly's education perspectives 45
downward behavioural expectations 11
downward envy condition 7
drawing (role in questioning) 157–8
duty of care code 106

E

education
approaches to middle years reform 46–9
boy's education 33–4
cultural context of 4–5
Donelly's education perspectives 45
educational reform context 135–7
educational outcomes and issues for Indigenous
students 36–8
experiences of young people and schooling 27–9
leadership within 132–4
and social geography 5–7
and social justice 30–2, 39–40, 45
sociopolitical context of 3–4
teacher education 108–13
emotional (effective) engagement 13
employer expectations (teachers) 106–7
engagement (student) 12–13, 70–5, 105, 159, 167
engaging with moral and social purposes 133
school factors affecting 70
teaching to extend student learning and engagement 71–5
see also disengagement
English language
language literacy 37
plain English report card 85–6
environments
class environment and relationships 75–6
supportive environments 12

equity 30–2, 33
Erikson's developmental theories 8–9
ethics
codes of ethics/conduct 106
and politics of difference 30–2
ethnicity, race and culture differences 28
evaluation
a framework for 150–1
student work as a basis for 158–61

F

families (social factor) 29, 37
focus groups (role in questioning) 155–6
formal knowledge 140
formative assessment 84–5
friendship groups 29

G

Gardner's multiple intelligences 68
gender differences 11, 28, 32–5
gender profile (of teaching profession) 101
generative professional learning culture 139–43
government
approaches to middle years reform 46–9
Australian Government Quality Teaching Program
(AGQTP) 124, 125
middle school programs of 124–5
and the plain English report card 85–6
policies for boy's education 34
role in curriculum 3–4, 44–9
and standardised testing—literacy and numeracy 36

H

heteronomy versus autonomy 134
high-stakes assessment 46
historical factors (educational experiences) 37, 38, 45, 133

I

identity 29, 62, 135, 167
Australian national identity 62–6
development of 8–10
professional identity 108, 113–14
responding to identity issues 9–10
self-identity (Indigenous people) 36–7, 76
inclusion – building inclusive practices 32–8
Indigenous students 7, 31–2, 76
case study: challenging the 'taken for granteds' 39–40
educational outcomes and issues for Indigenous
students 36–8
individuality 29, 39, 67–9
induction (teacher) 113–14
information age 135–6
inheritance/culture interaction 5
initiatives
addressing Indigenous students' needs 37–8
Australian government policies targeting boys 34
Changing Places – Making Links program 124